Ritualistic Crime

FIRST EDITION

Ritualistic Crime

EDITED BY Stephen Holmes

SAN DIEGO

Bassim Hamadeh, CEO and Publisher
John Remington, Executive Editor
Alisa Muñoz, Project Editor
Christian Berk, Production Editor
Emely Villavicencio, Senior Graphic Designer
Greg Isales, Licensing Associate
Natalie Piccotti, Director of Marketing
Kassie Graves, Vice President of Editorial
Jamie Giganti, Director of Academic Publishing

Cover image copyright © 2013 iStockphoto LP/manx_in_the_world.
copyright © 2013 iStockphoto LP/nkovac.

Printed in the United States of America.

3970 Sorrento Valley Blvd., Ste. 500, San Diego, CA 92121

CONTENTS

PART I

Introduction

Introduction

Stephen Holmes

This book is a culmination of readings on ritualistic crimes. It focuses on the causes, functions, and similarities of sacred forms of violence across the spectrum. For years people and larger groups have been engaging in ritualistic crime. However, many in the academic and lay community have not considered their actions to be part of this broad area of criminality. This is likely because ritualistic crime does not have a well-understood definition. Crimes of this genera include crimes committed by individuals or groups against another based on an errant belief that their acts will bring about a greater good. Thus, their crimes often involve acts of violence designed to suppress groups or individuals based on their beliefs, status, group affiliation, or identity.

Ritualistic crimes are based on a broad spectrum of individual acts and motivations. They may include offenses committed by fringe groups or even contemporary religions—the most prominent example being the crusades of the Middle Ages hundreds of years ago. They may consist of crimes committed by those who belong to groups that prescribe to extreme or hate ideologies. We often see these types of crimes committed by individuals belonging to different variants of the Aryan Nations or Christian Identity.

If we are to be inclusive, we must also include the acts and crimes of different types of cults and sects. If we look back just 20 or 30 years ago, it does not take long to come up with a list of groups fitting this description. Classic examples include the Manson family, the Temple of the People in Jonestown, the Branch Davidians, Aum Shinrikyo, and new age cults such as Heaven's Gate.

Most contemporary students may have heard of one or two of these groups but not all. However, once they become familiar with these groups, they are astounded by how each group was formed, organized, functioned, and, even more importantly, why individuals would follow leaders and commit heinous crimes on the word or whim of a charismatic leader who displayed clear psychological issues.

These groups and their members often start by engaging in small con games and, as they mature, move on to larger and more financially lucrative crimes such as gun and weapon smuggling, drug dealing, and even the harassment and murder of their vocal opponents and adversaries. Some such as Aum Shinrikyo even engaged in domestic terrorism when it killed government actors, killed judges, and committed a deadly chemical attack, releasing sarin gas in Tokyo's subway system in 1995.

Other readings look not so much at these cult-type groups but at established religions or their off shoots. These readings and topics include the Church of Satan and Goth groups and the Temple of the Vampire. Several of the groups under this head share many of the characteristics of our contemporary notion of cults or sects with the exception that they often do not espouse that their members strictly follow their teachings or any type of religious dictates. Instead, many of these groups provide members with general principles designed to give them a home and sense of belonging to a larger group of "outcasts and lost souls." Thus, these groups are often not considered criminal or having a criminal focus. However, it is often members of these groups, specifically youthful and unaffiliated actors that claim to be part of these groups, which are the biggest problem for law enforcement.

It is crucial for law enforcement and students of criminal justice to be familiar with these groups, their principles, and beliefs to be able to understand the classic signs of group affiliation. Typical examples of a loosely affiliated youthful group include Rod Ferrell and his loosely knit group of teenagers from Murray, Kentucky, that killed two in Eustis, Florida.

Other readings look at one of the fastest-growing semi-religious groups across America and Europe: Wicca and Neo-Paganism. During the last 30 years, we have seen a substantial increase in the number of youth and young adults who have begun practicing Wicca and other traditional nature-based religions, including Neo-Paganism. Many have speculated about why we have seen such a significant increase. Some say it was the result of the media that glorified the work and practices of white magic. There might be something to this, since witches are no longer seen as ugly women with large noses and green faces who cook children in their ovens. The contemporary group instead envisions themselves to be more like Harry Potter or Hermione Granger in J.K. Rowling's famous book series. Alternatively, for older adults, it may be exposure to the behavioral mimicking of Claire Randal, the compassionate time-traveling witch in Diana Gabaldon's *Outlander* series.

Regardless of the source, modern-day Wicca and practitioners of Neo-Paganism often do not commit acts that are of concern to law enforcement and other members of the criminal justice system. Justice system officials may, however, stumble across evidence of pagan worship in open spaces of public grounds where assemblies occur. Recognizing the classic signs of pagan worship often goes a long way in assuring the public and others that there is nothing to be concerned about. Many ceremonies in rural settings often focus on good harvests, rain, world peace, and other virtuous causes.

One of the most feared and misunderstood types of groups are syncretic religions. By definition, syncretic religions are those that blend two or more religious beliefs into one. This is the foundation of the faiths of Hoodoo, Voodoo, and Santeria. Initially formed by the victims of the slave trade, these religions date back to the early 1800s when slaves, attempting to keep a part of their culture, renamed their gods with Christian saints' names to avoid detection.

Most of the practitioners of syncretic religions practice what we currently understand as white magic. They have local *santeros* (or priests) that conduct ceremonies and pray for the sick and needy.

Practitioners often have an altar in their home, and during a quick drive through large cities such as Miami or New York, you are likely to see *Botanicas* where religious supplies, candles, and other paraphernalia of this craft can be purchased openly.

For the most part, the public has nothing to be concerned with for most practitioners of these types of religions. They are peaceful and are no more significant a threat than most of the dominant religious organizations. However, two things separate them from the more-established religions. First, they are very decentralized with no determined spiritual head or leader. Second, these religions routinely practice animal sacrifices. Thus, it is not all that uncommon for the public and even law enforcement to be alarmed when sacrificed animals are found in public places. Law enforcement or long-time residents of communities with large practicing Santeria constituencies quickly learn to spot the difference between the sacrifices of these groups and that of others intent on engaging in animal cruelty.

Although most syncretic religions are peaceful, some groups and individuals specialize in the dark side of this religion. These individuals practice what has now become known as Palo Mayombe. Palo Mayombe captured the attention of many Americans when Mark Kilroy, a student at the University of Texas, was killed after he crossed the border into Mexico from South Padre Island. He was abducted, attacked with a machete, and then ritualistically desecrated by Adolfo Constanzo, a Mexican drug dealer who practiced Palo. According to members of Constanzo's gang, they were not afraid of their enemies or even telling law enforcement what had happened because Constanzo's magic was so strong that he would protect them.

Practitioners of Palo Mayombe are often fearless, brutal, and violent. They use their religion and magic to curse enemies, and they use violence or other psychological intimidating techniques to assimilate power. Although there are those who claim that the power of Palo can be used to harness good and benevolent spirits, law enforcement must be aware of these practitioners and keep a close eye on any potential violent and criminal deeds committed by them.

The final set of readings focuses on new and emerging forms of religious groups and sects. These include the emergence of fictionally based religions and religious groups such as *Jediism* from the famous book and movie series *Star Wars*. While not commonly thought of as a threat or a criminally based syndicate, we must keep an eye on these groups. After all, no one thought that a bunch of individuals that thought the end of the world was coming would ever lend to mass suicide or the needless killing of women or children as in the case of Jonestown or the Branch Davidian complex in Waco.

Each of these readings provides context for the need to keep an eye on these groups and how each grows, flourishes, and prospers. Each has established similarities and relies on similar key elements. One of the most often cited key element is the reliance of a supreme or charismatic leader. Its membership can elect this leader or the leader may rise through the ranks and gain the trust and admiration of his or her followers. For instance, Marshall Applewhite and Jim Jones started their groups, while David Koresh attained his leadership position after a long power struggle with the former leader's son.

A second key element is that each relies heavily on ritualism. While not claiming that the Catholic Church and its affiliated groups are a cult, sect, or even engaged in criminal activity, most of the groups discussed in this book follow their lead or playbook by requiring members to participate in specific rituals. These rituals are used to reinforce a prevailing ideology and bond people of like mind and persuasion together.

A third key element is a set of established criteria that members must pass through to become self-actualized and a fully functioning member of the group. Just like Catholics must pass through and engage in each of the seven holy sacraments to be an adult member of the church and a "warrior for Christ," so must members of these groups pass through an established criteria. Common membership goals and elevation criteria include education, recruitment, trust exercises, and for some, the engagement in criminal deeds in the name of the group.

A crucial fourth element is a belief that members of the group are engaged in a rightful cause. That is, they believe that some group or segment of the population is sinful by nature, needs correction, and this correction must be performed in the name of an all-powerful entity. In the case of many right-wing extremist groups, that group may be racial or ethnic minorities or even those who choose a different lifestyle than their own. Thus, any act of violence committed can be justified in the name of a higher power.

The fifth element centers on the group's ability to maintain internal secrecy. What this means is that many of these groups do not want the general public to be aware of their beliefs and their internal rules and regulations. Such a premium is placed on secrecy that many members are discouraged from socializing with non-members or their own family. Those who do often face internal scrutiny, public humiliation, the threat of legal action, and in some cases, violence. Because of the tactics used, those who fail to follow the group's rules or separate and leave the group face a long and tough road, as exile or ex-communication from the group is difficult, especially for long-time members.

The final element is that many leaders of these groups profess to their followers that if they follow the tenants laid down and established by the group with fidelity, they will receive eternal salvation in the next life. This is also a common theme among many of the world's established religions. In some of the world's largest religions, it is commonly thought that participants will receive 72 "black-eyed virgins" following an act of martyrdom or walking through the pearly gates after living a life of "Christian virtue." World religions have used this promise to do their dirty work. The organizers and leaders of these cults and sects understand this and use similar assurances to their full advantage.

As you read through the articles in this book and learn more about these cults, groups, sects, and religions, keep these key elements in mind. Not all apply to each group, but most do. Further, it is important to understand that this book of readings only covers established groups. It does not include self-styled or loosely coupled spin-off groups or individuals. These individuals or actors are often the most dangerous since they do not report to anyone else or a higher-level bureaucracy. What is interesting is that as these smaller groups mature, they tend to take on many of these elements listed if they do not collapse under their own force.

As you learn more about each of these groups, and the crimes they commit, keep in mind how each element is used to not only grow the number of participants but also to keep its members in check. Not all sects or new religious groups are bad. Not all have evil intentions. In fact, most are formed due to objections with a larger group that professes dogma members consider to be objectionable. Further, if one studies history, it tells us that today's established religions were yesteryear's outlawed cults or sects.

On the Sacred Power of Violence in Popular Culture

Eric Bain-Selbo

Introduction to Violence in Religion and Popular Culture

Contemporary theorists of religion and violence have not looked so much at how religions or religious people can engage in violence in spite of religious beliefs and attitudes. There is no doubt that they can and have for millennia. Instead, contemporary theorists have focused on the *violence that is constitutive of religion*. In other words, religions are not institutions that may or may not engage in violence. They are institutions that are inherently violent. Religion and violence are intertwined. While all violence is not religious, much of it is or at least has religious overtones or dimensions. In this chapter, we will review some approaches to religion and violence and utilize them to interpret violence in popular culture, particularly in the films of Quentin Tarantino and in the sport of football.

Theory and Method

Violence by people in religious communities on the basis, and in the service, of religious beliefs or institutions has often been seen as something that happened only in "primitive" or tribal religions and cultures. But even the major religious traditions in more "civilized" areas of the world have been bound with violence. Krishna encourages the warrior Arjuna to engage in warfare in the Hindu ***Bhagavad Gita***. Krishna argues it is Arjuna's sacred duty. The Abrahamic traditions are punctuated with acts of violence, often by God. Whether it is Yahweh's wrath against the Egyptians (the story of the Exodus) or his own people (Exodus 32:25–35 describes the plague that the Lord inflicts on his people, even after his servants—the Levites—had slaughtered about 3,000 of them), God's brutal sacrifice of his own son in the Christian New Testament (not to mention the apocalyptic violence in the book of Revelation), or Allah's legitimation of military force and conquest against unbelievers (see surah 9:73 in the Qur'an), violence is central to the histories and narratives of the Abrahamic traditions. Today, religious adherents often turn to violence as a means of protecting or forwarding explicitly or implicitly religious objectives. In the following sections I explain three functions of violence in religious contexts. All three are interrelated. We then will see how these perspectives or functions can be used to interpret violence in seemingly secular contexts.

Cosmological Function: the Holy and the Damned

Central to understanding religious violence perpetrated between groups is to understand the dichotomy of "us versus them" in religious thinking. This dichotomy is part of a larger dualistic worldview in which there is good and evil. In such a **Manichean** worldview, "we" are good and "they" are evil. Regina Schwartz brilliantly illustrates the "us versus them" dichotomy that is central to the Biblical traditions. Central to her argument are the ideas of identity and scarcity (Schwartz 1997: 3–6).

All groups, by definition, go through a process of identity formation. There has to be some process by which those included in the group are conceptually and physically separated from those outside the group. But identity formation is not something that simply happens at the initial formation of a group. It must continue for as long as the group exists. The parameters and rules of the group must be affirmed continuously to distinguish the group from others. For example, the ancient Israelites formed a group characterized by physical marking (circumcision for the men), particular religious beliefs (e.g. belief in one God), and dietary restrictions (e.g. prohibitions against eating pork). This process of identity formation means that religion by definition *is* violent. It is not just that religion, through identity formation, *can* lead to violence. It is that religion, as a form of identity formation, always already is violent—if nothing else symbolically, in that it *cuts* one group off from another (in this case, the cutting literally of the male foreskin).

Schwartz also draws our attention to the fact that the physical world and human social structures are characterized by a scarcity of resources. Scarcity is a fundamental condition of group life, and it dramatically shapes relations among groups. There is only so much land or food or other resources to go around. Each group is in competition with other groups for limited resources. But there also are psychological or theological scarcities. God or the gods only can provide for some groups, not all. Only some groups will receive divine blessings. We see this most starkly in the identification of Jews as God's "chosen people." But the idea persists in Christianity and Islam. What complicates the matter even more is when the psychological or theological blessings are intertwined with tangible goods like land or food or other resources. So, for example, God's blessing on his people (Jews) entails their possession of the Holy Land (Israel).

When the "us versus them" conflict over scarce resources is understood in the context of a greater, **transcendent** battle between the forces of good and the forces of evil, then we have the makings for a cosmic war. Reza Aslan identifies a cosmic war as "a conflict in which God is believed to be directly engaged on one side over the other … a cosmic war is like a ritual drama in which participants act out on earth a battle they believe is actually taking place in the heavens" (Aslan 2009: 5).

An important aspect of cosmic war is the demonizing of the other—the opponent or combatant. Mark Juergensmeyer describes this as satanization. "The process of satanization is aimed at reducing the power of one's opponents and discrediting them," he writes. "By belittling and humiliating them—by making them subhuman—one is asserting one's own superior moral power" (Juergensmeyer 2003: 186). Satanization is part of the Manichean dualism that is central to cosmic war. In a cosmic war there is no room for compromise. As Bruce Lincoln notes, in cosmic war "Sons of Light confront Sons of Darkness, and all must enlist on one side or another, without possibility of neutrality, hesitation, or middle ground" (Lincoln 2006: 20). Thus, "the stage is set for prolonged, ferocious, and enormously destructive combat" (Lincoln 2006: 95). Even someone who suggests a compromise then is considered an enemy by his own side (Juergensmeyer 2003: 157). Ultimately, this mindset results in apocalyptic thinking—the final confrontation of good versus evil, with good prevailing in the end (Selengut 2008: 88).

Juergensmeyer notes that putting conflicts into a religious context ultimately is about meaning. Opposing the chaos and violence of the world (even with violence) is the *raison d'etre* of religion—and through religion that chaos and violence is given meaning.

Ethical Function: Justice, Order, and Vengeance

Combating the chaos and evil that the other represents is not just about restoring order for the sake of restoring order. The restoration of order is a matter of justice—divine justice to be exact. The universe is characterized by a moral order established by God—an order that occasionally can get "out of whack" and that requires the righteous actions of God's soldiers to restore it.

Individuals act justly or righteously when they use violence to establish or re-establish divine order. Such violence often is in response to previous violence, the latter being the source of the creation of disorder. Thus, the use of righteous violence to combat evil violence frequently is a matter of revenge—the revenge of the good (us) against the evil (them). It is an effort to strike back upon those who do harm to others and who disrupt the harmony of the divine order. So the violence is not simply a matter of retaliating against those who perpetrate evil (though such revenge can be sweet), it is a matter of serving a greater divine purpose. Ultimately, that divine purpose makes the use of violence a moral (because commanded—implicitly or explicitly—by God) action. In fact, we can take it a step further and insist that one is obligated morally to perform acts of violence in the service of a greater purpose or order. For example, Christian radicals who blow up abortion clinics or kill abortion providers frequently feel it is their moral and religious duty to engage in such acts. While this perspective is best represented in the Abrahamic traditions (i.e. Judaism, Christianity, and Islam), it also can be found in those major traditions from India (Hinduism and Buddhism) that are based on the **karmic** system. In the *Bhagavad Gita* the impending violence of the warrior Arjuna is justified both in terms of restoring divine order and by the fact that those who will die in battle are paying their karmic debt.

Social-Psychological Function: Sacrifice

Violence in religion is more than simply the acts of God or divinely ordained warfare. It includes that violence that we do to ourselves—self-imposed privations or sacrifices done for religious reasons. Emile

Durkheim, the early twentieth-century sociologist, provides good examples of the role of sacrifice in his analysis of aboriginal **totemic** religions in Australia (Durkheim 1995: 84–95). According to Durkheim, the totem, ancestor, or god for whom sacrifices are made ultimately is an expression of the collectivity. Thus, the sacrifices made symbolically for the totem, ancestor, or god reflect the real sacrifices that must be made by the individual for the good of the collectivity. We sacrifice something of ourselves (our freedom, our selfishness) and/or something that is good for us (an animal given for slaughter on the altar or part of our harvest burned to the gods) to forward the aims of the group.

Sacrifices raise us toward something that transcends our individual ego, but that transcendent thing is the collective itself. In this light, the sacrifices made by "primitives" may not seem so strange to us when we consider our own sacrifices (for example, in war) that we are willing to make for the good of the collectivity. In this sense, the fundamental nature of sacrifice has not changed for millennia (Durkheim 1995: 330–354).

A more contemporary scholar like René Girard also tries to make connections between the violence we find in religion (particularly ancient) and events and structures in the world today. Girard is interested especially in the sacrifice of the other, whether that be of animal or human. His hypothesis is that "society is seeking to deflect upon a relatively indifferent victim, a 'sacrificeable' victim, the violence that would otherwise be vented on its own members, the people it most desires to protect" (Girard 1977: 4). How does sacrifice do this? "The sacrifice serves to protect the entire community from *its own* violence," Girard writes, "it prompts the entire community to choose victims outside itself. The elements of dissension scattered throughout the community are drawn to the person of the sacrificial victim and eliminated, at least temporarily, by its sacrifice" (Girard 1977: 8). Any community necessarily will have tensions as individuals vie with one another for a limited amount of goods. By directing negative emotions and energy onto the shoulders of the sacrificial victim, the "**scapegoat**," members of the community are able to overcome those negative emotions and energy through the **ritualized** killing of the victim.

What Girard is getting at clearly has roots in religious life. Indeed, for Girard violence and the sacred are "inseparable" (Girard 1977: 19). Put more strongly, "the operations of violence and the sacred are ultimately the same process" (Girard 1977: 258). The purpose of religion is to prevent "reciprocal violence" (Girard 1977: 55). This continuous retaliation or revenge—fueled by the frustration of the necessary curbing of our egoism or selfishness and our competition for scarce resources—is the never-ending cycle of violence that eventually will destroy a society. Thus, instead of providing an unending cycle of revenge that produces real victims of violence, societies develop religions with sacrificial rituals in which surrogate victims suffer the violence of the community. As Girard concludes, there is no society without religion because without religion society cannot exist (Girard 1977: 221).

The function of ritual is "to 'purify' violence; that is, to 'trick' violence into spending itself on victims whose death will provoke no reprisals" (Girard 1977: 36)—"that is, to keep violence *outside* the community" (Girard 1977: 92). Girard looks across time and cultures to find ritualized behavior that supports his thesis. One of the most common rituals in which the surrogate-victim mechanism is operative is the festival (Girard 1977: 119). The festival will include a variety of behaviors that affirm the social norms via the ritualized practice of breaking those norms. In other words, by permitting *only through ritual practice* what is otherwise prohibited (e.g. sexual promiscuity), the norms of the society during everyday or profane times are affirmed for the members of the community. Festivals also are the events in which the surrogate-victim mechanism is operative. While killing is normally prohibited, during the festival it is permitted—either literally or symbolically.

While most of the examples that Girard uses are from more ancient times, he nevertheless affirms the role of sacrificial rituals in the formation of all societies and the continuing need for them. Girard believes that we more often than not are in a state of "sacrificial crisis" (Girard 1977: 39–67). This crisis is a consequence of the disappearance of sacrificial rituals, preventing the society's ability to find or create a surrogate-victim and perpetrate its violence against that victim. Girard argues that "the disappearance of the sacrificial rites, coincides with the disappearance of the difference between impure violence and purifying violence. When this difference has been effaced, purification is no longer possible and impure, contagious, reciprocal violence spreads throughout the community" (Girard 1977: 49). When all violence is condemned, then we are incapable of ritually affirming violence through the surrogate-victim mechanism. The consequence, ironically, is an increase in non-ritualized violence (including vendetta) throughout the society. This is why Girard writes:

> Sacrifice is the boon worthy above all others of being preserved, celebrated and memorialized, reiterated and reenacted in a thousand different forms, for it alone can prevent transcendental violence from turning back into reciprocal violence, the violence that really hurts, setting man against man and threatening the total destruction of the community.
>
> (Girard 1977: 124–125)

Sacrificial rituals are an effective way to prevent sacrificial crises and thus guard societies against excessive violence.

While sacrifice and promiscuity may be stereotypical aspects of festivals, so too is play. Durkheim argues that games originated in a religious context (Durkheim 1995: 385). Games or play also give rise to collective effervescence—the ecstatic bonding of individuals into a collectivity (Durkheim 1995: 385). Play, for Girard, is an expression of the sacred. It is another means by which genuine violence is avoided by virtue of the ritualized nature of the play itself.

> [W]e must subordinate play to religion, and in particular to the sacrificial crisis. Play has a religious origin, to be sure, insofar as it reproduces certain aspects of the sacrificial crisis. The arbitrary nature of the prize makes it clear that the contest

has no other objective than itself, but this contest is regulated in such a manner that, in principle at least, it can never degenerate into a brutal fight to the finish.

(Girard 1977: 154)

The play may be rough and even violent at times. There even is a victim in the form of the loser. But play never gives itself over to unwarranted violence or reciprocal violence. The rules of the ritual prohibit this possibility.

Case Studies

Play, Ritual, and Violence in American Football

American football is an exemplary intersection of religion, play, and violence. Michael Oriard, one of the most insightful scholars writing on the cultural history of American football, recognizes the integral role that violence plays in the sport:

> [Football is] the dramatic confrontation of artistry with violence, both equally necessary. The receiver's balletic moves and catch would not impress us nearly as much if the possibility of annihilation were not real; the violence of the collision would be gratuitous, pointless, if it did not threaten something valuable and important. The violence, in fact, partially creates the artistry: the simple act of catching a thrown ball becomes a marvelous achievement only in defiance of the brutal blow. Football becomes contact ballet.

(Oriard 1993: 1–2)

Violence is central to the beauty and power of the game. American football is ritualized violence—it is composed of prescribed and proscribed acts that serve a collective purpose and provide shared meaning. In this way it is religious in character.

In many locales, particularly university campuses, the ritual of American football is performed in the context of a festival, one characterized by the violation of norms that in turn affirms those norms for more profane times. For example, while many people on game day drink alcoholic beverages (sometimes to great excess) on the grounds of the university, they would be escorted off campus or even arrested if they consumed alcohol in the same place at other times. In this case, the exception (being allowed to drink publicly on campus) affirms the rule (no public consumption of alcohol on campus). The festival context sets the stage for the ritual violence.

Football certainly entails violent confrontations between players, but it is controlled violence nonetheless. Michael Novak argues that the controlled conflict "ventilates" our rage (Novak 1994: 84).

"The human animal suffers enormous daily violence," he adds, echoing both Durkheim and Girard. "Football is an attempt to harness violence, to formalize it, to confine it within certain canonical limits, and then to release it in order to wrest from it a measure of wit, beauty, and redemption" (Novak 1994: 94).

Sacrifice is a necessary element in football. This sacrifice is not only the "surrogate" or loser of the contest, but all the players. As Novak notes:

> Once an athlete accepts the uniform, he is in effect donning priestly vestments. It is the function of priests to offer sacrifices ... Often the sacrifice is literal: smashed knees, torn muscles, injury-abbreviated careers. Always the sacrifice is ritual: the athlete bears the burden of identification. He is no longer living his own life only.
>
> (Novak 1994: 141)

Examples of sacrifices abound. Whether it is broken bones or concussions or even death, American football players sacrifice themselves in the performance of the ritual. Novak concludes "football dramatizes the sacrifice, discipline, and inner rage of collective behavior" (Novak 1994: 207)—sacrifice, discipline, and rage that Durkheim and Girard would find to be fundamentally religious.

Football is a "revelatory liturgy," Novak explains. "It externalizes the warfare in our hearts and offers us a means of knowing ourselves and wresting some grace from our true natures" (Novak 1994: 96). We might not always want to know of our violent and aggressive selves, but at least some cultural creations can turn that violence and aggression into something that has some merit and beauty. American football perhaps is such a thing. It is, as Oriard describes it, "contact ballet."

"Since the earliest times," Michael Mandelbaum writes, "from gladiatorial contests in ancient Rome to public hangings in early modern England to boxing in the nineteenth and twentieth centuries—not to mention Hollywood movies of the twenty-first—staged events with violence at their core have commanded public attention" (Mandelbaum 2004: 176–177). Several questions emerge in our recognition of this historical fact of life. What does it tell us about sport? Is the "staged violence" of sports like American football what gives them their vast appeal? And what is it precisely that the spectator gets from witnessing such a violent spectacle?

Everyone seems to be in agreement that the catharsis theory of sports violence is not sufficient. The catharsis theory suggests that the violence we engage in or watch in sports relieves us of our excessive violent urges and thus allows us to function better psychologically and certainly socially. Robert J. Higgs argues that explanations like the catharsis theory may help to explain the "ubiquity" of sports, but they do not explain "the reverence paid to them" (Higgs 1995: 97). Michael Oriard insists that the catharsis theory may not be wrong, but it at least is "oversimplified" (Oriard 1993: 6). Higgs and Oriard are not social scientists, nor psychologists, but their conclusions are supported by such researchers. Daniel L. Wann and his collaborators note that "there is virtually no empirical evidence validating the existence of catharsis in sport ... The 'blowing off steam' theory of sport spectating may be attractive, but it is quite inaccurate" (Wann 2001: 198). John H. Kerr likewise is suspicious of a catharsis theory of sports violence, insisting that there is little experimental evidence to support it (Kerr 2005: 124).

These perspectives (especially those from Wann *et al.* and Kerr) would seem to contradict Girard and the application of his theory to sport. Girard's work seems to rely upon some notion of a catharsis theory—the sacrificial victim relieving us of the violence that we otherwise would commit against one another. But note that the catharsis theory is not completely and conclusively discredited.

Kerr argues for a more comprehensive psychological understanding of sports violence than simply a catharsis theory. He notes that contemporary life (at least in Europe and the United States) is not very exciting. The range of emotions, especially at the highest or most pleasant end, is fairly narrow (little wonder then that many Western cultures seem fixated on sex, particularly orgasms). Consequently, "people have to actively seek out thrills and vicarious risk-taking through, for example, watching sports" (Kerr 2005: 118). Anyone watching a crowd at a major sporting event can witness the intensity of the emotions that many fans experience. Fans attain high levels of arousal (akin to Durkheim's notion of collective effervescence), and this intense experience is a "pleasant excitement" (Kerr 2005: 98). This experience is particularly prevalent with violent sports like American football and ice hockey. Kerr concludes that "watching violent sports produces increases in levels of arousal, and ... people deliberately watch to achieve elevated arousal" (Kerr 2005: 118). Here then we might have an explanation not only of the psychological appeal of violent sports, but of certain stereotypical religious rituals (e.g. sacrifices) as well.

Is such arousal good or bad for us? The flip-side of the catharsis theory is that participating in or watching violent sports spurs people to act violently in other contexts. This argument is similar to ones made about violence on television or in the movies—that such violence encourages others (especially children) to act violently. Higgs, for example, tries to connect violence in sports with aggression or violence towards women in America (Higgs 1995: 320–322). Along with Michael C. Braswell, they argue that sports initiate a cycle of violence or aggression. "[I]nstead of ventilating aggression," they claim, sports "refuel it so that a loss or setback in sports as in war is a call for stronger retaliation. In the Church of Sports, there is no answer to this that we can see, only rivalry, revenge, and redemption from season to season" (Higgs and Braswell 2004: 107). We then have exactly the kind of violence that Girard claims religion helps to avoid. While such retaliatory violence usually is contained within the context of the rules of the game, there are instances in which the violence of a sport spills into the stands—leading to physical confrontations between players and fans or between rival fans. Kerr's work recounts many of these instances, including some (such as soccer hooliganism in Europe) that led to the deaths of non-participants.

Kerr notes that the research is split on the issue of the connection between violence in various forms of popular culture and among those who participate in or view them. He concludes that the "popular wisdom which suggests media violence and media sports violence has harmful effects on people, especially where those viewers are young children, may not be correct" (Kerr 2005: 130). So if sports violence perhaps does us no harm, does it do any good? The answer, for Kerr, is affirmative. The "pleasant excitement" of violent sports can be an important part of our overall psychological health. He concludes: "[T]here are situations where certain types of aggressive and violent acts are central to people's enjoyment of activities. These activities range from athletic contests to viewing violent sports as a spectator, or watching violent sports movies. Being a part of these activities does no psychological harm to the vast majority of those who participate and may actually benefit their psychological health" (Kerr 2005: 148). The argument that participating in or watching violence produces a psychological good may go a long way to explaining why violence has been such an integral part of our games and sports and religion through the centuries—perhaps redeeming (in some way) Girard's theory as well. The argument, in short, helps explain the pervasiveness of violence in popular culture and why we seem to like it so much (despite our occasional protestations to the contrary).

In addition to the social-psychological function, sports also facilitate "us versus them" thinking. "Our" team is better than "yours." Rivalries run across the athletic landscape—and perhaps none are more heated than those between college football teams and fans in the American South. The South is divided up into "us" and "them," Rebels and Tigers, Gators and Bulldogs.

In a college football game, only one team can win (college football's adoption of an overtime system in 1996 eliminated the possibility of ties). Even more, only one team can earn the honor and adulation that comes with victory. Only one team can have "bragging rights" after the game. In other words, there is a scarcity of goods to go around. This situation undoubtedly contributes to the fervor and even violence of the game. Not surprisingly, violence breaks out occasionally among fans. It is not unusual then to have stories like the one where the University of South Carolina fan shot his friend, a Clemson University fan, when they argued about a $20 bet on the game (the game having been won by South Carolina). One would imagine that it was not so much the sum of money that was in dispute, but what the money signified—victory, honor, superiority, etc. In short, college football in the American South is an exemplary model of how sports reflect a "cosmic war" perspective in which no compromise is possible and it is "winner takes all."

From its sacrifice and play to its "cosmic war" framework, it is little wonder why sports are such an important part of popular culture. The example of football shows how sports not only function religiously, but how violence is part of why that is the case.

Violence in Film (Quentin Tarantino, of Course)

With American football and many other sports, violence is ritualized in ways similar to religion. In both cases, the ritualizing of violence may be a way of coping with the inherent aggression and violence of individuals in society. The contesting of American football games and the violence that ensues also replicates a fundamental religious perspective (the Manichean divide between good and evil, "us and them," the prerequisite for a cosmic war). Another place where we see the ritualizing of violence is in film, and perhaps no contemporary filmmaker is as noted for his treatment of violence as Quentin Tarantino. Joshua Mooney describes Tarantino's early films as "ultra-violent crime stories [in which] almost everyone dies ... And they do not, as the poet said, go gently. Usually they have to be shot. Their blood doesn't spill so much as it gushes, spurts, splatters, soaks and coats. Sometimes it takes the stragglers an excruciatingly long time to die, but in the end, they get there too" (Peary 1998: 70).

Tarantino certainly is not afraid to take on religious themes or ideas in his movies. Take the example of *Pulp Fiction* (1994), a film written and directed by Tarantino. Hit man Jules (played by Samuel L. Jackson) not only quotes scripture before blowing away those who have wronged his boss, but also he claims to have experienced a miracle when he narrowly survives a shooting. In *From Dusk Till Dawn* (1996), written by Tarantino and directed by Richard Rodriguez, two dangerous criminals (played by George Clooney and Tarantino) hijack a family and its mobile home in order to escape into Mexico (where they end up at the infamous club The Titty Twister, fighting off vampires in a gory, graphic battle). The father (played by Harvey Keitel) is a preacher who, after his wife's death, has turned his back on God. Tarantino directed and wrote both *Kill Bill* movies (2003, 2004), starring Uma Thurman and David Carradine. The films are extremely violent and contain extensive martial arts sequences. The plot draws on magical and philosophical elements of Eastern religions (we might assume Buddhism and Taoism in particular).

Though films like *Reservoir Dogs* (Tarantino's first film from 1992) and *Inglourious Basterds* (his most recent from 2009) do not deal substantively with religious themes, they nevertheless include his trademark violence. The failed heist in *Reservoir Dogs* not only has ample gunshot violence, it also has a torture scene in which one of the criminals cuts off the ear of a police officer, prancing around his bound-to-a-chair body to the music of the 1972 pop classic "Stuck in the Middle with You" (originally performed by the band Stealers Wheel). The scene has been described as "perhaps the single most cited moment of violence in all of the 1990s American cinema" (Gronstad 2008: 171). *Inglourious Basterds*, on the other hand, features a renegade American military unit (made up mostly of Jews) that tracks down, kills, and scalps Nazis. It also features a young female survivor of a "Jew hunt" who plots the demise (in her Paris movie theatre nonetheless) of top Nazi brass (including, we find out, Hitler).

Thomas S. Hibbs argues that violence in film is both a symptom and cause of the aesthetization of evil (Hibbs 1999: 66). In other words, evil increasingly is becoming "art" or "cool" and violence is both one of the ways in which it is happening as well as a reflection that it is happening. Hibbs' argument is drawn from Hannah Arendt's notion of the "banality of evil"—the idea that evil that becomes ordinary or normal can no longer be fought against effectively (Arendt 1994: 287–288). For Hibbs, movie violence is part of our cultural drift toward the banality of evil.

Hibbs also claims that violence in film is both a symptom and cause of the pervasive nihilism in our culture. In part, we are becoming incapable of articulating ethical values—and thus increasingly incapable of living moral lives. All values and moral systems are relative. The values inherent in the moral system of an organized crime syndicate can be judged no better or worse than the values inherent in the moral system of the Amish. As he concludes, the "new problem is not that the meaning of evil is elusive, but that it is increasingly difficult for us to distinguish between evil and goodness" (Hibbs 1999: 49).

While Hibbs represents a common concern about the impact of media violence on culture, others have a particular concern with the impact on children. Psychiatrist Eugene V. Beresin cites studies that indicate that a typical American child will have viewed more than 200,000 acts of violence (including 16,000 murders) by the age of 18. Most of the viewing would be on television (the typical American child watches approximately 28 hours of television a week), but certainly film should be included as well as (more recently) video games and online gaming. Beresin notes that while the causes of youth violence are varied, the "research literature is quite compelling that children's exposure to media violence plays an important role in the etiology of violent behavior" (Beresin 2009).

Given the concerns of scholars, parents, and professionals, it is little wonder that Tarantino has been denounced for the violence in his films. Johann Hari credits Tarantino for the realism of the violence in *Reservoir Dogs*, but sees the use of violence in subsequent films to be morally dangerous. "I'm not saying it makes people violent," Hari argues. "But it does leave the viewer just a millimeter more morally corroded. Laughing at simulated torture—and even cheering it on, as we are encouraged to through all of Tarantino's later films—leaves a moral muscle just a tiny bit more atrophied" (Hari 2009). Concerns about the gratuitous or "hollow violence" in Tarantino's *Inglourious Basterds* are also at the core of the negative review of the movie by Lee Siegel (Siegel 2009).

But what the critics miss is that the violence in Tarantino's movies is far from gratuitous or "hollow." Aaron Anderson makes a compelling argument that violence in film, at least the kind of violence that Tarantino uses, is critical for creating meaning and developing the narrative and the characters. He argues that personal action "necessarily involves a wide array of inner thoughts, both conscious and unconscious. Actions that affect other people—as violence does—therefore constitute a type of pragmatic ethics in which inner views about how one actually interacts with the world become outwardly embodied" (Anderson 2004).

One of the central meanings or themes of Tarantino's violence is revenge. In this regard, he certainly is not an unusual case in American popular culture. As William D. Romanowski argues, "Violence has a central place in American mythology as a means of justice and retribution" (Romanowski 2007: 209). Romanowski consequently points us in an important direction. Revenge is never without meaning or a connection with the idea of justice. Thus, violence associated with vengeance or revenge—either in Tarantino films or as religious acts—is far from nihilistic (in other words, arbitrary or without meaning).

The problem, as we have seen with Girard, is that acts of violence (whether committed in the name of justice or not) simply give rise to more acts of violence. The cycle of revenge is never ending.

While Tarantino's films certainly reflect this idea of never ending violence, that is not the message of the films. As Bence Nanay and Ian Schnee claim, "Tarantino's films are concerned with ways to end violence ... the theme of the cycle of violence, and of breaking out of the cycle of violence, is perhaps strongest in *Pulp Fiction*" (Greene and Mohammad 2007: 185). In this regard, many of Tarantino's films can be read effectively through a Girardian lens. His films, like religious, sacrificial acts, seek ways to overcome the never ending cycle of violence.

In *Pulp Fiction*, many of the occasions for violence involve revenge—the administering of punishment or retribution, the meting out of justice. Hit men Jules and Vincent kill several men who betrayed the boss. The boss likewise seeks revenge on a boxer who double-crossed him—failing to throw a fight as agreed. Later in the movie, the boss prepares for revenge on two rednecks who anally raped him. Early in the movie, there also is a conversation between Jules and Vincent in which they consider the moral dimensions of a story they had heard about the boss throwing an associate off a building because the associate had massaged the boss' wife's feet. In short, almost all the violence in the film involves revenge. In all cases, there is an implicit or explicit understanding of justice, and from that understanding of justice violence is demanded (perhaps even morally demanded). Justice is not treated as simply a human construct, but as a given in the universe. In other words, it has a transcendent or religious dimension. While the characters may disagree about what constitutes justice, they are not nihilists. They talk and act as if justice *does* exist.

An important plot development in the movie is the dramatic religious experience of Jules—an experience that leads to a conversion of sorts. Early in the film, Jules recites a passage from the Bible (the claim is that it is Ezekiel 25:17, though only the last two lines are close to the Biblical verse). The passage he quotes is about the punishments that God will administer to evil men, and the shepherding and protection of others that is characteristic of the righteous man.

Given his murderous ways, the vengeful voice of God from this passage fits well with Jules' lifestyle. But after experiencing the "miracle" (Vincent has doubts about this) of having been shot at but having every bullet miss him, Jules identifies more with the first part of the passage—the part about shepherding "the weak through the valley of darkness." Jules realizes perhaps that his lifestyle simply perpetuates the cycle of violence. In the last scene of the film, Jules does not use violence to end violence, he simply walks away. Vincent, as we already have learned from the temporally disjointed nature of *Pulp Fiction*, does not walk away and is killed.

"At the end of the movie," Tarantino reminds us, "for all the talk about the film being violent and this, that and the other, the guy who actually becomes the lead character ... is a killer who has a religious epiphany! And it's played straight. It's not a big joke. That's supposed to be meaningful—and not in a sanctimonious way" (Peary 1998: 147). It is meaningful (whether or not Tarantino meant it this way) because Jules moves beyond the cycle of violence. But the power of that movement comes from the violent context of the film. The violence was needed for the epiphany to have any force.

David Kyle Johnson argues that "for a clear portrayal of revenge as morally justified, one need look no further than *Kill Bill*" (Greene and Mohammad 2007: 59). Uma Thurman plays Beatrix Kiddo, a member of a company of assassins who decides to leave the business and marry a record store owner. Her boss and former lover Bill, played by David Carradine, feels betrayed upon discovering her plans (he initially thought she was dead). He seeks revenge for his hurt feelings, and his band of assassins kills the wedding party at the rehearsal and mercilessly beats Beatrix. Bill then shoots her in the head. Unbeknownst to Bill, however, Beatrix survives the gunshot and after a lengthy coma seeks her revenge on the assassins and finally on Bill.

In the case of *Kill Bill*, the audience most certainly sides with Beatrix in her rampage of vengeance. She has been wronged terribly, and justice demands retribution. In this regard, her violent acts are a way of restoring order out of chaos—a typical function of religious action and central to creation mythologies. Revenge thus becomes a religious exercise. As Beatrix tells us, "When fortune smiles on something as violent and ugly as revenge, it seems proof like no other that not only does God exist, you're doing his will." Revenge then is a moral duty. It is righteous action, for it restores the divine and just order.

Anderson notes that "the film itself is not simply a revenge drama, but also a story of redemption. The only way that Kiddo can deserve a normal life is to pay penance for her own past life. This penance, however, takes the form of more violent actions, involving both Kiddo's ability to inflict harm upon others as well as her ability to endure pain and injury herself" (Anderson 2004). In other words, she must make certain sacrifices (including sacrificing others) in order to re-enter the collectivity.

By the end of the second film, after coolly killing Bill with the Five Point Palm Exploding Heart Technique, Beatrix ends her rampage of revenge and drives off with her daughter. The hope, of course, is that the cycle of revenge is ended. Maybe. In the first film we watch as Beatrix kills Vernita. When confronted by Vernita's young daughter Nikki, Beatrix says "It was not my intention to do this in front of you. For that I'm sorry. But you can take my word for it, your mother had it comin'. When you grow up, if you still feel raw about it, I'll be waiting." Here we see the prospect of the never ending cycle of violence.

In his review of Tarantino's most recent film, *Inglourious Basterds*, Charles Taylor notes that "the director wants us to relish the revenge taken on the Nazis." In the culminating scene of Nazi destruction, "it's the lust for vengeance that powers the film's most delirious and daring passage" (Taylor 2010: 105). As in other Tarantino movies, the dichotomy between good and evil is clear. Nazis, in fact, are a stereotypical symbol for evil incarnate. Their destruction brings justice to an otherwise chaotic and evil situation. The silver screen heroes of *Inglourious Basterds* (much like the football heroes on the gridiron) are warriors in contemporary cosmic wars—warriors who (hopefully?) judge the evildoers, destroy them, and restore order.

So, in Tarantino films we see extensive use of violence—but not violence that is completely disconnected from a conception of justice and righteous order. The violence at least implies a sense of justice, and often the connection is made explicit. While Tarantino's films seem to include a never ending cycle of violence, certain plot developments suggest ways of escaping that cycle (or, at least, the merits of doing so). In these ways, Tarantino's violence serves an ethical function.

Another way to think about the violence in Tarantino movies is related to the idea of sacrifice. As we saw with football, fans vicariously experience the violence of games. This experience is one of sacrificing the victim—the loser, the one being tackled or hit, etc. Such violent sacrifice of the victim compensates for the internal violence we must do to ourselves as members of a society (for example, repressing our instinctual desires). Through Tarantino films, we get to vicariously sacrifice victims—and even victims who really deserve such sacrifice. We particularly relish the destruction of the bad or evil characters, such as those who sought to kill Beatrix Kiddo. In a sense, these characters represent all those who have wronged us as well, and their destruction at least provides some psychological reckoning in the context of the film and perhaps also in our lives. This reaffirmation of order helps to maintain the communal value system—a system that helps to distinguish between right and wrong, good and evil.

We also are drawn to the personal sacrifices that characters make as they pursue their aims through the narrative of the films. Beatrix literally risks life and limb in order to exact her revenge. Similarly, the "basterds" in *Inglourious Basterds* are willing to risk everything in order to destroy the Nazis. As Durkheim notes, such risk-taking and willingness to bear pain raise these characters (and vicariously raise us) above our meager and profane selves (Durkheim 1995: 317–321). And, as Kerr observes, such risk-taking provides audiences with the opportunity to vicariously participate in it and thus to elevate our emotional lives out of the doldrums of contemporary existence (Kerr 2005: 118). In these ways and others, Tarantino films provide psychological benefits akin to those provided in religious settings.

Conclusion

As institutional religions come to have less influence on the majority of people in the West, popular culture comes to be the place where violence is ritualized and controlled. Whether we are watching violence in various sports or actors on television and film, violence continues to be central to our psychic and social lives. It is not gratuitous and barbaric, it is necessary and meaningful—whether that be in a religious or a secular context.

Summary

- Religion is inherently violent.
- The violence in religion serves important social-psychological functions.
- The violence in sports functions in similar ways to the violence in religion.
- The violence in popular media (television, film, etc.) functions in similar ways to the violence in religion.
- Violence in popular culture may serve as a substitute for stereotypically religious violence in an increasingly secular society.

Glossary Terms

Bhagavad Gita—literally "Song of the Lord"; an Indian religious text that is the sixth part of the *Mahabharata*; the text is approximately 2000 years old.

Karma—literally meaning action, it is the Indian law of cause and effect as these pertain to individual behavior and its consequences either in this lifetime or future ones.

Manicheanism—a view attributed to the Manichees (third century) in which the world is divided into the world of light and the world of darkness, good and evil, and history is the working out of the struggle between the two.

Ritual—prescribed actions or behaviors that express communal and/or religious meanings.

Scapegoat—a surrogate victim that bears responsibility for the evil or ills faced by a community.

Totem—a natural object (typically an animal or plant) that represents the community and/or its gods.

Transcendent—Referring to that which is qualitatively different and separate from this world; for example, God is transcendent (other-worldly) even if he/she/it also works in the world.

Points for Discussion

- Are human beings inherently violent?
- Is religion inherently violent?
- Is violence in popular culture a reflection of human violence or does it encourage human violence or both?
- Is violence in sports like ice hockey or football an important reason for why they are so popular?
- Is violence the key to why many films are so popular?

Further Reading

Girard, René (1977). *Violence and the Sacred*, trans. Patrick Gregory, Baltimore, MD: Johns Hopkins University Press.

A classic theoretical work that has influenced numerous scholars in regard to theories of religion, ritual, and violence.

Juergensmeyer, Mark (2003). *Terror in the Mind of God: The Global Rise of Religious Violence*, 3rd edn, Berkeley, CA: University of California Press.

Perhaps the most important and frequently cited book on contemporary religious violence. A standard in the field.

Lincoln, Bruce (2006). *Holy Terrors: Thinking About Religion After September 11*, 2nd edn, Chicago: University of Chicago Press.

A powerful critique of the discourse surrounding 9/11 and how it reflects upon the study of religion.

Schwartz, Regina (1997). *The Curse of Cain: The Violent Legacy of Monotheism*, Chicago: University of Chicago Press.

A powerful genealogy of violence in the Abrahamic traditions.

Selengut, Charles (2008). *Sacred Fury: Understanding Religious Violence*, Lanham, MD: Rowman & Littlefield.

An excellent introduction to various ways of interpreting religious violence, with ample historical examples.

Bibliography

Anderson, Aaron (2004). "Mindful Violence: The Visibility of Power and the Inner Life in *Kill Bill*," *Jump Cut: A Review of Contemporary Media*, no. 47. Online. Available HTTP: www.ejumpcut.org/archive/jc47.2005/KillBill/ (accessed 21 June 2010).

Arendt, Hannah (1994). *Eichmann in Jerusalem: A Report on the Banality of Evil*, New York: Penguin Books.

Aslan, Reza (2009). *How to Win a Cosmic War: God, Globalization, and the End of the War on Terror*, New York: Random House.

Beresin, Eugene V. (2009). "The Impact of Media Violence on Children and Adolescents: Opportunities for Clinical Interventions," American Academy of Child and Adolescent Psychiatry. Online. Available HTTP: www.aacap.org/cs/root/developmentor/the_impact_of_media_violence_on_children_and_adolescents_opportunities_for_clinical_interventions (accessed 13 August 2010).

Durkheim, Emile (1995). *The Elementary Forms of Religious Life*, trans. Karen E. Fields, New York: The Free Press.

Girard, René (1977). *Violence and the Sacred*, trans. Patrick Gregory, Baltimore, MD: Johns Hopkins University Press.

Greene, Richard, and Mohammad, K. Silem (eds) (2007). *Quentin Tarantino and Philosophy: How to Philosophize with a Pair of Pliers and a Blowtorch*, Chicago: Open Court.

Gronstad, Asbjorn (2008). *Transfigurations: Violence, Death, and Masculinity in American Cinema*, Amsterdam: Amsterdam University Press.

Hari, Johann (2009). "The Tragedy of Tarantino: He Has Proved His Critics Right," *The Independent*, London, 26 August. Online. Available HTTP: www.independent. co.uk/opinion/commentators/johann-hari/johann-hari-the-tragedy-of-tarantino-hehas-proved-his-critics-right-1777147.html (accessed 27 July 2010).

Hibbs, Thomas S. (1999). *Shows about Nothing: Nihilism in Popular Culture from The Exorcist to Seinfeld*, Dallas, TX: Spence Publishing Group.

Higgs, Robert J. (1995). *God in the Stadium: Sports & Religion in America*, Lexington, KY: The University Press of Kentucky.

Higgs, Robert J. and Braswell, Michael C. (2004). *An Unholy Alliance: The Sacred and Modern Sports*, Macon, GA: Mercer University Press.

Juergensmeyer, Mark (2003). *Terror in the Mind of God: The Global Rise of Religious Violence*, 3rd edn, Berkeley, CA: University of California Press.

Kerr, John H. (2005). *Rethinking Aggression and Violence in Sport*, New York: Routledge.

Lincoln, Bruce (2006). *Holy Terrors: Thinking About Religion After September 11*, 2nd edn, Chicago: University of Chicago Press.

Mandelbaum, Michael (2004). *The Meaning of Sports: Why Americans Watch Baseball, Football, and Basketball and What They See When They Do*, Cambridge, MA: Perseus Books.

Novak, Michael (1994). *The Joy of Sports: Endzones, Bases, Baskets, Balls, and the Consecration of the American Spirit*, rev. edn, Lanham, MD: Madison Books.

Oriard, Michael (1993). *Reading Football: How the Popular Press Created an American Spectacle*, Chapel Hill, NC: The University of North Carolina Press.

Peary, Gerald (ed.) (1998). *Quentin Tarantino: Interviews*, Jackson, MS: The University Press of Mississippi.

Romanowski, William D. (2007). *Eyes Wide Open: Looking for God in Popular Culture*, rev. and exp. edn, Grand Rapids, MI: Brazos Press.

Schwartz, Regina (1997). *The Curse of Cain: The Violent Legacy of Monotheism*, Chicago: University of Chicago Press.

Selengut, Charles (2008). *Sacred Fury: Understanding Religious Violence*, Lanham, MD: Rowman & Littlefield.

Siegel, Lee (2009). "Tarantino's Hollow Violence," *The Daily Beast*, 24 August. Online. Available HTTP: www.thedailybeast.com/blogs-and-stories/2009-08-24/tarantinos-hollow-violence/# (accessed 21 June 2010).

Taylor, Charles (2010). "Violence as the Best Revenge: Fantasies of Dead Nazis," *Dissent*, Winter (accessed 21 June 2010).

Wann, Daniel L., Melnick, Merrill J., Russell, Gordon W., and Pease, Dale G. (2001). *Sports Fans: The Psychology and Social Impact of Spectators*, New York: Routledge.

Filmography

From Dusk Till Dawn, Richard Rodriguez/Quentin Tarantino, dir. (1996)

Inglourious Basterds, Quentin Tarantino, dir. (2009)

Kill Bill, Quentin Tarantino, dir. (2003)

Kill Bill 2 Quentin Tarantino, dir. (2004)

Pulp Fiction, Quentin Tarantino, dir. (1994)

Reservoir Dogs, Quentin Tarantino, dir. (1992)

PART II
Cults, Sects, and Religious Crimes

Cults

History, Beliefs, Practices

Suzanne Newcombe

History of the Term "Cult"

There is no universally agreed definition of the word "cult"; it is only rarely used as a self-description and does not refer to any particular belief system. Since the 1920s, the word "cult" has most commonly been used to designate a minority religious group whose beliefs and practices an outside observer deems dangerous or strange.

Historically, "cult" was first recorded in English as reverence or homage to a deity or saint, for example, the "cult of Mary" in the Roman Catholic Church. From the nineteenth century, the word "cult" began to be associated with any religion "other" than Christianity. Specifically, it was used to describe the diverse beliefs of tribal peoples worldwide as well as the Druid revival in eighteenth-century Britain. In the 1890s, it was used to refer to the theosophical movement and the Church of Christian Science, among other groups. Overlapping with the original theological use of the word, in contemporary parlance cults are typically believed to have a charismatic leader who may be "worshiped." Also originating from this usage, a "cult" can refer to a group of people with an intense interest in a celebrity or nonmainstream band, game, book, or film.

Sociological theory on "cults" began with the work of Ernst Troeltsch (1931), who observed a growing tendency in German religiosity that emphasized a kind of "radical religious individualism" of personal experience while avoiding affiliation with traditional religious institutions. Expanding his theories, sociologists have debated various definitions of "cult" without any firm consensus on the meaning of the term. In sociological literature, "cult" is typically used as a technical term that must be specifically defined by the author at the outset of the work (e.g., Wallis 1976).

Characteristics of Cults/New Religious Movements

Some organizations have issued checklists with "characteristics" of "destructive cults." From a sociological perspective, many of these lists contain value judgments that are arguably a matter of opinion rather than fact; for example, a cult is a group with a manipulative leader who financially exploits the members. By using this description, any group that tithes could be seen as a cult. Such value-laden definitions tend to deflect attention away from specific aspects of beliefs and practices that may be causing problems for an individual or society.

Because of the difficulty in separating technical definitions from popular assumptions, many scholars have advocated avoiding the term "cult" altogether in favor of "emergent religions" or "new religious movements" (Richardson 1993). These alternative labels draw attention to more factual aspects of the new minority religions most frequently termed "cults," as well as highlight some of the tendencies such groups may display. Academic research has also focused on categorizing and understanding the various positions new minority religions take in relationship to society (e.g., Wilson 1970).

It is very difficult to make any generalizations that would apply to all new religious groups. Most new religious movements have quite small followings of committed members, often numbering in the dozens rather than thousands. These groups include a wide spectrum of beliefs and practices, appeal to different social groups, and have diverse ways of interacting with society. Many might be considered departures from Christian doctrine, while others combine beliefs of various world religions. Some groups that may be labeled "cults" do not consider themselves religious at all, perhaps having a basis in humanistic psychology or meditation. Some recruit primarily by face-to-face contacts, while others have their primary presence on the internet.

Sociologists argue that new religions have characteristics that do make them distinct from more established religious groups, for example, charismatic leaders and first-generation membership (Barker 2004). Those who convert to a movement are likely to have more zealous attachment to their faith than those who adopt the religion of their parents. This can lead to strong distinctions between "us" and "them" (often the "saved" and the "damned"), a theological position that can cause tensions with those outside the movement. An important element of charismatic leadership is the likelihood of rapid change of both doctrine and practice. Additionally, most new religious movements have atypical demographics; they usually appeal to one section of society more than others. But over time, members of the new movements that survive will have children, and the groups' membership usually begins to look more like that of the general population.

"Cults" in the Postwar Period

The relatively rapid social change that characterized the 1960s as an era was also associated with increased interest in new forms of religiosity. Although alternative religions and occult groups have to some extent been present throughout modern history, during the late 1960s and 1970s noticeable numbers of middle-class youths affiliated themselves with groups very different from the faiths of their parents. Sociologists have also described a culture of "seekership" among young people

Study Aid #180   Historical Development of Term "Cult"

The Christian church's worship practices

Any religion other than Christianity

Devotion to a particular celebrity figure—for example, the cult of Mary

Small breakaway religious group showing marked deviance

Highly authoritarian, separatist religious group

interested in exploring such groups (Campbell 1972). Many of the groups causing popular concern were reinterpretations of Christian doctrine, for example the Unification Church (popularly known as Moonies) and the Children of God, while others were affiliated with Indian spiritual leaders, for example the Maharishi Mahesh Yogi's Transcendental Meditation, Prem Rawat's Divine Light Mission, the International Society for Krishna Consciousness (ISKCON/Hare Krishnas), and Bhagwan Shree Rajneesh/Osho. Many of those who converted to these movements found that their relationships with their parents and relatives became strained as a result of their new beliefs and shift in priorities.

Concerns about cults became much more widespread after November 1978, when over nine hundred members of a religious group called the Peoples Temple, largely made up of US citizens, were killed and/or committed suicide in a remote area of Guyana. The scale of this tragedy inspired much more intense concern, particularly in the media, about those who have joined small and unfamiliar religious groups. The involvement of minority religious groups with several other highly publicized tragedies, for example, the release of toxic gas by Aum Shinrikyo on the Tokyo underground in 1995 and the group suicides of the Californian-based Heaven's Gate in 1997, has continued to emphasize the potential danger of some of these small and new minority religions. However, despite such well-publicized tragic cases, the majority of new religious developments are not violent.

Secular Reactions to Postwar "Cults"

Some relatives believe that their loved one may have been forcibly "brainwashed" into adherence to a cult's strange beliefs and practices. The term "brainwashing" originated from Robert Jay Lifton's work, which was based on reports of American prisoners during the Korean War who came to espouse the beliefs of their captors. Thus, those who joined "cults" were believed to have been coerced into membership rather than to have had a legitimate conversion experience. This explanation was also favored by some members who could not explain to themselves their radical changes in belief. However, Eileen Barker's seminal study argued that while social pressure to join a small new religion might be intense, the idea of irresistible and irreversible "brainwashing" could not be justified with evidence in the case of the Unification Church (Moonies). In her study, Barker found a low percentage of those contacted by the church joined, and among those who did join, there was a high turnover rate (Barker 1984).

During the late 1970s and 1980s, some families hired professional "deprogrammers" to forcibly abduct individuals from "cults." Some of those subjected to deprogramming tactics successfully brought charges against the deprogrammers for kidnapping and abduction. Although forcible deprogramming has become less common, some see a role for voluntary "exit counseling" in helping those who leave minority religions to reintegrate into society.

The growth of these new religious organizations inspired a variety of organized responses by worried friends and relatives. One distinct approach has been referred to as the "anticult" movement. Although anticult groups can be quite diverse in their membership, their primary aim is to identify and warn others of the potential harm "destructive cults" can cause to individuals and society. Perhaps the largest organization in this field is the International Cultic Studies Association (ICSA), which developed out of the American Family Federation (1979–2004).

Others have responded by forming research-oriented organizations that focus on clarifying and comparing the beliefs and practices of new and minority religions. For example, Inform was established in 1988 with funding from the United Kingdom Home Office to provide up-to-date, balanced, and reliable information on new and alternative religious movements to the general public.

Partially in response to the anticult activism, other groups have been established to champion the human rights of religious minorities and the right of individuals to have unpopular and nonmainstream religious beliefs. This approach is exemplified by the Ontario Consultants on Religious Tolerance (OCRT).

Conclusion

"Cults" and new religious movements have been appearing throughout history. Yet in the postwar period these groups have been subject to intense scrutiny from both the media and academic researchers. The rapid social changes of the era—increases in wealth, (arguably) decreasing social influence of institutional Christianity in Western countries, and the increasing accessibility of world beliefs and cultures—have all perhaps contributed to a visible public concern about "cults." In conclusion, it is

Study Aid #181 Common Characteristics of Cults	
Small	First-generation membership
Heterodox	Deviant/separatist
Charismatic leadership	

worth reiterating that although "cults" cause widespread anxiety, the majority of new religious groups do not have a history of violence and attract relatively little attention within their wider societies. As of early 2009, there were over thirteen hundred active new religious movements in Inform's files.

Further Reading

Eileen Barker. *The Making of a Moonie: Choice or Brainwashing?* Blackwell, 1984.

———. "What Are We Studying? A Sociological Case for Keeping the 'Nova.'" *Nova Religio* 8, no. 1 (2004): 88–102.

C. Campbell. "The Cult, the Cultic Milieu and Secularization." In *A Sociological Yearbook of Religion in Britain 5.* SCM, 1972.

J. T. Richardson. "Definitions of Cult." *Review of Religious Research* 34, no. 4 (1993): 348–56.

E. Troeltsch. *The Social Teaching of the Christian Churches.* Allen & Unwin, 1931.

R. Wallis. *The Road to Total Freedom: A Sociological Analysis of Scientology.* Heinemann, 1976.

B. Wilson. *Religious Sects: A Sociological Study.* McGraw Hill, 1970.

Cults

Sarah Sifers, Julene Nolan, and Daniel Houlihan

....

A t the young age of 15, Sean Sellers developed a fascination with satanic worship. Having at least a tacit grasp of Anton LaVey's philosophy as presented in the *Satanic Bible* (1969), Sellers developed his own interpretations, incorporated these into his desire to earn respect within the small cult group "the Elimination," and determined points could be earned by implementing an inversion of the Ten Commandments (Trostle & Green, 1996). On September 8, 1985, 16-year-old Sean Sellers shot and killed Robert Bower, a convenience store clerk who may have refused to sell Sellers' friend beer. Several months later Sellers murdered his mother and stepfather. In helping to construct his defense in a capital murder case, Sellers claimed he murdered to be in compliance with and gain respect within his cult (Thornton, 1999). Geraldo Rivera used the exceptionally well-spoken Sean Sellers as a cornerstone of his 1988 documentary *Devil Worship: Exposing Satan's Underground.*

Although Bard (1989) notes the existence of cults since the time of the ancient Romans (753 BC), the 1969 publication of LaVey's book (coupled with disenchantment with an unpopular war in Vietnam) and the occurrence of widely publicized high-profile cases of cult activity—the Jonestown mass suicide of 1978 and the 1989 Mexico cult murders—would place the issue of cults in the public focus. Geraldo Rivera's popular documentary would give adolescent cult members a face: Sean Sellers.

It could best be said that interest in cults has been inconsistent over the years and has waxed and waned. Rudin (1990) defines **cults** as small groups or ideological movements with an excessive dedication to some person, thing, or ideology. Cults often engage in deceptive practices and discourage questioning of the group's teachings. Cults engage in manipulative practices to retain members, including using guilt, making life choices for members, isolating members, keeping the inner workings of the group secret, and fostering excessive dependence. Cults focus on the survival of the group and benefit of the leader(s), including exploiting members. Following a spurt of interest in the late 1960s subsequent to the publication of LaVey's *Satanic Bible* in 1969, interest in cults seemed to peek in the 1980s. However, membership in cults is a subject that has lacked clarity and cults persist in significant numbers, although the overwhelming majority are not satanic and not as sensationalized as LaVey's.

LaVey's tome advocating rebellion against authority and embracing extreme independence reached a willing audience disillusioned with the ruthless violence associated with the Vietnam

War (Ellwood, 1997). As noted in Singer (1995), when elements of a social milieu unravel due to change that is sometimes forced or at other times welcomed, cults can emerge from the subsequent discontent. Unpopular wars are fertile ground for the emergence of cults (Ellwood, 1997).

Prevalence of Cults

In stating that cult involvement fell short of epidemic levels, Bard (1989) noted that cult activity had risen to higher levels than in the past. In 1998, Schadt suggested that organized cults numbered between 3,000 and 5,000 in the United States. These cults were believed to impact approximately 20 million people (Singer, 1995). Growth in the use of the Internet also appears to have concomitantly led to the establishment of thousands of cult websites. Schadt (1998) estimated the number of cult-oriented websites to be 10,000 and growing.

Types of Cults

Changing times bring changes in types of cults, as well as changes in those who might be attracted to them. Political cults have generally appeared at times of general unrest within the government. Many emerged in the 1960s as a result of the unpopularity of the war in Vietnam. The LaRouche movement had as its leader Lyndon LaRouche, a perpetual presidential candidate who used the movement as a public platform for his beliefs. Other movements were generally Trotskyist in nature and viewed as embracing communist ideals. These groups did not significantly reach youth (Tourish & Wohiforth, 2014). Other cult movements have been more focused on self-help or counseling. These are often quasi-religious in their presentation and ideology, but generally have financial gain for the cult originators as their ultimate goal. Again, these cults do not target youth in so much as vulnerable adults.

The cults that generally involve youth are those that are religious in primary function. Children and adolescents are sometimes drawn into cults because of the involvement of their parents. This is noted in the radical sects of Warren Jeffs, David Koresh's Branch Davidians, and the People's Temple of the Reverend Jim Jones. However, many youth go through a period of doubt or rebellion in their teens, and it is at this time that they may be singularly vulnerable to recruitment. Likewise, some children and adolescents have backgrounds of physical and/or sexual abuse that lead them to try to escape their home environments. These kids are particularly vulnerable to cult recruitment and are often targeted by these groups. Such was the case with the Manson family. Charles Manson was very adept at identifying these types of vulnerabilities within runaway or throwaway teens, and these became his recruits and subsequent followers (Guinn, 2014).

As noted by Marcia Rudin (1990), many cults share a similar make up and structure. Cults have charismatic leaders, such as Charles Manson, David Koresh, or Lyndon LaRouche. Cults play off peoples' fears and use fear mixed with deception in the process of recruitment. Cults rob members of their wealth, their relationships with family members and the outside world, and their ability to make autonomous, independent decisions. Lastly, cults claim to have access to universal truths and knowledge that transcend laws or society and necessitate separation of the cults from others. This can be seen clearly in the case of the Reverend Jim Jones and his People's Temple. Jones' paranoia led him to greater and more extreme efforts to avoid society, finally moving his most ardent followers to Guyana. On November 18, 1978, following the murders of Congressman Leo Ryan and members of his entourage at an airstrip near the cult headquarters, Jim Jones and over 900 of his followers committed suicide in an act that stunned the world and created a public dialogue on the existence and the dangers of cults (Moore, 1985).

Cults often use thought reform to control or persuade. Examples of thought reform techniques often used by cults include the following. Sacred science involves circular or confusing logic that explains "everything" and anyone who questions it obviously does not understand it, rather than the logic being faulty. Emphasis of doctrine over person suggests that doubt in doctrine is a sign of personal weakness. Demand for purity results in unrealistic demands and failure to meet these unreasonable demands result in shaming. Dispensing of existences indicates that non-believers are degenerates that deserve maltreatment or even death. Milieu control is a technique of controlling access to information and communication within and outside of the group. Loading language is a way of using language to minimize complexity of thought and discount objections. Mystical manipulation is used to manipulate the person through inducing exhaustion, spying to prove omniscience, or events planned to convince individuals of the powers of the leader of the cult or the tenants of the cult. Cult of confession involves group confession to create a bond that is difficult to break and dangling absolution that entices ongoing membership (Lifton, 1991).

Teenage Vulnerabilities

Phillip Zimbardo (1997) has noted that most people do not join cults in an attempt to fill voids within themselves. Zimbardo suggests that characteristics of the cult are secondary to the needs of the individual. Many who join have a history of alienation and low self-esteem (Hunter, 1998; Levine, 1984), abuse, neglect, and isolation (Hare, 1986). Many have poor interpersonal skills and lack empathy and understanding of how others feel (Hare, 1986). Deutsch and Miller (1983) have pointed to a tendency of female members to be idealists with a pattern of poor or distorted heterosexual relationships. Hunter (1998) has also pointed to a history of weak cultural and religious ties, as well as weak ties to their community. An irony noted by Hunter (1998) in the cult lifestyle is that it often leads to further estrangement from family and community as well as loss of individuality, despite these issues being what lead teens to the cults in the first place.

Ellwood (1997) has also noted patterns of mental illness, the use of hallucinogenic drugs, and a fascination with the paranormal and otherworldly associations as being behind the choices of some youth to join cults. Narcissism is also a factor, but is more relevant with leadership (Miller, Veltkamp, Kraus, Lane, & Heister, 1999). Narcissism is evident in the personalities of Charles Manson, David Koresh, and Jim Jones. It is also evident in the writing of Sean Sellers.

Nearly all high schools have some teens whose personalities, characteristics, or family backgrounds make them susceptible to cults. Because cults by description have to involve multiple people, Levine (1984) points to proximity as being an essential feature of cult involvement. Rudin (1990) has suggested that schools should be the first line of prevention for cults and that school staff should be educated in recognizing the signs of cult involvement and in having referral protocol in place, even if cults do not appear an imminent problem. Most young people who join cults have been actively seeking a group to meet their needs (Melton, 2013). Cults also can be viewed as exotic and provide a sense of feeling part of an elite group, which appeal to adolescents' desires for novelty, membership, and egocentric self-worth.

Indicators of Cult Involvement

Bard has suggested that those working with teens in schools and other settings be aware that the signs of cult activity might be subtle and transitory, and that outside professionals should be sought in cases of suspicion (Bard, 1989). Behaviors commonly seen in cult members include: submission to the cult leader(s), dissociative states, changes in behavior and appearance consistent with cult membership, breaking off associations with people outside of the cult in favor of those in the cult, and spending excessive time with the cult or in cult-related activities (Melton, 2013).

Religious Development

As noted by Bell (2009), personal identity can be seen to form along a continuum from lower levels of social acceptance to higher levels. Likewise, religious identities form in much the same fashion, from periods of passive acceptance to periods marked by significant doubt. In 1981, James Fowler proposed his stages in the development of faith, working from a platform advanced from the developmental theories of Piaget and Erikson [...]. Fowler presented seven stages representing the normal development of faith in individuals.

Stage 0 (age 0–2), which Fowler called primal/undifferentiated faith, corresponds closely with Erikson's first stage in that the focus is on trust and safety as well as learning self–other dichotomy. This forms basis of later faith. Stage 1 (3–7) is marked by intuitive/projective faith, which is learned through empathy-building experiences and stories with religious meanings. Beliefs often focus on a magical, higher power typically patterned after a parent. Stage 2 Fowler labeled mythical/literal faith, which covers the grade school years. Much in the fashion Piaget might have predicted, this stage is a time where religious stories and metaphors are interpreted in a rigid, concrete fashion. The children understand religion as being rule-governed and consequences both good and bad are associated with it. Stage 3 (age 12–adult), which Fowler labeled synthetic/conventional faith, is the most relevant to adolescence. Fowler notes that most adolescents conform to teaching at this stage, but many begin to entertain doubts related to perceived inconsistencies or misapplication of teachings or theory. It is at this stage that a personal relationship with a god is developed. Stage 4, which may occur in middle adulthood (if at all), is marked by individuative/reflective faith, and is a time marked by struggle in establishing personal beliefs, coping with the demands of faith, and critically examining one's belief and religious membership. This is a time where people become aware that many faiths claim to be the "true" faith, and their ability to think abstractly leads them to ponder the implications of that stance. The search for truth at this stage makes some vulnerable to the lure of cults. Stage 5, conjunctive faith, is where a person gains an acceptance of faith based on an understanding of strengths and weaknesses, followed by deciding to focus on strengths and tolerate weaknesses. During this stage people frequently move beyond reliance on symbols, and reconcile inconsistencies and human failings within religion. In Fowler's last stage (stage 6), universalizing faith happens as an individual ages and begins to believe in universal aspects of faith, acceptance of people as generally good and worthy of love and respect. This stage is characterized by self-forgetting, astonishing acceptance, and devotion to one's faith.

An alternative model based on psychoanalytic theories was developed by Genia (1990). In early childhood youth are in the egocentric stages where god is viewed as an extension of self and fluctuates based on the child's mental state. This stage is characterized by magical thinking. In middle childhood, the dogmatic stage involves an emphasis on rules and authority. God is viewed as a "pinch-hitter" to be relied upon when life gets difficult. In adolescence, the transitional stage is characterized by questioning, doubt, and trying on faiths. It is this phase of seeking and questioning that can open adolescents to cults. During the reconstructed–internalized stage in adulthood, faith provides structure and meaning for life, but thinking still tends to be dichotomous (black and white). Only some people ever reach the transcendent phase, which is open-minded and growth-oriented and involves a genuine and personalized faith.

Religion and the Formation of Cults

A Google search suggests that religious cults far outnumber any other type of cult. The most recognizable and prolific cults would fall under this heading. Part of the attraction of cults is their ability to fill a void or a need in individuals who are unfulfilled (Zimbardo, 1997). Religious cults aim directly at these vulnerabilities and their sales pitch usually comes from a highly charismatic individual. Examples of this type readily come to mind. For example, Warren Jeffs was the charismatic leader of a fundamentalist sect of the Church of Jesus Christ of Latter-Day Saints. It was found that Jeffs sexually abused young children, forced the wives of other members to be with him, and ruled the sect in a restrictive, authoritarian manner that abused the rights of most members. When he was arrested, what surprised authorities most was the blind and unwavering support most of his followers had for him (Singular, 2008).

The atypical appearance of the swoosh-shaped comet Hale-Bopp in the skies during March 1997 led to the high-profile mass suicide of 39 of the members of the religious cult Heaven's Gate. Charismatic leader Marshall Applewhite convinced members that the way to flee a faltering and doomed Earth was to ride a spacecraft that was following Hale-Bopp. With $5.75 in their pockets, which Applewhite claimed was the fee for space travel, the members consumed sedatives and suffocated themselves to follow their leader on the interplanetary journey (Ramsland, 2015).

The media coverage was intense in the standoff between the Branch Davidians, a breakaway sect of Seventh-Day Adventists, and the federal government. Again, the Davidians had a charismatic leader, David Koresh. Many in the cult were children and adolescents, many of whom Koresh sexually abused. On April 19, 1993, during a shootout with the Bureau of Alcohol, Tobacco, and Firearms, a fire broke out in the Mount Carmel Center, ending 51 days of standoff and leading to the deaths of 76 cult members, including Koresh and 17 children and adolescents (Linedecker, 1993).

Psychological Dimensions

Developing an Identity

Bell (2009) has conceptualized two modern challenges to **identity formation**: an emerging global culture that has challenged traditional patterns of identity formation, and rapidly advancing technology that provides a platform for the exchange of extreme ideas, as well as a platform to challenge the beliefs of others. The process of growing up and forming an identity might have been routine and mundane just a few years ago, but can now appear as a myriad of potential choices.

In articulating and crafting his theories of human development [...], Erikson tried to reconcile the turmoil and confusion of adolescence with the typical pathway to young adulthood (Erikson, 1968). Erikson's platform for this crisis and resolution was stage five of his stages of human development: **identity versus role confusion**. Olsson (1983) suggested that adolescents vulnerable to cults often suffer from role confusion.

Erikson suggested that this stage would be marked by rebellion, where the goals and objectives of parents would clash with those of the maturing adolescent (Erikson, 1974). For Erikson, childhood was a time for development, whereas adolescence was a time for **dissonance**. Van Gennep (1908) would explain this in his book *Les Rites de Passaege*. The **rites of passage** can be expressed in various ways, and in extreme cases (e.g., Sean Sellers) can lead to immersion into cults as the ultimate expression of rebellion from parents.

James Marcia (1996ref) would propose four identity statuses in attempting to establish a process where adolescent identity is lost or achieved. An adolescent in **identity diffusion** does not have a comfortable identity nor does he or she have well-defined interests, hobbies, ideals, career objectives, or affiliations (i.e., groups, clubs, teams, or cliques). These individuals are not seeking to develop an identity and as such are not typically looking to join a cult or other organization. Marcia's second identity status is **identity foreclosure**. Lacking his or her own initiative, the adolescent chooses the easiest path to identity, which is to follow the values of the parents or the cultural community. For example, a teen whose parents are members of a cult might default to that status also, even without the fundamental knowledge this stance might require. The third status, according to Marcia, is **identity moratorium**. Moratorium is marked by a search for one's true self, or what Erikson might have called a **crisis of identity**. To the confused youth, the search can lead many directions: a series of odd jobs, college, the military, or perhaps a cult. The search for one's self or identity is complex and confusing, but if the many questions of youth are comfortably answered, this is what Marcia termed **identity achievement**. When one has solved his or her confusion, answered pressing questions, and adopted a comfortable set of ideals and values, they have reached identity achievement. Although there is no way to be certain, there is some indication in his book, *Web of Darkness* (1990), that Sean Sellers might have achieved some level of identity achievement while in prison. However, it is at least theoretically possible to have identity achievement while still involved in a cult.

Social Dimensions

Researchers such as Singer (1979) have suggested that a sense of personal loss and interpersonal loss can directly influence the decision to join a cult. Others have suggested that joining is a search for community and belonging that is at times in short supply because of the demise of the family (Anthony & Robbins, 1980). If we look at Bronfenbrenner's bioecological system theory, these **socio-historical factors** mark the chronosystem and impact choices that are made in an attempt to return to a comfortable state (Bronfenbrenner, 1979). Schwartz and Kaslow (1979) suggested that children and adolescents joining cults often come from families going through transition (e.g., divorce) or who had poorly defined father roles. Subsequently, the choice to join a cult might signal an effort to reunite with a father figure.

Families that are at risk are those where children have not been allowed a level of independence significant enough for them to develop a proper sense of self-confidence. They also feel alienated within the family (i.e., black sheep) and search out situations that relieve this sense of detachment (Galanter, 1982; Levine & Salter, 1976). These are factors rooted in what Bronfenbrenner (1979) called the micro-system, and the decision to join a cult represents a search for community and belonging, which are in short supply in the deteriorating family.

Remember it was LaVey (1969) who suggested extreme independence. Teens and young adults choosing to try life in a cult are searching for a sense of autonomy or a greater sense of self. Cults often are led by charismatic and seemingly omnipotent leaders (e.g., David Koresh or Jim Jones). As is the case with some religions, leaders like Marshall Applewhite claim to have special knowledge and a unique pathway to some seemingly positive end point (e.g., Heaven's Gait). Cults restrict socialization by dominating free time and resources, and by actively discouraging free thinking and independent decision making. Within a cult, the worst thing one can do is question authority and its directives, and these behaviors are harshly prohibited. For the cult member, the dangers of being noncompliant or an agitator within the cult are always being weighed against the meager existence they had prior to joining. This pressure makes it extremely hard to leave a cult on one's own volition.

Interventions

Two general approaches to manage the dangers of child and adolescent cult involvement emerge in the literature. Miller and colleagues (1999) strongly promote the merits of prevention and early detection. Parents and schools must monitor children's access to cults or materials that might promote cult membership. It is also helpful to try to identify families where neglect might be occurring and intervene in an effort to get those families to function better. In particular, it is important to remedy situations where there is abuse as soon as possible. It is also important to monitor children and teens in families that are undergoing significant stress (e.g., parents going to prison, losing jobs, divorce). These are all antecedent approaches to try to stop cult involvement from happening. Hunter (1998) has noted that school districts and local organizations might be of particular help in monitoring for signs of concern (e.g., sudden decline in grades, withdrawal from friends, changes in dress, or incorporation of cult themes into writing or artwork).

It is sometimes hard to remove someone from a cult. Cults are skilled at isolating themselves and indoctrinating a fear or paranoia of family members or outside agencies. A detailed explanation of therapy to aid people struggling with leaving cults goes beyond the scope of this chapter. Suffice it to say that people thoroughly indoctrinated into cults are hard to persuade otherwise. One thing that professionals treating members who have left have to be mindful of is that they do not just have to deal with the emotional aftermath of the cult, they also have to address the problems associated with why the individual joined in the first place. This means a comprehensive and multisystem approach must be undertaken, and if the cult member resists, this presents a significant challenge.

Critical Thinking Question

In reviewing identity development and religious development in the chapter, you will note that in the stages of each there is one point at which adolescents appear most vulnerable to the enticement of cults. If you were the administrator of a high school, what steps could you take that would make these transitional periods for your students less uncertain, and why would you choose them?

Key Terms

Crisis of identity—A period of identity development where a teen has to choose between acceptable alternatives in life

Cults—Small groups or ideological movements with an excessive dedication to some person, movement, or ideology

Dissonance—Stress resulting from a clash of viewpoints or personal styles

Identity achievement—When the adolescent has solved his or her confusion and has adopted a set of ideals and values that he or she is comfortable with

Identity diffusion—Marcia's term for the state adolescents are in when they have not yet made a commitment in life or navigated any crisis

Identity foreclosure—Marica's term for the state adolescents are in when they have made a commitment (most likely following parents), but have not experienced a crisis

Identity formation—A time in youth growth critical for the developing characteristics that will be key to the personality

Identity moratorium—The period of uncertainty and search for the true self that adolescents are in when they are in a crisis. This is a period of vulnerability for cult involvement.

Identity versus role confusion—The fifth stage in Erikson's developmental stages. This is the stage where individuals search for meaning in their lives that corresponds to who they are and who they wish to become.

Rites of passage—Rituals or activities that mark the transition along the continuum from birth to adulthood, of movement from one stage to another

Sociohistorical factors—A combination of influences from one's social and historical background

Additional Resources

Rudin, M. R. What Parents Need to Know about Cults, F.A.C.T.Net http://factnet.org/what-parents-need-know-about-cults

Dakss, B./CBS (2005). Spotting Teens Who Are into Cults http://www.cbsnews.com/news/spotting-teens-who-are-into-cults/

References

Bard, E. M. (1989). Satanic cult indicators for the psychologist. *NASP Communique, 18*(2), 10.

Bell, D. M. (2009). *Religious identity: Conceptualization and measurement of the religious self* (Doctoral dissertation). Emory University, Atlanta, GA.

Bronfenbrenner, U. (1979). *The Ecology of Human Development: Experiments by Nature and Design.* Cambridge, MA: Harvard University Press.

Deutsch, A., & Miller, M. J. (1983). A clinical study of four Unification Church members. *American Journal of Psychiatry, 140*, 767–770.

Ellwood, A. L. (1997). Assessment of adolescents in cults. In L. K. Hamberger (Ed.), *Violence issues for healthcare educators and providers* (pp. 223–242). New York, NY: Haworth Press.

Erikson, E. H. (1968). *Identity: Youth and crisis.* New York, NY: Norton.

Erikson, E. H. (1974). *Dimensions of a new identity.* New York, NY: Norton.

Fowler, J. (1981). *Stages of faith.* New York, NY: Harper Collins.

Galanter, M. (1982). Charismatic sects and psychiatry: An overview. *American Journal of Psychiatry, 139*, 1539–1548.

Genia, V. (1990). Religious development: A synthesis and reformulation. *Journal of Religion and Health, 29*, 85–99.

Guinn, J. (2014). *Manson: The life and times of Charles Manson.* New York, NY: Simon & Schuster.

Hare, R. D. (1986). Twenty years of experience with the Cleckley psychopath. In W. H. Reid, D. Dorr, J. I. Walker, & J. W. Bonner III (Eds.), *Unmasking the psychopath* (pp. 3–27). New York, NY: Norton.

Hunter, E. (1998). Adolescent attraction to cults. *Adolescence, 33*, 18–23.

LaVey, A. S. (1969). *The Satanic bible.* New York, NY: Avon Books.

Levine, S. (1984). *Radical departures: Desperate detours to growing up.* New York, NY: Harcourt, Brace, & Javanovich.

Levine, S. V., & Salter, N. E. (1976). Youth and contemporary religious movements: Psychosocial findings. *Canadian Psychiatric Association Journal, 21*, 411–420.

Lifton, R. J. (1991). Cult formation. *Harvard Mental Health Letter, 7*, 1–4.

Linedecker, C. L. (1993). *Massacre at Waco, Texas.* New York, NY: St. Martin's Press—Macmillan.

Marcia, J. E. (1966). Developmental and validation of ego-identity status. *Journal of Personality and Social Psychology, 3*, 551–558.

Melton, J. G. (2013). *Encyclopedic handbook of cults in America* (revised and updated edition). New York, NY: Routledge.

Miller, T. W., Veltkamp, L. J., Kraus, R. F., Lane, T., & Heister, T. (1999). An adolescent vampire cult in rural America: Clinical issues and case study. *Child Psychiatry and Human Development, 29*, 209–219.

Moore, R. (1985). *A sympathetic history of Jonestown.* Lewiston, NY: Edwin Mellen Press.

Olsson, P. (1983). Adolescent involvement with the supernatural and cults. In D. Halperin (Ed.), *Psychodynamic perspectives in religion, sect and cult* (pp. 235–252). Oxford, UK: Butterworth-Heinemann.

Ramsland, K., & Kuter, R. (2008). *Multiple personalities: Crime and defense.* Retrieved from www.crimelibrary.com/criminal_mind/psychology/multiples/6.html

Ramsland, K. (2015). The Heaven's Gate Cult: The Real End. *Crime Library.* Archived from the original on February 10, 2015.

Rudin, M. R. (1990). Cults and Satanism: Threats to teens. *National Association of Secondary School Principals Bulletin, 74*, 46–52.

Schadt, A. L. (1998). Cults, youth, and counselors: An overview. *The Journal for the Professional Counselor*, *13*, 31–39.

Schwartz, L. L., & Kaslow, E. (1979). Religious cults, the individual and the family. *Journal of Marital and Family Therapy*, *13*, 80–83.

Sellers, S. (1990). *Web of Darkness*. Tulsa, OK: Victory House.

Singer, M. (September, 1979). Coming out of cults. *Psychology Today*, 72–82.

Singer, M. T. (1995). *Cults in our midst: The hidden menace in our everyday lives*. San Francisco, CA: Jossey-Bass Publishers.

Singular, S. (2008). *When men become gods*. New York, NY: St. Martin's Press.

The Geraldo Rivera Show. (1988, October 22). *Devil Worship: Exposing Satan's Underground*.

Thornton, A. (1999, January 22). Condemned killer's mental diagnosis draws skeptics. *The Daily Oklahoman*.

Tourish, D., & Wohiforth, T. (2014). *On the edge: Political cults right and left*. Abingdon, UK: Routledge.

Trostle, L. C., & Green, M. S. (1996). The devil made me do it: Adolescent attraction to Satanism. *In Society: An Alaskan perspective*. Dubuque, IA: Kendall/Hunt Publishing.

Van Gennep, A. (1908/1960). *The rites of passage*. Chicago, IL: University of Chicago Press.

Zimbardo, P. (1997). What messages are behind today's cults? *American Psychological Association Monitor*, *28*, 14.

Religion or Cult?

Phil Zuckerman

....

Whenever I teach my sociology of religion class, one of my assignments is to have students go out into the "real world" and participate in, carefully observe, and then write a report about a religious service not of their own tradition. For some students, especially those who have never attended a religious gathering before, it can be a terrifying experience. They fear that they will stick out or be stared at or somehow be awkwardly ostracized as an unwelcome outsider, an obvious nonbeliever, or worse yet—an interloping spy from a sociology class! Usually, nothing happens to my fearful students other than that they end up meeting very friendly people or hearing beautiful music or tasting bland wafers or listening to provocative sermons or overhearing typical daily-life chitchat, and ultimately learning a bit about how contemporary Americans worship.

Sally and Ted were both in my class a couple of years ago. They each went out on their own to observe a church service of a religious denomination that they had had no previous connection with. And they were both exasperated by what they experienced.

Sally came to my office one Monday morning, wanting desperately to discuss her experience. She told me the following:[1] "Oh, my goodness, Professor Zuckerman. My observation experience was freaky! What a weird and strange religion! I went to their house of worship and was there for the whole service and all I can say is that it was really disturbing. Everyone felt like they were all mindless zombies! People just stood up and down on cue like robots, mindlessly repeating words over and over again in unison. There was no joy on anyone's face. They were all so stiff and deadpan. And the leader would say these weird, monotone words and then everyone would all just repeat things back to him in unison and without any feeling. Like they were brainwashed. No one seemed alive. They all felt totally programmed. It was like they were just doing everything out of some sort of memorized repetition. It was really, really weird. I swear, *it felt like a cult!*"

Sally was describing a Catholic mass at a local Catholic church in town. Sally had grown up in an evangelical-charismatic, nondenominational Protestant congregation and, to her, this traditional Catholic style of worship was cultlike.

But wait—here's what Ted had to tell me about his experience only a few days later:[2]

Phil Zuckerman, "Religion or Cult?" *Invitation to the Sociology of Religion*, pp. 61-73, 131-149. Copyright © 2003 by Taylor & Francis Group. Reprinted with permission.

"Professor Zuckerman—my observation experience was totally bizarre! It really freaked me out! I went to the building and was there for several hours. Everything was so chaotic. People were literally screaming and singing out and shouting all over the place almost the entire time. It felt like spiritual mayhem. The preacher was sweating and prancing about the stage for an hour, yelling and howling, while people shouted randomly back at him the whole time. Lots of people had their arms over their heads during the service, with their hands open like they were feeling warm light on their palms or something. When they sang they would hold their hands high and sway them back and forth—like at a rock concert. Many of them would sing with their eyes closed and with this weird smile—it felt like a Grateful Dead show or something. And then at one point some people started mumbling in this strange way—making weird, incomprehensible sounds like they were in a trance or something. One woman behind me fell down mumbling with her eyes rolling back—I thought she was having an epileptic seizure or something! But people just sort of acted like it was no big deal. There was a lot of energy, but it felt scary. People just seemed like they were on drugs or under a spell. I swear, *it felt like a cult!*"

Ted was describing an evangelical-charismatic, nondenominational Protestant service at a local church in town. Ted had grown up Catholic and, to him, this exuberant style of worship was cultlike.

The point of all this should be obvious: *one person's religion is another person's cult.* And that is exactly what I say whenever I am at a party, standing by the chips and guacamole, sipping my beverage, talking to somebody about what I do. The conversation usually runs as follows:

New acquaintance says: "So my company ... *blah, blah, blah* ... and what do you do?"

"I teach at a small liberal arts college ... *blah, blah, blah* ... so, yeah, I'm a sociologist of religion."

"Oh, really? That's fascinating. Say, what do you think of those Zen meditation people—they're a cult, right?" *Note:* for "Zen meditation people" one could easily insert just about any religion. I've heard Catholics, Hasidic Jews, Scientologists, Mormons, Baptists, Muslims, Sikhs, Buddhists, Jehovah's Witnesses, Baha'is, Seventh-Day Adventists, and a whole slew of other religious organizations referred to as "cults" by various people in the course of various similar conversations. And in most instances, what people seem to be wanting me to say is, "Oh sure, they are definitely a cult, and they are really weird. Take it from me, I'm a scholar, an expert. You don't want your son/daughter/boyfriend/mother-in-law associating with them!"

Instead, much to the disappointment of my new acquaintance, I shrug my shoulders and say that I don't really use the word "cult"—that is has very little meaning for me as a sociologist of religion and that, well, *one person's religion is another person's cult.* At that point, the topic of conversation either switches to the weather, or my new acquaintance starts in on me about cults: "How can you say there are no such things as cults? Surely cults are not the same thing as *real* religions!"

What is so fascinating to me is that, at root, the whole issue concerning whether this or that group is a "cult" or a "religion" is an excellent example of the social construction of religious legitimacy versus religious illegitimacy.

The first question, of course, is: What does the term "cult" actually mean? What makes one group a religion and another group a cult? What do these commonly thrown around terms such as "cult," "sect," "denomination," "religion" actually signify? Unfortunately, the disappointing fact is that these terms are not empirically derived descriptions of static phenomena. Rather, they are malleable, contested, and ever-changing social constructs. Don't misunderstand me: there is a long, rich, and respectable history in the sociology of religion of defining and substantiating these terms in a deliberate, scholarly manner (Troeltsch 1931; Johnson 1963, 1971; Swatos 1981; Bainbridge 1997; Stark and Bainbridge 1985; Wilson 1993; Zablocki and Robbins 2001). But the definitions that scholars concoct, while intelligent, sound, and theoretically useful, are not the definitions that most people are familiar with (Richardson 1993b; Richardson and van Driel 1997). For most people, the term "cult" is essentially a pejorative label used to deprecate or delegitimize a given group (Bromley and Hadden 1993, 6). The term "religion," on the other hand, is basically a label designating acceptance and respect, or at least denoting legitimacy. And depending on whether the one doing the describing wants to put down and insult a group or respect and support a group, they'll use whichever word suits their given ideological, political, or theological purposes. Thus, regardless of what we academics may declare in our journal articles and conference presentations, my general sense is that for most contemporary Americans, these terms mean the following:

- A *cult* is a small religious group that is bizarre at best, deadly at worst. Cults are something to be suspicious of. They are dangerous and certainly not "legitimate" religious organizations.
- A *sect* resembles a cult—small and kind of weird, different, perhaps troublesome—but is not as bad, bizarre, or dangerous. Sects may or may not be "legitimate" religious groups; their status is somewhat borderline.
- A *denomination* is just a subsection of a larger religion, and is generally considered a legitimate religious body.
- A *religion* is a large religious group that is unquestionably legitimate.

Again, these are *not* the definitions that professional scholars of religion subscribe to. They are rather definitions which merely reflect my personal sense of what people out in the world think of and say when they hear or use these terms.

So now back to my conversation over chips and guacamole. My new acquaintance is disgruntled by my not agreeing that this or that group should be labeled a cult, and he is even more curious/annoyed as to how I can just completely write off the term "cult" itself. So I ask him what makes a group a cult, and he rattles off various typical characteristics and selected phenomena people commonly associate with cults. I then proceed to explain that these characteristics can be found all over the religious map and can be associated with just about any religious tradition/organization at one time or another, to one degree or another.

Here, then, are the more common associations people have with cults, along with my discussion of how they are not so strictly limited, that they can often apply to the most "noncultlike" religions.

First is the notion that *cults are religious groups led by a charismatic leader.* Surely when people think of cults, they think of masses of adherents pledging their allegiance to some single powerful individual. They think of followers devoting their souls and wallets to some head honcho, powerful guru, master, or supposed prophet. These devotees willingly submit to his or her authority, soulfully abide by his or her decisions, dutifully obey his or her rules and guidelines. They look to this charismatic leader for wisdom, spiritual counsel, enlightenment. They accept and value his or her insights concerning not only the cosmos but mundane aspects of their daily lives. This leader is seen as personally holy. He or she is somehow closer to the Divinity—maybe even a direct spokesperson for the Divinity. Maybe even God incarnate. Such a leader can be found among many religious organizations that people might consider to be cultlike. We can immediately think of Bagwan Sri Rajneesh and his group of followers (the "Rajneeshies"). Or David Berg and The Family/Children of God. Or Elizabeth Clair Prophet and Church Universal Triumphant. Or the Reverend Sun Myung Moon and the Moonies/ Unification Church. But—and here's where I try to sock it to my party friend—we could also throw in Roman Catholicism! After all, if there ever was a charismatic leader who held sway over his faithful followers and was considered by many to be holy/close to the Divinity and whose teachings and insights are granted sacred weight and whose very being commands holy reverence, it would be the pope. And yet surely most people don't think of Roman Catholicism—the single largest Christian denomination in the world, with hundreds of millions of followers—as a cult.

What religion hasn't at one time or another been under the leadership of a strong, powerful, charismatic figure who demanded unfailing allegiance and personal sacrifices of his or her followers? It could be argued that Islam—the second-largest religion in the world today—began as a "cult" around Muhammad. The Church of Jesus Christ of Latter-day Saints began as a "cult" around Joseph Smith. And the list goes on and on: Bahu'u'allah and the Baha'is, John Knox and Presbyterians, Martin Luther and/or John Calvin and their Protestant Christian progeny, Guru Nanak and the Sikhs, The Ba'al Shem Tov and Hasidic Judaism, Charles Taze Russell and Jehovah's Witnesses, Mary Baker Eddy and Christian Science, Ellen Gould White and the Seventh-Day Adventists, Emanuel Swedenborg and Swedenborgianism, John Wesley and Methodism, George Fox and the Quakers, Aimee Semple McPherson and the Foursquare Gospel Church, Ernest Holmes and Religious Science.[3] And many religious bodies today continue to be led by charismatic or authoritative or divinely inspired leaders, including Roman Catholicism (as mentioned above), various Jewish Hasidic sects, Sikhs, The Nation of Islam, Mormons—again, the list goes on and on. In sum, virtually every major, "legitimate" religion today was at one time—or continues to be—led by a charismatic leader.

A second association people have with "cults" is *brainwashing.* Many people believe that cults are religious groups that somehow have the mysterious ability to brainwash unsuspecting, gullible members through some rigorous and perfected method of psychological "mind control" (Bromley and Hadden 1993, 30). [... S]ociological research has revealed that there is simply no such thing as brainwashing. We have no empirical proof that people can systematically and tactically control the minds of others to get them to do or believe things explicitly against their will (Robbins 1984).

Of course, people can be manipulated. People can be swayed, cajoled, coaxed, seduced, deceived, duped, pressured, pushed, prodded—just go out and try buying a new car! There are certainly religious groups out there that apply social-psychological pressures on their members to conform, or to accept hard-to-swallow beliefs, or to make monetary or emotional sacrifices. But you will find these same mechanisms at play in an army boot camp. Or in your own family. The fact of the matter is that social-psychological manipulation and dynamics of social pressure are commonplace and abundant, permeating endless arenas of our social world: in the military, in college dormitories, in high school friendship cliques, in business environments, in education, in politics, in sex, in advertising, in sports, in the courtroom, in the family, in fraternities, in the workplace, and so on. And more important, one can observe that various forms of social-psychological manipulation are a typical ingredient in almost any mainstream or "legitimate" religious tradition. Children in almost every "legitimate" religion are socially and psychologically pressured into accepting all sorts of beliefs and engaging in all sorts of activities they wouldn't necessarily choose on their own were it not for the guiding force they experience (often unconsciously) from their parents, friends, and teachers. And yet isn't it interesting that when a twenty-year-old joins the Hare Krishnas, people suspect he has been brainwashed, but no one speaks of sending five-year-old children to Sunday school as brainwashing. And yet who is more susceptible to psychological manipulation? Who has less life experience and intellectual capacity to measure truth from falsehood? Who is more likely to succumb to the influence of teachers and peers: the twenty-year-old on the streets of San Francisco or the five-year-old in Sunday school? Without question, the five-year-old. As Catherine Wessinger (2000, 6) has observed:

> The "cult" stereotype conveys the belief that members of unconventional religions are "brainwashed." The brainwashing theory provides a simplistic explanation of why people adopt strange beliefs that are unbelievable to members of main-stream society. The brainwashing theory overlooks the fact that mainstream social and religious institutions also indoctrinate and socialize people. Children are indoctrinated in Sunday and church schools, in catechism classes, and by homeschooling. Individuals attending military schools are socialized in brutal hazing processes ... We are all socialized by our parents, teachers, ministers, friends, spouses, and peers ... the processes utilized by members of NRMS [New Religious Movements/cults] are not different from those used in mainstream families and institutions.

Again, while we can acknowledge that social-psychological manipulation does take place in various religious circles—and that some religious leaders or organizations may be qualitatively better at it than others—this does not mean that certain religious groups have mastered a mysterious, proficient form of mind manipulation and that they have it down to such an exact science that they can get people to do or believe things completely against their will to a degree unparalleled by other religious communities.

A third common phenomenon that people associate with "cults" is that *they urge their members to do illegal, criminal, or murderous acts.* We can immediately think of Jim Jones and his Peoples Temple and their suicide/murder of nearly a thousand people in Guyana in 1978. Or of David Koresh and his Branch Davidians and the deadly inferno in Waco, Texas, in 1993. Or of Shoko Asahara and his Aum Shinrikyo movement of Japan, responsible for gassing subways in Tokyo in 1995. Or the suicide of thirty-five members of the Heaven's Gate group in San Diego in 1997. While some contemporary religions clearly engage in murderous or criminal activities, an even cursory perusal of the history of nearly all major "legitimate" religions will reveal that they too, at one time or another, have exhibited morbid, unethical, brutal, and/or suicidal tendencies (Juergensmeyer 2001). Judaism, Islam, Catholicism, Protestant Christianity, Hinduism, Sikhism—all of these religions have had periods in their history in which violence and/or lawbreaking and/or seemingly unethical or apparently self-destructive conduct was expected, condoned, deemed holy, and actively engaged in by various adherents and leaders. Thus, designating a religious body as "cultlike" because some of its members or leaders engage in criminal, bloody, or suicidal activity is historically blind; again, almost all religions, at one time or another, have done the same.

A fourth and final association people have concerning "cults" is that *they have weird beliefs.* Consider the Raelians, whose charismatic leader—a former French journalist and race car driver named Claude Vorilhon, also known as Rael—claims to have had contact with aliens. According to Raelian belief, humans were created by alien scientists and we are soon approaching the time when our alien creators will return to earth.[4] While such beliefs may strike one as odd, an unbiased perusal of the foundational beliefs of almost every religion will reveal equally bizarre or weird tenets. The unavoidable sociological bottom line when studying religions is that what constitutes beliefs as "weird" is always a matter of subjective opinion. I may think Scientologists have weird beliefs. But Scientologists may think Baha'is have weird beliefs, and Baha'is may think Lutherans have weird beliefs, and Lutherans may think Wiccans have weird beliefs, and Wiccans may think Muslims have weird beliefs, and it just goes on and on and on. Again, from Wessinger (2000, 5):

> The comparative study of the world's religions shows that beliefs and practices that are regarded as strange in one religion are normative in another. For instance, Hindus and Buddhists believe in reincarnation, while reincarnation is viewed by most Christians as an unusual belief associated with "cults." Conversely, Christians

believe that Jesus's resurrection from the dead is true, but this doctrine is viewed by members of other religions as fantastic and unbelievable.

The very word "weird"—like "beautiful" or "deviant" or "successful" or "rational"—is one that has no empirical, scientific foundation, but only subjective, socioculturally determined meanings that are ever-changing and ever-contested.

In sum, the supposedly unique or distinguishing characteristics people associate with religious organizations they wish to delegitimize by labeling them as "cults"—charismatic leadership, brainwashing, destructive behavior, weird beliefs—can be found in almost any religion in one way or another, to one degree or another, or at one time or another, rendering the whole distinction between "cult" and "religion" intellectually indefensible.

Despite my protests outlined above, most people out there are still going to differentiate between "religions" and "cults." Most people are still going to use terminology to put down some religious groups, while supporting (legitimizing) others. My fascination is to try to understand how and in what ways this plays itself out. And I believe that it has little or nothing to do with the actual content of the organization's beliefs, rituals, or structure.

In listening to the way people talk about religions/cults, in watching the way the media depict and discuss religions/cults, in observing how religious groups are accepted or denounced in political and other cultural arenas, and in studying religious sociohistorical dynamics, I've come to the conclusion that the social construction of religious legitimacy generally boils down to two basic factors: (1) the amount of time the religious group has been in existence and (2) the sheer number of members involved.

First, the time factor. The longer a religious group exists, the less likely it is going to be characterized as a "cult" and the more likely it will be accepted as a legitimate religion. Whenever new religious movements first arrive on the scene, they are often regarded suspiciously, especially by other religions. But in time, if they aren't snuffed out, they become more and more accepted. For example, there was a time in British history when being a Quaker was synonymous with being a social and theological criminal, a deviant religious outlaw. Quakers were ruthlessly persecuted. And yet, over time, Quakerism became accepted as a respectable and even benign religious organization. Or another example: the Church of Jesus Christ of Latter-day Saints—Mormons. There was a time in this country when being a Mormon was synonymous with being a social and theological criminal, a deviant religious outlaw. Mormons suffered extensive persecution and violence at the hands of those who considered them a dangerous and illegitimate religious organization. And yet today, most Americans view Mormonism as just another established religion—after all, we have elected representatives in the House and the Senate who are Mormons. In short, the sheer passing of time seems somehow to confer religious legitimacy. The group's beliefs can remain virtually the same, the style of worship can remain the same, the leadership hierarchy can stay in place, the basic raison d'être of the religious group need not alter. The group just needs to stick around long enough, and societal acceptance will eventually result.[5]

A second factor in the construction of religious legitimacy involves nothing more than numbers. I call it the numbers rule of religious legitimacy. It goes like this: If one lone individual firmly believes in something that no one else believes in (and for which there is little or no empirical evidence), people generally call such an individual "insane" or "crazy." Now, if, say, ten or fifty people firmly believe in something that no one else believes in (and for which there is little or no empirical evidence), people might refer to such a group as a "cult." But if five hundred or five thousand people firmly believe in something which no one else believes in (and for which there is little or no empirical evidence), such a group might be referred to as a "sect." And if the number gets up into fifty thousand or maybe five hundred thousand then we're talking "denomination." And if the numbers are, say, five million or more, we've got ourselves a bona fide "religion." Of course, I am picking these numbers arbitrarily. The point I am simply trying to make is that religious legitimacy often boils down to how many people are members of a given organization, and nothing more.

This can also be seen in the use of the word "myth" versus the designation of "religious narrative." The use of these words/descriptive labels plays into the whole social construction of religious legitimacy/illegitimacy. A myth commonly means something that isn't factually true, a folk legend, an old tale, a story that isn't really historically accurate. We often speak of Greek myths or Native American myths, implying that these ancient and fantastical descriptions of the world's origins and various gods and goddesses are clearly and enjoyably fictitious. But people seldom if ever speak of Jewish myths or Buddhist myths or Christian myths. Why? What makes one ancient, fantastical tale a "myth" and yet another equally ancient and fantastical tale a "religious narrative" whose factuality cannot be questioned? Again, it all boils down to numbers. A "myth" is simply a religious narrative without any sizable number of people believing in its historical validity anymore. The ancient Jewish/Christian story of the earth's origin (as described in Genesis of the Bible) and the ancient Sumerian story of the earth's origin are both equally "mythological" and manifestly unbelievable from an empirical point of view. And yet one is deemed a religious narrative and the other a myth. Why? Because one has millions of people believing it as truth and the other doesn't.

Of course, there are multiple factors which are at play in the social construction of the legitimacy or illegitimacy of a given religious organization, beyond the two I have highlighted, time and numbers. We could speak of power; often the labeling of a group as a cult comes down to who in a given society has the power to do such labeling, that is, the government, the media, or professors of religion. And it is crucial to remember that each religious movement has its own particular story embedded in its own particular sociohistorical context, the details of which would require careful study to understand how the designation as cult or religion occurs in that specific instance. And finally, it is crucial to recognize that the labels "religion" and "cult" are often nebulous and seldom fixed; for example, while most Americans seem to accept Mormonism as a legitimate religion, there are certainly those who still would label it a cult. And there are many religious organizations that tread a fine line between cult and religion, hovering precariously between societal acceptance and suspicion, between religious legitimacy and illegitimacy—for instance, Scientology (Aldrige 2000; Stark and Bainbridge 1985).

Scientology is currently waging an international public relations campaign to disassociate itself from the label "cult" and gain acceptance as a "real" religion, for a variety of reasons—legal, financial, and otherwise. I was recently sent a big, handsome, hard-back book (unsolicited) by the Church of Scientology International; the chapters and appendices are devoted to "proving" that Scientology is a "real" religion. And the stakes are quite high for Scientologists. If they are deemed a "real religion" by those in power, they can enjoy everything from tax breaks to societal respect. But if they are deemed a "cult," they risk lawsuits, legal persecution, and societal rejection. In the case of Scientology, it may not be sheer numbers of adherents or time in existence that establishes its legitimacy but savvy public relations and successful lawyers.

Personally, having read *Dianetics* and having gone through some elementary Scientology therapy and having studied the beliefs and practices of the movement, I find its truth claims about this world and beyond, its basic philosophies and teachings, and its common techniques in human betterment uninviting and rather dubious. To put it simply, I don't buy it. But I also personally have no reason or need to label them a "cult." And as a sociologist, I am certain that such a designation is ultimately meaningless.

"But they take lots of money from their members!" says my aggravated acquaintance standing by the chips and guacamole.

"What religious organization doesn't?" I reply. "My Baptist in-laws give 10 percent of their income to their church. It would cost me $2,000 a year to belong to my local synagogue!"

"But they have really weird beliefs! And their whole thing was founded by this charismatic leader who just manipulated people, and they brainwash their members ..."

"Yeah, *whatever.*"

And that's when I excuse myself to go outside for a breath of fresh air.

Notes

1. I didn't record the conversation, and am thus paraphrasing her words from memory. However, her concluding sentence (about their being a cult) is accurately etched in my brain.

2. Again, I am paraphrasing from memory.

3. Even though it could be argued that the New Testament portrays early Christianity as a "cult" around the charismatic leadership of Jesus, I am not including Jesus or Christianity in my list above because a substantial and growing body of scholarship has successfully called into question the historical accuracy of the New Testament, particularly concerning the biographical details of the character Jesus (Doherty 2000, 2001; Helms 1988; Wells 1975, 1988; Price 2000; Leidner 1999; Freke and Gandy 1999; Ellegard 1999).

The same goes for Buddha and Buddhism (Price 1999). Additionally, the accurate historical origins of Hinduism and Judaism are too obscure to be certain of any specific charismatic leader(s).

4. See www.rael.org for more information.

5. This discussion directly relates to why many sociologists of religion prefer to use the designation "new religious movement" instead of "cult." Aside from recognizing that "cult" has a derogatory ring which the term "new religious movement" avoids, use of this designation implicitly acknowledges that the "novel" or "odd" aspect of the given organization is really only a result of its limited time on the scene (i.e., being a *new* religion), and nothing more.

References

Aldridge, Alan. 2000. *Religion in the Contemporary World*. Cambridge, England: Polity Press.

Bainbridge, William Sims. 1997. *The Sociology of Religious Movements*. New York: Routledge.

Bromley, David, and Jeffrey Hadden. 1993. "Exploring the Significance of Cults and Sects in America: Perspectives, Issues, and Agendas." In *Religion and the Social Order: The Handbook on Cults and Sects in America,* edited by David Bromley and Jeffrey Hadden. Greenwich, Conn.: JAI Press.

Doherty, Earl. 2000. *The Jesus Puzzle*. Ottawa, Canada: Canadian Humanist Publications.

———. 2001. *Challenging the Verdict: A Cross-Examination of Lee Strobel's "The Case for Christ."* Ottawa: Age of Reason Publications.

Ellegard, Alvar. 1999. *Jesus: One Hundred Years before Christ*. Woodstock, N.Y.: Overlook Press.

Freke, Timothy, and Peter Gandy. 1999. *The Jesus Mysteries*. New York: Harmony Books.

Helms, Randel. 1988. *Gospel Fictions*. Amherst, N.Y.: Prometheus Books.

Johnson, Benton. 1963. "On Church and Sect." *American Sociological Review* 28: 539–549.

———. 1971. "Church and Sect Revisited." *Journal for the Scientific Study of Religion* 10:124–137.

Juergensmeyer, Mark. 2001. *Terror in the Mind of God: The Global Rise of Religious Violence*. Berkeley: University of California Press.

Leidner, Harold. 1999. *The Fabrication of the Christ Myth*. Tampa, Fla.: Survey Books.

Price, Robert. 1999. "Of Myth and Men." *Free Inquiry* 20(1): 24–36.

———. 2000. *Deconstructing Jesus*. Amherts, N.Y.: Prometheus Books.

Richardson, James. 1993b. "Definitions of Cult: From Socioligical-Technical to Popular-Negative." *Review of Religious Research* 34: 348–356.

Richardson, James, and Barend van Driel. 1997. "Journalists' Attitudes toward New Religious Movements." *Review of Religious Research* 39 (2): 116–128.

Robbins, Thomas. 1984. "Constructing Cultist 'Mind Control.'" *Sociological Analysis* 45(3): 241–256.

Stark, Rodney, and William Sims Bainbridge. 1985. *The Future of Religion: Secularization, Revival, and Cult Formation*. Berkeley: University of California Press.

Swatos, William. 1981. "Church-Sect and Cult: Bringing Mysticism Back In." *Sociological Analysis* 42:17–26.

Troeltsch, Ernst. 1931. *The Social Teaching of the Christian Churches.* New York: Macmillan.

Wells, G. A. 1975. *Did Jesus Exist?* London: Pemberton.

———. 1988. *The Historical Evidence for Jesus.* Buffalo, N.Y.: Prometheus Books.

Wessinger, Catherine. 2000. *How the Millennium Comes Violently.* New York: Seven Bridges Press.

Wilson, Bryan. 1993. "Historical Lessons in the Study of Sects and Cults." In *Religion and the Social Order. The Handbook on Cults and Sects in America,* edited by David Bromley and Jeffrey Hadden. Greenwich, Conn.: JAI Press.

Zablocki, Benjamin, and Thomas Robbins, eds. 2001. *Misunderstanding Cults: Searching for Objectivity in a Controversial Field.* Toronto: University of Toronto Press.

PART III

Millennial Religions

New Religious Movements

Their Incidence and Significance

Eileen Barker

....

Introduction

The subject of the incidence and significance of New Religious Movements is enormous, and the necessity to select a few points from the many that could be raised is but an invitation to anticipate at a superficial level what others will be exploring in far greater depth. I can hope to do no more than raise some of the more obvious (though sometimes forgotten) questions that relate to the challenge of the movements and to the responses to which their presence has given rise.

Statistical Significance

Despite the fact that there is a surprisingly large number of NRMs peppering the free world at the present time, and that a considerable number of persons have been affected by the movements, the real significance of new religions in modern society is not a statistical significance. Certainly, there is no indication that I have come across in the West which suggests that any one movement is showing signs of becoming a major religious tradition during the life of its first-, second- or even third-generation members. This argument is less forceful in Japan, where it has been estimated that between 10 and 20 per cent of the population are followers of one or other NRM,[1] and where a movement such as Soka Gakkai claims several million followers—but even its impressive growth seems to have reached a plateau, at least at the present time—and it should be remembered that at least 80 per cent of the population are not followers of any NRM.

How Many NRMs Are There Now?

The short answer is that we do not know with much accuracy what the incidence of new religions is. A somewhat longer answer starts with the simple truth that, of course, it all depends on what is meant by an NRM. Do we include each and every New Age group or do we lump them together as a single 'movement'? Do we include movements within mainstream traditions (Opus Dei, Folkalore, the House Church movement—*each* House Church)? What about the African Independent Churches? What about the United Reform Church? Are the 'self-religions' or Human Potential groups really new *religious* movements? How new is new? What about Subud, Vedanta or possibly Jehovah's Witnesses which is the first 'sect' that comes to mind in a country such as Italy when the phrase New Religious Movement is mentioned? Might we include even the anti-cult movement—sections of it certainly exhibit several of the characteristics that 'anti-cultists' themselves attribute to 'cults'?

Definitions of Movements

There is, of course, no 'right' answer. Definitions are more or less useful, not more or less true. The definition from which I personally start—for purely pragmatic reasons—is that an NRM is new in so far as it has become visible in its present form since the Second World War, and that it is religious in so far as it offers not merely narrow theological statements about the existence and nature of supernatural beings, but that it proposes answers to at least some of the other kinds of ultimate questions that have traditionally been addressed by mainstream religions, questions such as: Is there a God? Who am I? How might I find direction, meaning and purpose in life? Is there life after death? Is there more to human beings than their physical bodies and immediate interactions with others?

Numbers of Movements

INFORM has over 2,600 different groups on its computer, the majority (but not all) of which might be called NRMs.[2] Given that there must be a good many groups about which we have not heard, it would not be unreasonable to assume that, including schisms but not branches of the same group under different names, there could be over 2,000 discrete groups in Europe. Gordon Melton, who uses a much narrower definition, which excludes the human potential groups, can provide some information on nearly 1,000 groups in America.[3] Shimazono says that scholarly estimates of the number of NRMs in Japan vary from 800 to a few thousand.[4] Several years ago, Harold Turner estimated that there were 10,000 new religions with 12 million or more adherents in among the tribal peoples of the Americas, Asia, Africa and the Pacific.[5] He would include the African Independent Churches, but untold numbers of new religions may be found in India; several hundreds exist in South America, Australia and New Zealand and in places such as the West Indies, Korea and the Philippines.

In short, while clearly dependent on the definition used, the number of NRMs according to my broad definition is likely to be in the order of four figures (two or more thousand) in the West and five figures (probably somewhere in the lower tens of thousands) world-wide.

How Many Members?

Attempting to assess the incidence of the movements seems like child's play when one turns to questions concerning membership numbers. Many of the movements do not count, keep secret or distort (usually upwards) their membership figures. We know that some NRMs have only a handful of members—a score or less—while others have hundreds or thousands, with a few (but only a very few with any credibility) claiming millions.

Definitions of Membership

There is, moreover, a vast range of levels of membership: there are totally committed members who (like monks or nuns) devote their lives to their movement, living as a community and working full time for it; there are associate members (similar to congregational members), who may come to a centre on a weekly basis for worship or a course; and there are sympathisers (or 'nominal' members) who may be in general agreement with an NRM's beliefs and practices, but whose lives are not very widely or deeply affected by their somewhat peripheral affiliation. While for some purposes it is only committed members who are counted, at other times or in different movements, one can find included even those who have done little more than sign a piece of paper saying that they are in general sympathy with some of the movement's beliefs.

Double-Counting

Further confusion may arise as the result of double-counting. It is not impossible—indeed, as one moves toward the New Age end of the NRM spectrum, it is quite common—for individuals to have overlapping memberships, happily hopping from one 'self-religion' to another. It would not be impossible for committed seekers in California, Amsterdam or Highgate to spend twenty minutes in Transcendental Meditation each morning before embarking on their Tai Chi, then going on to attend a channelling session on Monday, to meet with their Co-counsellor on Tuesday, have an Alexander lesson on Wednesday, watch an Osho video on Thursday and participate in a Forum Seminar throughout the weekend. Two months later one might find them chanting 'Hare Krishna', 'Om Shanti' or, perhaps, 'Nam Myoho Renge Kyo'.

Turnover

There is, furthermore, the complication of high turnover rates. Both the movements and their opponents tend to play down this characteristic of many of the better-known NRMs. On the one hand, few new religions are eager to publicise the fact that a sizeable number of their members have found the movement wanting; on the other hand, anti-cultists who are eager to defend 'the brainwashing thesis' do not wish to publicise the fact that the 'victims' not only can, but do, of their own free will, leave those very NRMs that are accused of employing irresistible and irreversible techniques of mind control.[6]

So far as our present interests are concerned, this means that it is frequently the number of people who have passed through a movement, rather than the current membership, that is counted. Being familiar with the phrase 'Once a Catholic, always a Catholic', we should not be surprised that the Church of Scientology considers all those who have ever done one of their courses to be a Scientologist, and counts them as such even if they have not been in touch with the movement for years—even, presumably, if they are among the movement's most vitriolic opponents.

And it cannot be denied that there is no way in which I, having done the course (albeit for purposes of research), cannot be an *est* graduate—or, rather, a Forum graduate. (In *that* sense—and, let me insist, in that sense only—the anti-cultists who, as a result of my participant observation, accuse me of being 'numbered' among cult members are, doubtless, correct.)

The Cultural Milieu

A further point that ought to be raised so far as incidence is concerned, but which, at the same time, propels us towards the 'significance' part of my remit, is something about which Colin Campbell has written extensively: the cultic milieu.[7]

One of the features of modern society which sociologists of religion, such as Durkheim, Weber and Wilson, have frequently pointed out is that organised religion no longer has the kind of hold over social institutions that it has enjoyed in earlier periods. Religion has become increasingly a leisure pursuit that may be 'privatised', 'individualised' or even, to borrow Luckmann's term, 'invisible'. Mainstream religious organisations have suffered significant losses of membership in most of Europe and, according to some, though not all, commentators, in the United States. Anyone who has made but the most cursory of enquiries about people's religious positions in Western society will be all too familiar with the sentiment: 'You don't have to go to church to be a good Christian.'

Concomitantly, in place of a relatively homogeneous, coherent, and more or less shared culture, we have witnessed the growth of religious pluralism, interwoven with numerous social changes such as increased social and geographical mobility, universal franchise, universal education and the break-up of a traditional occupational structure, traditional values and authority structures—all of which can contribute to a dissatisfaction with, or at least a second look at, the beliefs and practices that might otherwise have been passed on by parents or others in roles of authority—thus creating a potential 'demand' (in the economic sense) for alternative ways of satisfying spiritual and religious requirements.

On the 'supply' side, although it should be remembered that most of the traditional Churches still supply more people with their religion than does any NRM, we have expanding missionary activity and escalating migration—a factor that Melton has repeatedly pointed to is the relaxing of the US immigration laws in 1965, which allowed a number of gurus to enter the United States and thus promote the growth of religions with Eastern origins. And, of course, there has been the development of a mass media (supplemented by all manner of electronic, satellite and Internet devices) swelling the variety of (broadly defined) religious resources that have become available to any one individual participating in the cultural milieu. All sorts of ideas are out there. And many of these ideas originate from, are carried by, and/or are reinforced by New Religious Movements.

This is particularly obvious with a number of New Age ideas such as person-centred spirituality and/or the potential of individual development. And, while fifty years ago none but a very small proportion of Christians would have seriously countenanced the idea of reincarnation, the European Value Surveys, the International Social Survey Programme and several other research projects tell us that anywhere between a fifth and a quarter of Europeans and North Americans now believe that we shall return to this world in another body when we have shuffled off this mortal coil. Such a belief was reported by 24 per cent of Britons—though it might be noted that several of these respondents *also* reported believing in the resurrection of the body.[8]

The point that I want to make here is that, when attempting to chart the incidence and/or significance of NRMs, we might want to be at least aware of, even if we do not include, those who are not officially members of any particular NRM. There are people who might be horrified at the thought they could be in any way connected with a 'cult', but who are, none the less, 'recipients', even carriers, of ideas and practices that are borne by, if not always born in, NRMs.

And while we are considering this category of persons loosely adding to the social significance of the movements, may I suggest that we might also recognise the existence, first, of members of the media who use and promote NRM ideas; second, of members of the mainstream religions who have picked up ideas and practices originating or transmitted by NRMs; third, of managers and other personnel in business corporations who invite and/or attend courses liberally imbued with NRM ideas and practices; and, fourth, members of the anti-cult movements who have played such a significant role in promoting the high profile that certain NRMs and their members have achieved in the past three decades or so. It is, indeed, members of the Evangelical wing of the counter-cult movement who can be credited with spreading certainly the idea, and arguably some of the practices, of ritual Satanic abuse in North America, Western and Eastern Europe, Australia and elsewhere around the world.[9]

Generalising about NRMs

One cannot generalise about NRMs. The only thing that they have in common is that they have been labelled as an NRM or 'cult'. The movements differ from each other so far as their origins, their beliefs, their practices, their organisation, their leadership, their finances, their life-styles and their attitudes to women, children, education, moral questions and the rest of society are concerned. Attempts to produce typologies have been limited, and even relatively useful distinctions (such as Roy Wallis's distinction between world-affirming, world-rejecting and world-accommodating religions)[10] do not really help us to anticipate with much certainty the *empirical* characteristics that might follow from the *defining* characteristics of each category. Assuredly, there is nothing to match the elegant types that Bryan

Wilson elaborated for the earlier, predominantly Christian-based, sects.[11] The ever-increasing range of alternatives from all corners of the world (from relatively new philosophies such as psychoanalysis or the development of science, electronic innovations and science fiction, and the increase of UFO sightings and 'strange encounters of the third kind') have made neat, predictive models out of date almost before the ink has dried on their author's paper—or the laser has printed from their author's PC.

None the less, the anti-cult movement, much of the media and a sizeable chunk of the population continue to provide us with facile check-lists of the characteristics of NRMs as dangerous, manipulative, exploitative, and deceptive sex maniacs—or, in depictions where descriptive rather than evaluative detail is given, frequently making it difficult to distinguish 'destructive cults' from many traditional mainstream religions.

There are, however, some characteristics that make an NRM more visible and, thereby, significant *as* an NRM. One may find, for example, the first-generation enthusiasms, the unambiguous clarity and certainty in the belief systems, the urgency of the message, the commitment of life-style, perhaps a charismatic leadership, and, possibly, strong Them/Us and/or Before/After distinctions—all of which are, of course, liable to undergo significant change within a single generation.

Who Joins NRMs?

Just as there are all types of NRMs, so there are all types of people who join the movements. However, those who have joined the better-known of the current wave of NRMs in the West have been dispro-portionately white and from the better-educated middle classes. There are exceptions—indeed, it is worth pointing out that many of the ill-fated members of the Branch Davidians and of the People's Temple were blacks from the lower classes,[12] and that they were not as disproportionately young as those joining movements such as the Children of God, the Unification Church or ISKCON. Even the somewhat older people who have become involved with the 'self-religions' (and who may need a respectable income to pay for courses) have tended to be disproportionately in their thirties or early forties. As with other aspects of NRMs, however, we have to remember that all kinds of people of all kinds of ages, occupations, classes, ethnic groupings, educational attainments and from all kinds of religions have joined and will doubtless continue to join NRMs. And now, of course, there is a growing number of persons who have been born into an NRM. Two-thirds of the current membership of The Family are second- or even third-generation members.

Temporal Differences

The first thing that might be noted arises out of what I have already intimated: NRMs change over time. Merely the fact that time has passed means that founders have died, that young, idealist converts with few dependants or other responsibilities have grown into middle-aged parents—and a new 'born-into' generation, demanding the allocation of such resources as time and money, will have to be socialised and accommodated. Thus, like all new religions before them, the present wave of NRMs have, during the past quarter of a century, undergone changes which are all too often forgotten when the media, the anti-cult movement and, as a consequence, members of the general public talk, write or merely think about NRMs.

In a special edition of *Social Compass* that Jean-François Mayer and I recently put together to highlight changes that have occurred in NRMs over the past twenty years,[13] I argue that such changes tend to result both in the movements becoming less like each other, and, at the same time, in their becoming more like the wider society—the apparent paradox resting on the fact that modern society is a pluralist society into which the movements may merge in a number of different forms.

But it is not only the individual NRMs that change with the passage of time. Given that the structures and cultures of society are continually altering, we would expect, and do indeed find, that the 'cult scene' *as a whole* will change. The balance of public attention and the popularity of particular kinds of NRMs will vary at different times. Furthermore, these shifting scenes differ in different parts of the world.

Spatial Differences

In discussing the incidence of NRMs in Europe, Stark and Bainbridge draw a distinction between sects (schisms of mainstream traditions) and cults (innovative groups). They argue (and claim that the evidence supports the argument) that sects are likely to appear when traditional religions are strong, while cults emerge only when the traditional religions are weak.[14] Other contributors to this book provide international data, but let me, for comparative purposes, offer three very brief sketches.

England

In England (and I am referring to England rather than to Britain or the United Kingdom), the emergence of a youth culture after the Second World War did not immediately translate into a new religious scene. Indeed, with a few exceptions such as young black males who became Rastafarians, the youth culture of the working class was and remains notable for its lack of religious manifestations—unless we were to extend our definition to include Teds, Mods, Rockers and, later, Punks and Skinheads.

Middle-class youth roughly followed the paths that their peers in North America were treading. It was not until the 1960s, towards the end of the period of militant student unrest, that a religious—or spiritual—alternative became visible to any but the few who were already involved in such an alternative. The demos faded into squats in the inner cities, into communes in sacred centres such as Glastonbury, and along the ley lines of the United Kingdom. Then the hippies started to move into more structured, but none the less religious or spiritual (rather than political) organisations—some of them of a strictly authoritarian nature. The dawning of the Age of Aquarius mingled into the Human

Potential movement, which has continued to flourish—reaching into those parts of mainstream society from which other religions have been increasingly banished since the onset of a desacralization of society—or secularisation, in the Bryan Wilson meaning of the concept.[15]

Then we could observe the rise of enthusiastic religion (the charismatic, neo-pentecostal and/or restoration movements) filtering into mainstream Churches, thereby increasing the supply of one of the scarce resources—religious enthusiasm—that NRMs such as the Children of God or the Unification Church were offering in the 1960s and 1970s when many of the young people who were to join such movements were typifying the Churches as cold, hypocritical, apathetic and dominated by old ladies. It is, however, not without significance that the Holy Spirit used an NRM—the Vineyard movement—as its medium for the introduction of the 'Toronto Blessing' to certain sections of the more evangelical wing of the Church of England—a phenomenon that has become decidedly controversial in other, more conservative, sections of the Evangelical church.[16]

Japan

As is well known, the Japanese had its modern 'Rush Hour of the Gods'[17] some time before the West had its—the former's influx of new religions occurring immediately after the Second World War, while the latter's did not really take off until the mid-1960s. There are numerous historical reasons for the differences between Japanese and Western NRMs.[18] Furthermore, since the 1970s, Japan has witnessed a new wave of movements, commonly referred to as the New New or Neo-New Religions. Aum Shinrikyō is one such NNRM, typical of the NNRMs in so far as it seems to have appealed disproportionately to young, well-educated people rather than to the less educated, lower-middle class and/or, especially, housewives who have been attracted to many of the earlier, post-war NRMs. The general shift, according to Shimazono, is that, while the former new religions were concerned with salvation and good community living in this life, the New New Religions have been less concerned about practical and *communal* problems (such as poverty, disease and family conflicts), and have placed less emphasis on altruistic ethics, concentrating more on the transformation of, and control over, the *individual*'s mind and body. In order to attain further salvation for the soul in future lives, the process of enlightenment may be pursued with the help of mystical knowledge and magical practices.

But while Shimazono typifies Aum Shinrikyō as an NNRM, he also classifies it as a somewhat atypical 'isolationist' movement, and argues that the most significant development in contemporary Japan is the emergence of a magico-religious popular culture that is disseminated not through religious organisations so much as through comic books, magazines and computer games which can be read or played at any time—'producing an instantaneous private space'.[19]

Eastern Europe and the Traditionally Christian Former Soviet Union (FSU)

There were NRMs in Eastern Europe and the Soviet Union before 1989. Frequently they were more or less underground, and, when exposed, they sometimes suffered quite severe consequences. Several

Krishna devotees were imprisoned and a couple died in Soviet jails. On the other hand, several Buddhist and New Age/Human Potential groups, while not exactly flourishing, were able to meet and practise quite freely in Poland, and I even managed to meet two Transcendental Meditators in the middle of the main square in Tirana before Albania's socialist regime collapsed.

But, of course, the incidence of NRMs was minute—until, that is, the Wall came down. And when it did come down the NRMs were there—several of them literally there, handing out literature with all manner of offerings. Since then, the movements have been particularly successful in Russia, and have not done badly in East Germany, Hungary and the Ukraine. There are quite a few to be found in Poland and the Czech Republic, several in Romania, Slovakia and Belorussia, and a few in Bulgaria and in the Georgian and Armenian Republics. Some intrepid members of NRMs have been found offering humanitarian aid along with salvation in the war zones of Croatia and Ngomo Karabakh.

Although there are indigenous new religions and revivals of older, folk, pagan or esoteric religions to be found in Eastern Europe and the FSU, the majority of the NRMs are from the West, many of them offering as many capitalist as spiritual wares to anyone who will listen: Unificationists offer English language classes and travel to the West, Scientologists offer management courses; but it would seem to be some of the new evangelical groups, such as the Churches of Christ planted from Boston, the Word of Life from Sweden, the Vineyard Church in the Czech Republic, or the amazingly successful Faith Church in Hungary that are really thriving.

Yet while it looked at first as though the newfound freedoms of Eastern Europe and the Former Soviet Union were presenting the new religions with a field day, whatever success they have enjoyed has generated increasing antagonism from the traditional Churches who see the movements as one of the main reasons for their lack of success in retaining what they consider to be rightfully their flock. New laws have been introduced or are in the process of being proposed to curtail the activities and, in some cases, to forbid the presence of foreign, non-established small religions. [20]

One of my doctoral students, Marat Shterin, who is comparing the NRMs in England and in Russia, is finding the difference between the reactions of the Russian Orthodox Church and the Church of England one of his most significant variables. None the less, both his and my own observations suggest that the development of the movements in Eastern Europe and the FSU differs in a number of ways from their development in the West. Perhaps this is not altogether surprising, given that they are now more experienced and, in several cases, it is a second-generation membership that is trying to establish a foothold in what are totally different surroundings. And, of course, the fact that so many of the potential converts have been brought up in an atheistic socialist state obviously has a considerable effect on what seekers are seeking.

Cultural Adaptability

The interplay between an NRM and the culture in which it originates is a familiar subject of study. A more recent interest has been investigating the way that particular movements 'travel'. In some respects, the transported NRM might appear only marginally different in whatever country it is operating. When, for example, I visit a community-based group such as the Unification Church, the Hare Krishna or The Family (all three of which I have stayed with or visited in a dozen or more different countries), I sometimes find it difficult to remember where I am, apart from being in a Moonie centre, an ISKCON Temple or a Family home—in this respect, staying with a particular NRM is rather like staying in, say, the Tokyo, Lagos or Washington Hilton—one is in a Hilton hotel—and Tokyo, Lagos or Washington just happen to be outside. One might, perhaps, notice that *some* of the other residents happen to speak a different language or have skin of a different hue—but one finds that also in the London Hilton, the Lancaster Gate Unification Centre, the Soho Krishna Temple and the Dunton Bassett Family home.

But clearly the different social contexts do, to a greater or lesser degree, affect the movements' *modus operandi* and the reception that they are given. Some manage to preserve their original beliefs and practices pretty well intact world-wide; others succeed only to the extent that they adapt—more or less—to the host culture. I have been told that there are Unificationists who are allowed to keep more than one wife in some African countries with Islamic influences.

It has already been intimated that some movements of Japanese origin are relatively successful in the West—Soka Gakkai International provides one such example—while others make less of an impression on the natives. Louis Hourmant attributes changes in the Japanese NRMs he has observed in France, such as a playing down of the magical-religious component in Reiyūkai, to responses to the differences between Western and Japanese society.[21] However, Jean-François Mayer, in a Swiss context, notes that the adjustment of Mahikari has not been accompanied by a parallel diminution, although the integration of values and of the ideology promoted by Mahikari seems to be a very lengthy process for its Swiss followers.[22] Interestingly, just as the New New Religions in Japan incorporate a negation of some modern values, Mahikari members in Switzerland tend to think that their new religion brings them the sense of the sacred which they feel the conventional Churches in the West have lost.

The Significance of NRMs for Individuals

Members

It is obvious, but none the less worth mentioning, that the significance of an NRM—the scope and the intensity of the experience for its membership—will obviously vary from individual to individual and from movement to movement. It will also vary according to the position that individuals occupy in the movement—whether, for example, they are new converts or seasoned leaders—or, perhaps, whether they are male or female.[23] For some, joining an NRM will become and will remain the most important thing to happen in their lives—they may find direction, meaning, the hope of salvation, a sense of belonging to a like-minded community, the opportunity to develop a relationship with

God, to develop their spirituality, to find their true selves or all manner of other possibilities that they felt they were denied in the 'outside world'. For others, the experience may have seemed wonderful at first but has since soured through disappointment and, perhaps, disillusionment. A few will have extremely unpleasant experiences and feel that they have been deceived, manipulated, exploited and/or robbed not only of money and material goods but also of their time and, perhaps, their innocence and, maybe, their faith in God and/or in humanity.

Members' Relations and Friends

Sometimes it seems as though NRMs have an even greater significance for the relatives and friends of members than for the members themselves. While there are friends and relatives who rejoice in converts' finding a new happiness, contentment or fulfilment in an NRM, there is also a significant number of people who have had their lives profoundly and adversely affected by a friend or relative joining a new religion—and some of these people have become involved with the anti-cult movement. The metaphor of death has frequently been employed by parents who talk about feelings of bereavement; a few have even claimed that they would prefer their son or daughter to be dead rather than in 'the cult'. Husbands or wives have talked about an NRM coming between them and their partner, producing a rift that cannot be breached. One partner taking on new interests that exclude the other is not, of course, a phenomenon confined to NRMs, but it should be recognised that it can be as fraught a situation as that which arises when people discover that their partner is being unfaithful and intends to remain so.

The Significance of NRMs for the Rest of Society

Fifteen or so years ago, I edited a book called *New Religious Movements: A Perspective for Understanding Society*.[24] Had I the time, I would like to bring out a second volume for we have learned so much more in the intervening period about the ways in which NRMs can contribute to our understanding of society. Some of the points have already been covered and there is no space here to discuss many others. But I would like to conclude by introducing some of the ways in which sociologists of religion may be alerted to features of the wider social context in which the movements flourish or wither.

The NRMs of the Gaps

One of the ways NRMs have been seen as being of significance is that they may occasionally function as a barometer of what at least some members of a society feel they need but is not being supplied by other means.[25] This is not so much a God of the Gaps theology as a movements of the gaps sociology. Such a perspective could—indeed has—sensitised us to perceived lacunae. There are, however, methodological problems. First, in pluralist societies, it would be foolhardy to generalise too much from particular innovations in particular NRMs. However, a rush to NRMs which are offering, say, enthusiastic rituals of worship, healing, interpretations of religious experiences might suggest a significant perceived need, rather than a chance gap or even acceptance of something because it is there rather than because it is sought. Second, while the movements might want to offer alternatives in more totalitarian societies, it would be difficult to argue that it was the positive suggestions of the NRM, rather than the repressive nature of the regime, that were responsible for the attractiveness of the 'offer'—which could, equally well, come from any dissident source—including those of a purely secular nature. But none of this is to deny that NRMs can have a significant role to play as a dissenting force in society. They can.

Media and Anti-Cultists

An enormous amount of work has now been done on the ways in which the media and the anti-cult movement (ACM) have responded to the NRMs and the significance of the interaction between the various institutions. Melton explores this subject in further detail, but I would like to take two recent examples to illustrate the significance that members of a society may attach to NRMs as the result of media and anti-cult constructions of their image. In other words, what I want to highlight is the *significance of the significance* that the media and the ACM attach to the movements.

The first example illustrates how a democratic society (in this case, England) can give 'permission' to its citizens to carry out a criminal attack on a person *merely* on the grounds that s/he is the member of a 'cult'. It is the case of Kathy Wilson, a 23-year-old member of the Church of Scientology whose erstwhile friends decided that she had been brainwashed and needed rescuing. They took matters into their own hands and tried to grab her, taking a knife and a Rottweiler to assist in the kidnap. Kathy screamed. There ensued some ugly and violent exchanges as passing Scientologists came to Kathy's rescue. Despite the fact that Kathy maintained—and still maintains—that she is happy and wants to remain a Scientologist, in March 1995 a British jury unanimously acquitted the man who admitted that he had intended to 'snatch her' against her will. It was reported that his counsel had argued that:

> even though she claimed in court she did not consent to removal, it was possible her free will had been removed by the processes she had undergone in the cult and she did not have 'sufficient intelligence and understanding' to decide if she consented.[26]

What is of particular significance for our purposes is that the would-be kidnapper, who maintained that although Kathy's abduction would be 'probably against her will because she's been brainwashed and she'll be on drugs', cited as the sources of his information 'taxi drivers, a local newspaper journalist, others involved in the "rescue" of members of religious cults, as well as his own investigations'.[27] Furthermore, in a recorded interview with police, just after the incident in November 1992, he declared: 'I know I would be liable to criminal prosecution now, but no jury in the country … would see me guilty'.[28] It would seem that he was right.

My other example is from the United States, and it illustrates how the public image of an NRM can lead not to *ad hominem* but to *ad NRMinem* arguments being employed to judge something as wicked *solely* on the grounds that there is even a very slight NRM connection. It concerns the use of a slide presentation on AIDS that laid emphasis on teenage celibacy and which was promoted for use (in public and private schools, churches and doctors' offices) by such worthy citizens as a nun, a chapter leader of Concerned Women of America and a leader of Project Respect. These women then learned, at a meeting of the True Light Educational Ministry (a group 'advising people leaving cults'), that the two men who had put together the programme which they had considered so excellent happened to be Unificationists. Despite the fact that there was no evidence whatsoever that the slides had been or would be used to promote any Unification beliefs apart from that shared by the erstwhile promoters—that pre-marital sex is not a good idea—the women immediately started to advise those to whom they had previously promoted the programme that the programme should not be used.[29]

Did one of the Unificationists have a point when he suggested that it would be foolish to refuse the use of polio vaccines because one disliked their inventors' religions?

The Law

If one had to select one criterion that might indicate the extent to which a society was 'open' or 'closed', the legal position of NRMs would be a not altogether ridiculous choice. For somewhat finer tuning, the second criterion could well be the legal treatment of NRMs. I believe that this is an area where NRMs can be of particular significance in both reflecting and affecting the society in which they exist. One might look, for example, at the position of NRMs in Islamic and Soviet countries and the new legislation that has been introduced and is being contemplated in Eastern Europe and the Former Soviet Union (in Moscow, Kiev and Yerevan); one can examine the mounting number of cases that have gone to the Supreme Court in America, providing a remarkable forum for debate about the nicer points of law concerning the relative balance of freedoms between (a) individuals, (b) groups and (c) society.[30]

Mainstream Traditions in the West

There are several different issues that could be pursued so far as the significance of NRMs *vis-à-vis* traditional religions are concerned. I have already touched briefly on Stark and Bainbridge's theory about the significance of the religious situation to the growth of cults and sects, and I have briefly mentioned both the positive way in which a tradition may use the 'challenge' of the movements to incorporate changes in their own practices, and the negative reactions of the Mother Churches in Eastern Europe and the FSU. This is, of course, an area which invokes a wide range of questions about the functioning of pluralistic societies.

NRMs as an Indicator of Perceived Vulnerability

A further, related point of potential significance concerns not only which societies and groups within society get more or less worried about the NRMs in their midst (until recently, Finland was relatively unconcerned—and still is, compared with, say, Belgium), but also what aspects of which movements are selected for condemnation. I am not sure what the situation is now, but at one time it looked as though Britain was particularly concerned with brainwashing allegations, France with political intrigue, the United States with the break-up of the family and financial considerations, Germany with social security payments, and Japan with the effect on young people's career prospects. There are ways, as Beckford and others have suggested, in which we can learn about a society by analysing what is seen as particularly threatening.[31] Different perceptions and interpretations of the 'Satanist scare' might prove a fruitful starting point for further study in this area.[32]

The Significance of NRMs for the Sociology of Religion

Finally, the study of NRMs has introduced numerous methodological challenges and has taken not a few sociologists out of the ivory tower of academia into a marketplace of fierce competition in the business of social construction of reality in government circles, in the courts, the popular media and in various other venues in our pluralist society.[33]

Concluding Remarks

New Religious Movements come in a vast variety of forms. They are successful or they fail for a multitude of reasons. Facile generalisations are bound to be wrong. Some of the beliefs that are held by members of the general public are true about some of the movements some of the time but, through their studies of NRMs, social scientists have found that many of the statements in the popular media are blatantly untrue about the majority of the movements, and others refer to only a tiny proportion of their number. Much more detailed work needs to be carried out to understand the processes that occur within the movements and between them and the wider society. And, possibly more importantly, the knowledge that we have of the movements needs to be disseminated and understood more widely. Not only the NRMs, but societal reaction to them have significantly greater significance than their relatively small numbers might suggest.

Notes

1. Susumu Shimazono, 'New Religions and the New Spirituality Movement: Two Types of Religious Movements in Advanced Industrial Societies', paper given at the Santa Barbara Center for Humanistic Studies conference, 'New Religions in a Global Perspective', Buelton, California, 16 May 1991, p. 3.

2. INFORM (Information Network Focus on Religious Movements) is a charity, based at the London School of Economics, which I founded with the support of the Home Office and mainstream Churches in 1988 in order to provide information that is as accurate and up to date as possible about new religions. It can be contacted at INFORM, Houghton St, London WC2A 2AE, England; tel. 0171-955 7654, fax 0171-955 7677, e-mail INFORM@LSE.AC.UK.

3. J. Gordon Melton, *Encyclopedia of American Religions,* 4th edn, Detroit: Gale, 1993.

4. Shimazono, op. cit.

5. Harold Turner, 'New Religious Movements in Primal Societies', in John Hinnells (ed.), *The Penguin Dictionary of Religions,* Harmondsworth: Penguin, 1984, p. 232. Second edition: *A New Dictionary of Religions,* Oxford: Blackwell, 1995, p. 350.

6. See Eileen Barker, *New Religious Movements: A Practical Introduction,* London: HMSO, 1989. Fifth impression with amendments 1995, pp. 104–5.

7. Colin Campbell, 'The Cult, the Cultic Milieu and Secularization', in Michael Hill (ed.), *Sociological Yearbook of Religion in Britain,* London: SCM Press, 1972, pp. 119–36.

8. This is not necessarily a contradiction in terms—there are a number of theologically minded people (often with Theosophical leanings) who see the two concepts as entirely complementary. It is, however, doubtful whether many of the 24 per cent have such well-worked-out beliefs.

9. See James T. Richardson, Joel Best and David Bromley, *The Satanism Scare,* New York: De Gruyter, 1991.

10. Roy Wallis, *The Elementary Forms of the New Religious Life,* London: Routledge and Kegan Paul, 1983.

11. Bryan Wilson, *Religious Sects: A Sociological Study,* London: Weidenfeld, 1970.

12. James T. Richardson, 'People's Temple and Jonestown: A Corrective Comparison and Critique', *Journal for the Scientific Study of Religion, 19*(3), 1980, pp. 239–55.

13. *Twenty Years On: Changes in New Religious Movements,* special edition of *Social Compass, 42*(2), June 1995.

14. Rodney Stark and William Sims Bainbridge, *A Theory of Religion,* New York: Peter Lang, 1987. Republished in 1996 by Rutgers University Press, New Brunswick.

15. 'The Process Whereby Religious Thinking, Practice and Institutions Lose Social Significance', *Religion in Secular Society: A Sociological Comment,* Harmondsworth: Pelican, 1969, p. 14.

16. See *Religion Report,* 20 March 1995, *9*(7), 1.

17. H. Neill McFarland, *The Rush Hour of the Gods: A Study of New Religious Movements in Japan,* New York: Macmillan, 1967.

18. See, for example, McFarland, op. cit. and Shimazono, op. cit. and 'New New Religions and This World: Religious Movements in Japan after the 1970s and the Beliefs about Salvation', *Social Compass, 42*(2), 1995: pp. 193–206; Susumu Shimazono, M. R. Mullins and P. Swanson (eds), *Religion and Society in Modern Japan,* Berkeley. CA: Asian Humanities Press. 1993.

19. There are quite a few signs that similar manifestations are beginning to become more prominent in the West. One of my students recently took the members of our graduate seminar on a journey through the Internet 'in search of God'. It was, as one of my other students remarked, 'something else'.

20. See Eileen Barker, 'But Who's Going to Win? National and Minority Religions in Post-Communist Society', in Irena Borowik and Grzegorz Babinski (eds), *New Religious Phenomena in Central and Eastern Europe,* Kraków: Nomos, 1997, pp. 25–62.

21. 'Les Nouveaux Mouvements religieux japonais en France', *Social Compass, 42*(2), June 1995, pp. 207–20.

22. Jean-François Mayer, *Social Compass, 42*(2), June 1995, pp. 180–92.

23. See Susan Palmer, *Moon Sisters, Krishna Mothers, Rajneesh Lovers: Women's Roles in New Religions,* Syracuse, NY: Syracuse University Press, 1994.

24. Lewiston, NY: Edwin Mellen Press, 1982.

25. Warren Lewis, 'Coming-Again: How Society Functions Through its New Religions', in Eileen Barker (ed.), *NRMs: A Perspective for Understanding Society,* Toronto: Edwin Mellen Press, 1982, pp. 191–215.

26. *Daily Telegraph,* 15 March 1995.

27. *Daily Telegraph,* 11 March 1995.

28. Ibid.

29. *New York Times,* 22 March 1995. pp. B1 and B6.

30. James T. Richardson, 'Minority Religions ("Cults") and the Law: Comparisons of the United States, Europe and Australia', *University of Queensland Law Journal, 18*(2), 1995, pp. 183–207.

31. James A. Beckford, *Cult Controversies: The Societal Response to the New Religious Movements,* London: Tavistock, 1985.

32. See, for example, Richardson *et al., op. cit.*

33. Eileen Barker, 'The Scientific Study of Religion? You Must be Joking!', *Journal for the Scientific Study of Religion, 34*(3), 1995, pp. 287–310.

Peoples Temple

Mass Murder-Suicide, the Media, and the "Cult" Label

Hugh B. Urban

O n November 18, 1978, more than nine hundred people died in a series of murders and suicides in Guyana, South America, most of them members of an American-born religious movement called Peoples Temple. Founded by the Reverend James Warren (Jim) Jones ([...]), Peoples Temple was for a time one of America's most innovative, progressive, and successful religious movements, blending charismatic Christianity with a powerful message of social justice and racial integration. However, the group and its leader faced intense criticism from the American media, politicians, and anticult groups, and so relocated to Guyana in 1977 in order to build a progressive agricultural project based on racial harmony and a form of Christian socialism.

Peoples Temple also had a powerful streak of Christian millenarianism, or the expectation of the imminent end of the world (informed in part by the Cold War threat of nuclear holocaust and in part by the growing persecution the community faced). The group had in fact been preparing for some sort of cataclysmic end, going through several "practice suicides" in the 1970s. However, the final tragic events were triggered when California congressman Leo Ryan flew down to Jonestown on behalf of a group called Concerned Relatives in order to bring any members of the group who wished to leave back to their families. While Jones initially allowed several members to leave voluntarily, gunmen from Peoples Temple ambushed the group at the airstrip, killing the congressman and four others. Then, back at Jonestown, Jones gave his community the order to commit an act of what he called "revolutionary suicide," protesting an inhumane and intolerant world that would not leave them in peace to pursue their communal ideal. Most members died by drinking Flavor-Aid mixed with cyanide, Valium, and chloral hydrate—though not all did so voluntarily, and many were reportedly injected with the poison (leading some to call this a mass murder rather than a mass suicide).[1] Meanwhile, a radio communication was sent to another Temple member, Sharon Amos, in Georgetown, who killed her two youngest children and then, together with her oldest daughter, took her own life. Overall, the deaths represent the largest mass murder-suicide in modern history and the largest loss of American civilian lives in a deliberate act prior to the terrorist attacks of September 11, 2001.

While the Jonestown tragedy of 1978 is the most spectacular example of a self-destructive new religious movement in modern times, it is by no means the only one. The final decades of the twentieth century and the years leading up to the new millennium witnessed a proliferation of end-times movements, such as Heaven's Gate [...], the Order of the Solar Temple (an apocalyptic movement originating in Geneva, whose members committed mass suicide in 1994), the Branch Davidians (whose members had a violent showdown with the Bureau of Alcohol, Tobacco and Firearms in Texas in 1993 [...]), Aum Shrinrikyo (a Japanese group that spread sarin gas in Tokyo subways in 1995), and many others.

The idea of an approaching end times or apocalypse is obviously not unique to contemporary new religious movements. Indeed, it is deeply embedded in the much older Christian concept of the "millennium" (literally, a thousand-year period) and is first mentioned in the book of Revelation or Apocalypse of St. John, which describes a millennium after Satan is defeated and the righteous will reign with Christ for a thousand years. Throughout Christian history—particularly during the late medieval and early modern periods—there have been a number of millenarian movements, such as the Free Spirit, the Münsterites, and many others. During the 1840s, a huge millenarian movement called the Millerites spread across the northeastern United States, inspired by William Miller's calculation that the Second Coming of Jesus would occur sometime in 1843–44. However, it does seem that the final decades before the year 2000 inspired a fresh wave of religious groups anticipating the catastrophic end of the world and the transition to something radically new.

In this and the subsequent chapters, we will look at just a few examples of millenarian movements—two that ended in violent tragedy (Peoples Temple and the Branch Davidians) and one that has a more optimistic view of the coming millennium (the Raëlians). Because of its catastrophic end, Peoples Temple raises a number of profound issues and debates for the study of new religions and of religion more generally. Perhaps most importantly, it raises the debate surrounding the "cult" label, which, as we have seen, has often been applied to many new religious and alternative groups from the Mormons onward. Dubbed "the Cult of Death" by *Time* magazine in 1978, Peoples Temple became the media poster child of a dangerous, murderous cult and has informed much of the popular representation of new religions ever since. As the *Time* article put it, "The Jonestown story, like some Joseph Con-rad drama of fanaticism and moral emptiness, has gone directly into popular myth. It will be remembered as an emblematic, identifying moment of the decade: a demented American psychopomp in a tropical cult house, doling out cyanide with Kool-Aid. Jonestown is the Altamont of the '70s cult movement."[2]

[... M]ost scholars in the United States today reject the term *cult* in favor of more neutral terms such as *new religious movement*. However, this still leaves us with the question of how to talk about and make sense of groups that might be violent or self-destructive. How can we examine such groups both sympathetically and critically in ways that will take them seriously as genuine quests for religious meaning, while at the same time also seriously analyzing their more problematic and self-destructive elements?

Jim Jones and the Formation of Peoples Temple

Like those of other new religious leaders we have discussed so far, the biography of Jim Jones is difficult to write, since there are relatively few sources, and the few that we have tell very different stories about the man. According to some accounts, he was a "bad seed" and a troublemaker from his childhood onward, known as the local "Dennis the Menace,"[3] but others describe him as a spiritually gifted young man with an innate calling to the church.[4] However, at least the basic facts do seem to be generally agreed upon.

James Warren Jones was born on May 13, 1931, in Crete, Indiana, and then moved with his family to the small town of Lynn, Indiana, three years later. Struggling in the midst of the Great Depression, the Jones family was poor. The family farm failed shortly after Jim's birth, his father was largely disabled from a war injury, and his mother worked various jobs to support them. At the time, this was a part of the country that was not only deeply divided by racial segregation but also pervaded by Christian fundamentalism. Although his family was not particularly religious, Jones became interested in various local churches as a young man and was quickly drawn to the lively and charismatic services of the Pentecostal Church. Pentecostalism would leave a lasting impression on his own preaching style and the later Peoples Temple, particularly its vibrant, expressive worship, manifestations of the Spirit, faith healing, and communal ideal of mutual sharing and support. By age sixteen, Jones had already begun preaching on his own, traveling to predominantly African American neighborhoods to spread a message of revival and brotherhood.

In 1949, while attending Indiana University–Bloomington, Jones married Marceline Baldwin. Marceline came from a Methodist background, and although Jones was critical of Methodism as an organized church he found that reading the Methodist social creed was a life-changing experience. Here was a church that believed in real issues of social justice, such as alleviating poverty and promoting free speech, prison reform, and racial integration. At the same time, he was repelled by the racism and intolerance that he encountered in places such as Bloomington, which was a center of Ku Klux Klan activity and, in his view, "besieged by redneck mentality from the South."[5] Thus Jones developed two passions that would drive him for the rest of his life: racial integration and socialism.

In 1954, Jones set up his own church, called Community Unity, in Indianapolis. With his charismatic, energetic preaching style, he began to attract a growing congregation and also the interest of local Pentecostal church elders. However, his insistence that his congregation be racially integrated was both unusual and controversial among the racially divided churches of Indianapolis. In 1955, he moved his community to a larger building in the city and took the new name Peoples Temple; then in 1959, the congregation voted to affiliate itself with the Disciples of Christ, a mainline church already known for its commitment to progressive issues and social justice.

"A Black Church": Religion and Race in Peoples Temple

Perhaps the most remarkable aspect of Peoples Temple was its attitude toward race, which was in many ways radical and well ahead of its time. Several of the movements we have discussed in this book were racially separatist—including the Nation of Islam and early Rastafari—calling for blacks to have their own homeland in Africa, free of white oppression. Jones's vision was quite the opposite. At a time when most churches in the United States were still segregated, Jones's commitment to social justice was closely tied to an ideal of a racially integrated congregation, and he actively sent missionaries out into black communities to draw in new members. In turn, many African Americans were drawn not simply by his charismatic preaching style but also by his fiery message of justice and unity. While its leadership remained largely white, Peoples Temple was, in many ways, a "black church"—that is, its preaching style, energetic worship, music, and commitment to social and political ideals had much in common with African American churches. In the words of Rebecca Moore, a religious studies scholar and relative of former Peoples Temple members, "Peoples Temple really was a black church. It was led by a white minister, but in terms of the worship service, commitment to the social gospel, its membership, it functioned completely like a black church."[6] The exact demographics of Peoples Temple are a bit uncertain, but various sources state that it was between one-fifth and one-half black by 1960.

Interview with Tim Carter

Tim Carter joined Peoples Temple in 1972 and was one of the few members who survived the tragedy in Jonestown. In this interview he talks about what drew him to the community, his reflections on Jim Jones as a person, and how he was able to move on after the events of 1978. Carter served in the military in Vietnam and then explored a variety of spiritual, social, and political ideas in the early 1970s. He found many of his own spiritual and political views embodied in the unique community of Peoples Temple.

As soon as I walked into the Temple, I was home, and I knew it. It felt like I had known those people forever. We've all experienced that, where you meet somebody and it just feels like you've known them for a long time, even if you've only known them for an hour. I hadn't met Jim Jones, I had no idea who he was, I had no idea really what the Temple was about. I had no concept of joining the Temple or living with them. But I knew that I had found a home for me. It felt like a synthesis of everything that I believed in spiritually and politically. One of the first things that Jones talked about was the Sermon on the Mount, which resonated with me.

There was no color. That was a thing you could feel and literally see in the Temple—*there was no color.* From my experience in Vietnam, I was one of the few whites that was totally accepted by the brothers over there. But there weren't that many of us. There were race deaths in Vietnam. Race deaths were real. Racism always has been real, but it was very real in Vietnam. So the contrast of that with the Temple was there.

One of the first things I heard Jones say was "Be still and know I am God," which is from the book of Psalms. A lot of people interpreted it as "*He* is God." Maybe that's what he meant, but I never interpreted it like that. I interpreted it as "I am" equals God, Universe, Source, whatever that is. Later on in the meeting they started passing around the bucket, and I had very little money. I was working whatever jobs I could find. In the Redwood Valley, I spent two days chopping wood so I had money to date with. The plate came around, and I put in my last sixty-eight cents. I leaned over to my sister and said, "I hope you got smokes, because that was all my money." About ten minutes later, Jones pointed to the balcony where my sister and I were sitting, and he said, "You who just gave your last 68 cents, that means more than these people who have a hundred dollars and only gave ten." I thought, "Wow, this guy is legit in terms of being psychic."

In terms of why people stayed in the Temple and what attracted them to the Temple, I do believe that there was a huge dichotomy between the younger and the older members. The younger members, both black and white, were much more politically oriented. I think that for the older black folks and white folks it was more religious, even though in the Temple religious faith meant helping other people, putting into action the Sermon on the Mount. That was an incredibly powerful thing for me. I could actually see with my own eyes that we were making a difference in the community. The Temple was helping people. For a lot of my liberal friends, it was a lot of talk and not a lot of do. And I felt good about the "do" part.

Jim Jones was brilliant, he was charismatic, he was a genius—and that's not an exaggeration. He was the best speaker that I ever heard in my life to this day. He was better than Jesse Jackson when Jesse was at his best. He was also manipulative, he was cunning, he was controlling. If I had seen all those things when I was first there, I probably wouldn't have ended up in Guyana. My reason for staying in the Temple for the last two years was my loyalty to the people. That was genuine and is genuine. It didn't have to do with following Jim Jones, because I hated the son of a bitch for about the last year and a half. I really did not like him, but I believed in what we were doing. And if you take away Jim Jones, I believe in my heart that Jonestown would still exist in some form or fashion. It might only be two hundred people, but I think it might be two thousand people or five thousand. I'm almost certain that it would still be in existence today.

I didn't know he was a drug addict. From what I've learned since, he was doing drugs back then. He was doing speedballs. I also learned that he was actually giving out bennies (Benzedrine) to some folks. There was a clear devolution in his personality, although I did not

(continued)

know that it had to do with drugs. The person that existed as a being when I first joined the Temple was not the same person that existed when everything came down. Was he a good man gone bad, was he a bad man gone worse? The light and the darkness existed equally. It's just that we only saw that which was more of the light.

People want to focus on Jim Jones. But the story of Peoples Temple is the people. It's not Jim Jones. He's a part of it. He added them all together. But what made the Temple dynamic and successful and *mainstream* was the people—because we were as mainstream as it could get in terms of the progressive movement in the Bay Area. We were not freaks. We were not cultists. We were mainstream. When the focus is on Jones, then all we are is "cultists." We are "them." For anybody to actually begin to learn anything about Peoples Temple, it has to become a "we."

There are a lot of people who feel that Jonestown really was just a concentration camp and nothing more, and others who feel that it was a real opportunity. Both realities are true, and that's one of the mind-fucks of Peoples Temple, is that everything about it is *contradictory*. The more I learn about what went on in Jonestown, though, the more I get sick to my stomach.

If the only story that somebody focuses on is that, well, there was this underground sensory deprivation chamber, and people had to work twelve hours a day, and the diet was horrible, and people couldn't leave—well, that's an accurate image. Is it the whole image? No. For everything in the Temple there are contradictions. At the same time that that's going on, we were building a city in the middle of the jungle. I saw kids that were sociopathic in the States. One of them was a black albino kid. He was out of place everywhere. He had been teased and given a hard time to the point where he was torturing animals. There was another kid who had watched his mother's brains blown out by his father. He was an angry kid. When I got to Jonestown I could see that these were completely different human beings—and I'm not talking about robot automatons. One of them was in charge of the animals; the same kid that had been torturing animals had a great relationship with them.

There were things that make me want to swell my chest with pride. Then I think, what difference did it make? Everybody died. If you look at the ending as suicide, then it really was a waste. But if you look at the ending as *murder*, then some of the things that we did do still have meaning.

They knew that people didn't want to die. There might be some, but most didn't. So they actually created the means to murder everybody. But it's one of those concepts that is so insane that even if you're there, you, and it looks like it's a threat, you ignore it because it's so crazy. It's like nuclear war—neither side fired the shot, thank God; it doesn't make any sense to destroy everything, because you gain nothing.

People say, "How did you survive?" And I say, "I survived, number one, because I know that there is a Source that is more than this physical realm, that nothing is lost in God or the Universe, whatever appellation you want to apply to that Energy." But mostly it was just that I willed myself to survive. I just don't believe in suicide. I don't know if it was because of my Catholic upbringing, or because of whatever Jewish genes I still have left in me. Everything that I have ever read spiritually says that whatever lessons you were supposed to learn in this life, you're going to be back in that position to learn them again. I thought to myself, I can't ever go back again to that blackness that was Jonestown on that final day. Maybe that was a selfish reason, but it kept me going.

For me, personally, it was all about not putting my faith in anybody but myself. Now, if the Dalai Lama walked into my house I would be thrilled, and I would sit and listen, and it would be wonderful. I would consider him a teacher—but not *the* teacher. So for me, it was not putting faith in anybody else. Am I still spiritual? Extremely. But in terms of putting my energy into any specific group? No, I can't do groups anymore, including the church.

Much of Jones's style and message was directly influenced by one of the most charismatic black preachers of the twentieth century, Father Divine, and his Peace Mission. As early as the 1930s, Father Divine had begun an interracial community in New York, preaching a message of racial integration and self-help for blacks and whites alike. Jones visited the Peace Mission several times in the 1950s and was so impressed by the church that he wrote a short booklet praising its principles of "cooperative communalism," which would become central to the vision of Peoples Temple.[7] Like Father Divine, Jones would encourage his congregation to call him "Father," and he began a housing and feeding program modeled on the Peace Mission. After Father Divine's death in 1965, Jones attempted to take over the organization, and while he failed to do so, Peoples Temple members did recruit many from the Peace Mission.

Cold War Nuclear Anxieties and Christian Socialism

In many ways, Peoples Temple was a complex mixture of a highly optimistic form of Christian socialism and a darker anxiety about the imminent end of the world. From at least the early 1960s, Jones had deep concerns about a coming Armageddon—concerns that were neither unique nor very surprising considering the Cold War context of the movement, at a time when many Americans were building bomb shelters and preparing for nuclear war. In 1962, Jones read an article in *Esquire* magazine that recommended "Nine Places in the World to Hide" in order to survive nuclear war. Following the article's advice, Jones moved his family to Brazil and lived there during 1962–63—during the very period when the Cuban missile crisis occurred, confirming his belief that the world was on the brink of nuclear holocaust. After returning to the United States, Jones also had a vision in which he saw a nuclear flash hitting Chicago. In 1965, Jones and about seventy of his followers relocated to the Redwood Valley in California—another site mentioned as a safe haven in the *Esquire* article. As Jones put it in a sermon in 1973, mixing biblical passages with nuclear fears: "So we have to be prepared to take our flight to the valley in the case of great desolation or Armageddon that would spring forth in a nuclear hell, as Peter said, when the elements melt with a fervent heat."[8]

In California, the community began to draw a mix of young, college-educated whites who were attracted by its progressive spiritual and political mission and lower-income blacks who were drawn by the church's urban ministries in San Francisco and Los Angeles. Peoples Temple also engaged in a wide range of social services, establishing nine residential homes for the elderly, six homes for foster children, and a forty-acre ranch for the mentally handicapped. By the mid-1970s, Jones's social service programs had begun to attract very positive media attention. Thus he was named one of the nation's one hundred outstanding clergymen by *Religion in Life* magazine in 1975; he won the *Los Angeles Herald*'s Humanitarian of the Year award in 1976; and he was one of four recipients of the annual Martin Luther King, Jr., Humanitarian of the Year award at Glide Memorial Church in San Francisco in 1977.

However, Jones's religious beliefs and teachings appear to have evolved significantly over time. From his early roots in Pentecostalism, Jones began to preach ideas that departed more and more from mainstream Christianity. After his contact with Father Divine, he increasingly began to emphasize his own divinity and godlike powers—not simply as a pastor but as a prophet or even a newly anointed being. As Jones described himself in a sermon delivered in San Francisco, he was not simply a man but really a manifestation of the "Christ Principle" or "Christ Revolution." Embodying the same egalitarian love as Jesus himself, Jones claimed the same power to heal and perform miracles:

> I have put on Christ, you see. I have followed the example of Christ. When you see me, it's no longer Jim Jones here, I'm crucified with Christ, nevertheless, I live yet not I, but Christ that lives here. Now Christ is in this body.
>
> You will not get Christ's blessing in Jim Jones' blessing until you walk like Jim Jones, until you act like Jim Jones. ... *I* am no longer a man, but a Principle. I am the Way, the Truth, and the Light. No one can come to Father but through me.[9]

Jones's divine claims appear to have been accepted by many in the Peoples Temple community. As Harold Cordell put it in a letter of 1965, "Jones is certainly a deliverer and the same anointed Spirit or Christ Spirit that we know resided in Jesus. ... [He is] one of the greatest prophets and messengers that have ever appeared on this earth."[10] Faith healings were often a key feature of the church's services, as Jones claimed to restore sight to failing eyes, remove pain, and allow the crippled to walk.

At the same time, Jones's sermons progressively incorporated a more socialist message—or rather, a kind of Christian communalism. At a time when the United States was still very much in the grip of the Cold War and communism was widely perceived as the ultimate enemy of the American way of life, Jones was remarkable for his outspoken criticism of American capitalism and his embrace of socialism. Jones was also critical of traditional Christianity, which he dismissed as a kind of "fly away religion" based on a vague faith in a "Sky God." Instead, Jones taught a form of Christian socialism based on the more practical goal of liberating and uplifting all people—particularly women and people of color—here on earth. American capitalist culture was, in his view, an "irredeemable Babylon" and an "Antichrist system" that was bound to destroy itself through nuclear war. In contrast, Jones offered the hope of creating an egalitarian, racially integrated society and a kind of "socialist millennial" vision of a new Eden. As he put it in a sermon delivered in San Francisco in 1973, "If you're born in capitalist America, racist America, fascist America, then you're born in sin. But if you're born in socialism, you're not born in sin."[11] Peoples Temple was thus presented as a kind of "apostolic socialism," a nonviolent revolution that would sweep the world like a hurricane:

> I am the only fully socialist. I am the only fully God. ...
>
> We could invite people then into other main services and up in our valley, beautiful projects and our senior homes, and let them see what we've done through cooperative, *non-violent,* true *apostolic* socialism, as an alternative to totalitarian fascism. ...
>
> I am going to establish a *hurricane.* I'm going to shake the whole nation with my spirit and my mind socialism. I'm going to *shake* the whole creation.[12]

In other sermons, Jones launched a scathing attack on mainstream Christian churches and their imaginary "Sky God." At times, Jones even attacked the Bible itself, which in his view had been used throughout history to support and reinforce rather than to fight racism, slavery, genocide, and other social injustices. As he put it in another sermon from 1973, this book had become another idol, and a dangerous one at that:

> Never in the history of mankind has a black book done so much infamy as this book. It brought blacks back in chains, it murdered the Indians, till there's not one hardly left. Their tribes are done. Their religion is gone. ... The Mexican people, their whole nation was *robbed* from them ... in the name of this black book. It is a paper idol. It's a destroyer. It's a *killer.* ...
>
> Your Bible is *full* of lies. Your Skygod makes no sense. If he was all-perfect, why doesn't he heal 'em all?[13]

In place of the dead letter of the Bible, with its vain promise of a distant heaven after death, Jones promised the more immediate rewards of divine socialism—food, shelter, comfort, and community here and now on this earth.

Growing Tensions from within and outside Peoples Temple

Peoples Temple had in many ways two very different sides to it—a popular public face and a more complex and darker internal dynamic. Publicly it was seen as a compassionate, caring, socially engaged church concerned with poverty, integration, and social justice, but inwardly it had a more authoritarian and disciplinary structure. Members were kept in check by a system of rewards and punishments and by catharsis sessions that focused heavily on sexuality and confession of sexual transgressions. After the move to Guyana, the disciplinary nature of the community became even more intense. Members who tried to flee were beaten, humiliated, or sentenced to heavy labor; some who broke rules were placed in sensory deprivation chambers; and finally, some were kept sedated with drugs.[14]

Jones himself had an extremely active and complicated sexual life. Not only did he often control and arrange the sexual lives of members—by deciding who would marry whom and who would be encouraged to procreate—but he also made himself the primary object of the members' sexual desires. While still married to Marceline, he had numerous relationships with both female and male members and fathered two sons with other women. Various observers have interpreted Jones's sexual life in rather different ways. Some scholars such as Catherine Wessinger offer a fairly generous interpretation of Jones's sexual relations, viewing them as an important part of the social dynamics of this religious community, and particularly as a means of offering women new roles in the church hierarchy. As she suggests, this was a means of "empowering them as his delegates to perform administrative duties ... in the establishment of their ideal socialist community."[15] Others, however, see Jones's sexual affairs as primarily a matter of power and a way of asserting control over every facet of members' lives and all levels of the community as a whole. As Rebecca Moore concludes, "Sex was an important way Jim Jones controlled individuals. ... Jones' management of relationships was not about sex, but about power, and he used his power to control all aspects of life inside the Temple."[16]

The Move to Guyana: Building Jonestown as Heaven on Earth

Despite the success of Peoples Temple in California and the recognition that Jones received as a humanitarian leader, the church faced increasing pressure from all sides. Because of its racially integrated community, the church was targeted by white racists and threatened by neo-Nazis, who sent hate mail and slashed members' tires. At the same time, Peoples Temple became the target of a number of extremely negative news stories concerning its "cult-like behavior" and investigations by various federal agencies. In 1972, the *San Francisco Examiner* published a series of articles attacking

Jones's messianic pretensions and the authoritarian structure of the movement; and in 1977, *New West* magazine published an exposé suggesting that Peoples Temple should be investigated for financial misdealings, coercive practices, and questionable involvement in San Francisco politics.

Finally, the movement also came under attack from former members, who had begun to speak out publicly against Jones in the early 1970s. Perhaps the most vocal opponents were Grace Stoen, who left Peoples Temple in 1976, and her husband Timothy Stoen, who left in 1977. The Stoens were a particular problem for the community because they were fighting for custody of their young son, John Victor Stoen, who was under Temple guardianship. Together with other ex-members and parents of members, the Stoens formed a group called the Committee for Concerned Relatives, which saw Peoples Temple as a "dangerous cult that had to be dismantled."[17] Later in 1977, Jones learned that the allegations of ex-members had helped prompt an investigation by the Treasury Department, and he feared that Peoples Temple might also be scrutinized by the IRS, as many other new religious movements had been during the 1970s.

Feeling himself attacked on all sides, and already deeply critical of American-style capitalism, Jones began to look for a new home for his church outside the Babylon of the United States. Jones had already visited Guyana in 1973, and in 1975 he stationed fifty members of the church there to begin clearing the jungle and building houses. As pressures in the United States escalated, Jones began to refer to Guyana as a "promised land" and a "socialist paradise" for the exodus from America; here they would attempt to bring their vision of an egalitarian, integrated socialist community to fruition in the new city of Jonestown. As former member Tim Carter recalled, the United States seemed to them to be a place of "creeping fascism" and intolerance where they were no longer at home: "It was apparent that corporations, or the multinationals, were getting much larger, their influence was growing within the government, and the United States is a racist place." Jonestown, conversely, "was a place in a black country where our black members could live in peace."[18]

By September 1977, nearly one thousand members had been transferred to the new site, which was imagined as a kind of heaven on earth, a paradise in the jungle where racism, sexism, and classism would be eliminated and where people who had been discriminated against in America could live in peace and freedom. As Harriet Tropp argued in a radio broadcast in defense of Jonestown, Peoples Temple was an amazing "democratic socialist cooperative," with a long list of valuable accomplishments: it had eliminated class distinctions, achieved a socialist lifestyle based on cooperation and sharing, and established successful medical, educational, and agricultural projects.[19] For many participants in Jonestown, this utopian vision would be valued up until the very end of the experiment. In the words of Annie Moore, who was apparently the last person to die at Jonestown,

> Jim Jones showed us all this—that we could live together with our differences, that we are all the same human beings. Luckily, we are more fortunate than the starving babies of Ethiopia, than the starving babies of the United States.

What a beautiful place this was. The children loved the jungle, learned about animals and plants. There were no cars to run over them; no child molesters to molest them; nobody to hurt them. They were the freest, most intelligent children I had ever known.[20]

Despite this tremendous optimism and hard work, however, Peoples Temple faced a number of serious challenges in their new location. First, a large percentage of the population at Jonestown—about half of the over nine hundred members—were either elderly or children, which meant that the able-bodied adults had to struggle to provide material support, health care, and education for the entire population. At the same time, there were growing suspicions that, even after leaving the United States, the community was still under scrutiny by the US government. Residents were convinced that the CIA was watching them and working to undermine the community; in fact, the heavily excised documents released by the CIA do indicate that agents were working in Guyana, and the agency was the first to notify the US Defense Department of the deaths. However, this is not particularly surprising, given that this was an American movement espousing socialism and criticizing the United States—all in the midst of the Cold War and the larger paranoia about communism, cults, and brainwashing.[21]

Jones himself, meanwhile, declined rapidly during the period in Guyana, both physically and mentally. In addition to mental exhaustion, Jones developed serious health problems by mid-1978, including high fever and a fungal disease in his lungs. At the same time, he appears to have been using large amounts of drugs, which increasingly impaired his ability to lead the community. Embassy officials who visited Jones in May and November of 1978 stated that he was clearly on drugs, noting his slurred speech, erratic behavior, and mental confusion.[22] After the murder-suicide, the autopsy report would show that Jones had toxic levels of pentobarbital in his system. Overall, as Jones's physical and mental state declined, the morale of the Jonestown community appears to have declined rapidly as well.

Practice Suicides, White Nights, and the End of Jonestown

The final tragic events of November 1978 were not the first time Peoples Temple had discussed the idea of mass suicide. Even as early as 1973, Jones appears to have suggested the idea that the leadership might need to take their own lives. In 1976, Jones ordered a suicide drill, in which members of his inner circle were asked to drink wine and were then informed that they had consumed poison that would kill them within forty-five minutes. Finally, when no one questioned the decision or rebelled, he informed them that it had simply been a test. As one former member, Bonnie Thielmann, recalled, collective suicide was seen by many members as the logical and necessary alternative to dehumanizing, self-destructive, and increasingly fascistic American society: "We expected to move to a safe haven in another country before America collapsed, but if we didn't, we all agreed that, yes, we'd commit suicide."[23]

Another suicide drill took place in Jonestown in February 1978. In this case, members of the community were given a drink they were told was a mixture of juice and potent poison. As one member, Edith Roller, recalled in her journal from this period, there was little protest as the members of the community lined up for the drink. While she didn't personally believe that the current situation called for such a radical decision, she also reflected that she "had to die sometime."[24] Other members even wrote publicly about their willingness to die for Jonestown. According to a letter sent by Pam Moton to all members of the US Congress in March 1978, it is evident "that people cannot forever be continually harassed and beleaguered by such tactics without seeking alternatives that have been presented. I can say without hesitation that we are devoted to a decision that it is better even to die than to be constantly harassed from one continent to the next."[25]

As real and perceived threats from both within and without the community mounted, Peoples Temple began to prepare for attack. Jones used the term *White Nights* to refer to moments of "severe crisis within Jonestown and the possibility of mass death during, or as a result of, an invasion."[26] While White Nights had taken place earlier in California, they became far more intense after the move to Guyana. For example, in September 1977 the attorney of former member Timothy Stoen traveled to Jonestown to serve court papers to Jones and then persuaded a Guyana court to issue an arrest warrant. Believing that the community was threatened, members armed themselves with farm implements and stood waiting on the periphery of the compound for days, ready for an attack. In January 1978, Jones announced another White Night, claiming that they were under attack from the Concerned Relatives and the CIA. On this occasion—an eerie foreshadowing of the final suicides—members of the community lined up to take poison in order to prevent their children from being taken and tortured. Before anyone actually died, however, Jones announced that the crisis was over.

November 18, 1978, was the final White Night. When Congressman Ryan arrived in Guyana to meet with Jones and members of Peoples Temple that day, he was initially received very politely and was even allowed to take fourteen members who wished to leave along with him to the airplane. Shortly after Ryan and most of his party were gunned down on the airstrip, however, Jones announced that this was the time to end this social experiment, and a large batch of Flavor-Aid mixed with cyanide, valium, and chloral hydrate was prepared for the community. In Jones's final words, this was not to be a mere suicide but a kind of revolutionary act, a protest against an intolerant, racist, and inhumane world. It was in his view preferable to the persecution they would face from the US government and an act of defiance against a society that would not leave them in peace:

> We're not committing suicide—it's a revolutionary act. We can't go back; they won't leave us alone. They're now going to tell more lies, which means more congressmen. There's no way, no way we can survive. ...
>
> They'll pay for it. This is a revolutionary suicide. This is not a self-destructive suicide. So they'll pay for this. They brought this upon them.

It's been done by every tribe in history. Every tribe facing annihilation. All the Indians of the Amazon are doing it right now. They refuse to bring any babies into the world ... because they don't want to live in this kind of a world. ...

We said ... we don't like the way the world is. Take our life from us. We laid it down. We got tired. We didn't commit suicide, we committed an act of revolutionary suicide protesting the conditions of an inhumane world.[27]

At least some of the members on the final day seemed to agree with Jones. In the words of one woman, recorded on the same tape with Jones as the suicides began, "This is nothing to cry about. This is something we could all rejoice about. ... They always told us that we could cry when you're coming into this world. So we're leaving it, and we're leaving it peaceful. ... I have been here one year and nine months, and I never felt better in my life. ... I had a beautiful life. We should be happy."[28]

However, these recordings from the final hours of Peoples Temple reveal that not all of the members were in agreement that the situation was entirely hopeless. Some challenged Jones's decision, suggesting that it was senseless to throw away all of their hard work and the amazing community they had created. "I look at all the babies, and I think they deserve to live," one member, Christine Miller, said to Jones, asking if it was too late for the movement to follow a proposed plan to move to Russia for safe haven.[29] But she was quickly shouted down amid the escalating rhetoric. Moreover, not every member of Peoples Temple chose to drink the Flavor-Aid willingly; and at least five who were meant to be poisoned survived by hiding, pretending to be dead, or fleeing the scene. Tim Carter, who fled Jonestown but only after watching his own wife and infant son die, recalls that many were either injected with poison or forced to drink the Flavor-Aid at gunpoint. As we will see in more detail below, Carter argues that this was not a "revolutionary suicide" at all but largely an act of mass murder, in which hundreds of children, seniors, and adults were executed against their will.

Key Issues and Debates: Destructive New Religions and the Media—"Cult," "Revolutionary Suicide," or "Mass Murder"?

[... O]ne of the key problems in the study of new and alternative religious groups has been the "cult" label. Many of the movements discussed so far in this book—such as ISKCON, the Church of Satan, and the Church of Scientology, in particular—were regularly branded as cults in the mainstream media, becoming part of a larger "cult scare" that spread across American during the 1970s and '80s.[30] Yet Peoples Temple arguably became the most infamous poster child for the popular stereotype of the dangerous, destructive cult.

Literature on cults had been around long before Peoples Temple, dating back at least to the 1920s, with books such as Gaius Atkins's *Modern Religious Cults and Movements* (1923). But the real flood of anticult publications began in the 1960s and '70s—not surprisingly the very period in which the American spiritual marketplace was growing rapidly and providing a variety of new religious offerings—with books such as Jan Van Baalen's *Chaos of the Cults* (1962) and Walter Martin's *The Kingdom of the Cults* (1965). By the late 1960s, anticult paranoia combined with the growing fears about the alleged phenomenon of brainwashing during the Cold War [...]. This paranoia was only exacerbated by the media sensation of the Charles Manson family and its murder spree in 1969, leading to widespread fears that destructive groups were waiting to capture the minds of vulnerable young people and lead them to commit heinous acts. And by the 1970s, the fear of new religions had blossomed into a widespread "cult scare" and given rise to a wide array of anticult groups—the Individual Freedom Foundation, Love Our Children, the Citizens Freedom Foundation, the Spiritual Counterfeits Project, Cults Exodus for Christ, and the Cult Awareness Network, among many others— dedicated to saving America's youth from dangerous mind-control groups. These cult anxieties were clearly tied to a wide range of other anxieties, tensions, and obsessions of post-1960s America—not simply the fear of communism spreading on US soil but also the countercultural movement, the civil rights movement, the sexual revolution, experimentation with mind-altering drugs, shifting gender roles, and radical new social experiments.

With its explicitly socialist rhetoric, its radical racial politics, its complex sexual dynamics, and its catastrophic end, Peoples Temple became the quintessential cult in the American popular imagination. Major publications such as *Time* and *Newsweek* burned the image of Jonestown into American's collective consciousness with cover stories such as "The Cult of Death" and luridly detailed descriptions of the suicides. [... M]any new religions such as ISKCON had been described as dangerous "brain-washing" groups, and Peoples Temple quickly became the poster child for the idea of mind control—a movement so total in its domination of members' minds that it could lead them to self-destruction. As *Time* magazine put it immediately after the deaths in Jonestown, "In an appalling demonstration of the way in which a charismatic leader can bend the minds of his followers with a devilish blend of professed altruism and psychological tyranny, some 900 members of the California-based Peoples Temple died in a self-imposed ritual of mass suicide and murder."[31] In its analysis of the psychology of Peoples Temple, the *Time* article draws upon well-known "cult experts" such as Margaret Singer, whom we encountered in our discussion of ISKCON and the brainwashing debate. Once again, the members of Peoples Temple are portrayed as mind-controlled dupes who have become entangled in the cult's poisonous web and have given up all free will to the powerful, seductive cult leader:

> Why did they join an organization like the Peoples Temple? And why did they stay in it? ... Social scientists who have studied these groups agree that most cult members are in some sort of emotional trouble before they join. Says Dr. Margaret Thaler Singer, a psychologist at Berkeley: "About one-third are very psychologically distressed people. The other two-thirds are relatively average

people, but in a period of depression, gloom, being at loose ends." Such people are vulnerable to well-planned recruitment techniques. These usually involve displays of effusive affection and understanding, or "love bombing," as one psychiatrist puts it. Once recruits start going to meetings, they are frequently subjected to various drills and disciplines that weary them both physically and emotionally, producing a sort of trance.

Cut off from family and friends, the new member gets repeated infusions of the cult's doctrines. The lonely, depressed, frightened and disoriented recruit often experiences what amounts to a religious conversion. ... At this point, the cultist's life is no longer his own. Personalities change from the lively and complex patterns of normality to those of an automaton reciting what he has been taught. The usual problems of living have been replaced by a nearly childish existence in which the cult and its leaders supply all rules and all answers.[32]

In sum, Peoples Temple is portrayed as the epitome of a deadly mind-control group at the terrifying intersection between spirituality and madness: "Religion and insanity occupy adjacent territories in the mind; historically, cults have kept up a traffic between the two."[33]

Today, Jonestown is a kind of cultural reference point for the stereotype of the "crazy cult," to which we repeatedly return in popular discourse. Thus "drinking the Kool-Aid" has become common slang for someone who has given up rational thought and adopted a group mentality and/or a crazy idea (even though the beverage consumed at Jonestown was actually the knock-off brand Flavor-Aid, not Kool-Aid). Jim Jones's face with his large dark sunglasses now adorns T-shirts, lunchboxes, album covers, and other pop culture material. And virtually every subsequent movement that has been thought to be potentially dangerous or self-destructive has been described in the popular media as "another Jonestown" waiting to happen. As such, Peoples Temple is a particularly acute example of the problem of the "cult" label and the question of how we *should* describe movements that have such a history of destructive and ultimately self-destructive behavior.

For most scholars of religion today [...] the term *cult* is so biased and loaded with negative connotations as to be largely useless in the serious academic study of these controversial movements. As Rebecca Moore put it in her study of Peoples Temple, "Cult is never a value-neutral word, since it always carries an implicit criticism. We do not call Baptists or Catholics or Jews cultists; we only call religions of which we disapprove cults."[34] Most often, the cult label is used for groups that challenge or reject mainstream social norms by changing their dress and hairstyle or living in alternative communal or family arrangements or dropping out of school or jobs: "One thing they all seemed to have in common was a rejection of the lives their parents led, discarding worldly success and traditional markers of middle-class achievement such as careers, families, homes."[35]

As an alternative to the cult label, more sympathetic scholars have tried to humanize Peoples Temple by taking it seriously as a legitimate religious movement and placing it within the broader framework of American history and comparative religion. As John Hall suggests, Peoples Temple was not just some weird aberration from mainstream society but in many ways a deeply *American* movement. With its commitment to the Social Gospel, its charismatic worship, and its progressive politics, Peoples Temple was very much a reflection of American religious life, particularly during the volatile decades of the 1960s and '70s.[36]

Going still further, other scholars such as David Chidester suggest that Peoples Temple and its tragic end need to be understood in the broader context of comparative religions. Mass suicide, Chidester points out, is by no means unheard of in the history of religions, and he cites numerous other examples of religiously sanctioned suicide, including *seppuku* or *hara kiri* in Japan, *sati* or widow's self-sacrifice in India, and the ritual suicides by the Cathar Christian sect in medieval France. After examining a variety of different traditions, Chidester identifies four main religious uses of suicide, all of which were found in Jonestown: (1) to *reinforce* the purity of the community in relation to the perceived defilement of the outside world; (2) to find *release* from a world of misery, suffering, and pain; (3) to exact *revenge* against a government, news media, and traitors to the movement who have provoked the final suicidal act; and (4) to enact *revolution* in the face of what members regard as a dehumanizing and intolerant larger society. In this sense, Chidester suggests, collective suicide might be not so much a bizarre result of cult "brainwashing" as a logical outcome of this community's religious worldview and its unique commitment to apostolic socialism.[37]

However, while Chidester's more sympathetic approach does help us understand Peoples Temple within the broader framework of the comparative study of religions, it seems perhaps less helpful for understanding the complex power relations and internal dynamics between Jones and his followers. Many religions may include the possibility of some form of ritual suicide, such as *hara kiri* in Shinto or *sati* in Hinduism; but not all of them involve the complex sexual relations, the severe discipline, and the drug abuse that we see in Peoples Temple. As we saw above, it is also not at all clear that all or even most of the members died voluntarily.

Others have therefore argued that the Jonestown deaths should not be called "revolutionary suicide" at all and were in fact largely an act of *mass murder*. Tim Carter was one of the few surviving members who witnessed the events firsthand, and he believes that by far the majority of those who died were killed involuntarily—by being either injected with poison or forced to drink the Flavor-Aid at gunpoint. By his count, 246 of those who died were children, who could not be considered to have committed suicide voluntarily; roughly 180 were seniors, who were unable to defend themselves; and somewhere around 125 were injected with poison, on the basis of the abscesses Carter claims that he saw on their bodies. In sum, in his words, "We were just fucking slaughtered. … There was nothing dignified about it. Had nothing to do with revolutionary suicide, nothing to do about making a fucking statement. It was just senseless waste, senseless waste and death."[38]

In Carter's view, the fact that Peoples Temple members were victims of murder rather than suicide is actually evidence that they were *not* brainwashed dupes in some mind-control cult. Rather than robot automatons under Jones's will, they were a group of individuals dedicated to working together and building a genuine spiritual community. The fact that most of them died against their will, in Carter's opinion, proves that they did not give up on this social and spiritual ideal but struggled for it until the end:

> People want to focus on Jim Jones. But the story of Peoples temple is the people. It's not Jim Jones. ... What made the temple dynamic and successful and *mainstream* was the people—because we were as mainstream as it could get in terms of the progressive movement in the Bay Area. We were not freaks. We were not cultists. We were mainstream. When the focus is on Jones, then all we are is "cultists." We are "them." For anybody to actually begin to learn anything about Peoples Temple, it has to become a "we." ...
>
> There were things that make me want to swell my chest with pride. Then I think, what difference did it make? Everybody died. If you look at the ending as suicide, then it really was a waste. But if you look at the ending as *murder,* then some of the things that we did do still have meaning.
>
> They knew that people didn't want to die. There might be some, but most didn't. So they actually created the means to murder everybody.[39]

To make sense of Peoples Temple, Carter suggests, we have to take seriously its complex and often contradictory nature; we have to examine *both* its darkest, most disturbing elements—its authoritarianism and violence—*and* its most positive elements—its often remarkable commitment to building a progressive spiritual community.

In sum, taking a movement such as Peoples Temple seriously as a legitimate "religion" rather than dismissing it as a "cult" does not mean that we should not *also* look critically at the more problematic aspects of the group. Calling something a religion does not mean that it is entirely good. After all, we can think of many examples of "mainstream" religions that have also been involved in horrible acts, from the Christian Crusades and Inquisition, to child sexual abuse in the Catholic Church, to acts of terrorism carried out by various Muslim, Christian, Hindu, and even Buddhist groups. [... R]eligious discourse is uniquely powerful, precisely because it involves an appeal to a transcendent, supra-human, and eternal source of authority. As such, it can inspire acts of both great goodness and great evil. It can help lead movements of social justice (the civil rights movement, Gandhi's nonviolent resistance to British colonial rule, Mother Teresa's campaign to help the poor, etc.), but it can also be used to legitimate acts of violence and terror (flying airplanes into skyscrapers, justifying preemptive wars, covering up cases of pedophilia, etc.). So by taking controversial groups such as Peoples Temple seriously as "religions" rather than branding them as "cults," we are not thereby glossing over their negative, darker, or destructive aspects. Rather, we are simply saying: they are as capable of exploiting their claims to religious authority as adherents of "mainstream" religions.

Because Peoples Temple is such a complex and painful example of a religious movement that ended in tragedy, it highlights this point in a particularly acute way. It therefore deserves to be studied, examined, reflected upon, and taken very seriously, not simply reduced to a Jim Jones T-shirt or dismissed as just another weird anecdote from the 1970s. In the words of an anonymous letter, left by a member of Peoples Temple and found after the deaths: "To whomever finds this note. Collect all the tapes, all the writing, all the history. The story of this movement, this action, must be examined over and over. We did not want this kind of ending. We wanted to live, to shine, to bring light to a world that is dying for a little bit of love."[40]

Questions for Discussion and Debate

1. Where should we begin if we're trying to make sense of a movement as complex and tragic as Peoples Temple? Should we begin with a psychological profile of Jones himself? With an analysis of racial issues in America of the 1950s and '60s? With a sociological study of the members themselves?

2. Peoples Temple obviously had roots in mainstream Christianity, particularly in Pentecostalism and Methodism, yet it quickly went in a more radical and socialist direction, which included criticisms of the Bible and of the traditional Christian idea of God. Should it still be considered a form of "Christianity," or was it something else? Or could one argue that Jones was reasserting the radical socialist message inherent in the Gospels themselves?

3. Do you accept the argument of scholars such as Chidester that Peoples Temple should be viewed as a genuine religious movement that engaged in a form of "religious suicide" comparable to other examples in the history of world religions? Is it possible that these scholars might be bending too far over backward to portray Peoples Temple in a positive light—and thus perhaps are minimizing the fact that this was an extremely controlling and manipulative movement that ended in terrible tragedy?

4. What do you think of the arguments of former members such as Tim Carter, who believe that this was primarily an act of *murder*, not suicide? Do you find his argument persuasive? Also, what difference does it make—for survivors, family members, and students of religion—whether we call this a murder or a suicide?

Suggested Classroom Activity

Analyze the final audio recording of Jim Jones and Peoples Temple on November 18, 1978. How is Jones himself describing the decision to end this religious experiment by mass murder-suicide? What sorts of religious imagery is he using, what sorts of comparisons to other cultures and examples—and why? How are the other members of the community reacting? Does it seem as though there is general consensus, or confusion, or debate among the members? Finally, what should we call a document like this? A religious message? A suicide note? The ravings of a mentally disturbed individual?

Suggested Video

"Jonestown: The Life and Death of Peoples Temple." *PBS Frontline,* 2006.

Suggestions for Further Reading

Alternative Considerations of Jonestown and Peoples Temple. Department of Religious Studies, San Diego State University, 2014. http://jonestown.sdsu.edu/.

Chidester, David. *Salvation and Suicide: An Interpretation of Jim Jones, the Peoples Temple and Jonestown.* Bloomington: Indiana University Press, 1988.

Hall, John R. *Gone from the Promised Land: Jonestown in American Cultural History.* New Brunswick, NJ: Transaction, 1987.

Moore, Rebecca. *Understanding Jonestown and Peoples Temple.* Westport, CT: Praeger, 2009.

Moore, Rebecca, and Fielding McGehee III, eds. *New Religious Movements, Mass Suicide and Peoples Temple: Scholarly Perspectives on a Tragedy.* Lewiston, NY: E. Mellen Press, 1989.

Moore, Rebecca, Anthony B. Pinn, and Mary R. Sawyer, eds. *Peoples Temple and Black Religion in America.* Bloomington: University of Indiana Press, 2004.

Reiterman, Tim. *Raven: The Untold Story of Rev. Jim Jones and His People.* New York: Penguin, 2008.

Smith, Jonathan Z. "The Devil in Mr. Jones." In *Imagining Religion: From Babylon to Jonestown.* Chicago: University of Chicago Press, 1988.

Thielmann, Bonnie. *The Broken God.* Elgin, IL: David C. Cook, 1979.

Wessinger, Catherine. *How the Millennium Comes Violently: From Jonestown to Heaven's Gate.* New York: Seven Bridges Press, 2000.

Notes

1. Tim Carter, "Murder or Suicide? What I Saw," in *Alternative Considerations of Jonestown and Peoples Temple,* Department of Religious Studies, San Diego State University, 2006, http://jonestown.sdsu.edu/?page_id=31976.

2. Lance Morrow, "The Lure of Doomsday," *Time,* December 4, 1978, 6.

3. David Chidester, *Salvation and Suicide: An Interpretation of Jim Jones, the Peoples Temple and Jonestown* (Bloomington: Indiana University Press, 1988), 2.

4. Rebecca Moore, *Understanding Jonestown and Peoples Temple* (Westport, CT: Praeger, 2009), 9–10.

5. Jim Jones quoted in Chidester, *Salvation and Suicide,* 3.

6. "Jonestown: The Life and Death of Peoples Temple," *PBS Frontline,* 2006. See also Moore, *Understanding Jonestown,* 15.

7. Moore, *Understanding Jonestown,* 16.

8. Jim Jones, 1973 Sermon, transcript Q 958, in *Alternative Considerations,* 2014, http://jonestown.sdsu.edu/?page_id=60665.

9. Jim Jones quoted in Rebecca Moore, *Sympathetic History: The Moore Family Involvement in Peoples Temple* (Lewiston, NY: E. Mellen Press, 1985), 155.

10. Moore, *Understanding Jonestown,* 20.

11. Jim Jones, "San Francisco Sermon," 1973, transcript Q1053, in *Alternative Considerations,* http://jonestown.sdsu.edu/?page_id=27318.

12. Ibid.; see also Chidester, *Salvation and Suicide,* 5.

13. Jim Jones, Sermon of 1973, in *Alternative Considerations,* 2014, http://jonestown.sdsu.edu/?page_id=60680.

14. Moore, *Understanding Jonestown,* 34; see Catherine Wessinger, *How the Millennium Comes Violently: From Jonestown to Heaven's Gate* (New York: Seven Bridges Press, 2000), 47.

15. Wessinger, *How the Millennium Comes Violently,* 35.

16. Moore, *Understanding Jonestown,* 35; see also Laurie Efrein Kahalas, *Snake Dance: Unraveling the Mysteries of Jonestown* (New York: Red Robin Press, 1998).

17. Wessinger, *How the Millennium Comes Violently,* 40.

18. Deborah Layton, *Seductive Poison: A Jonestown Survivor's Story of Life and Death in the Peoples Temple* (New York: Anchor Books, 1999), 111–16. See also Tim Carter, interview on *The American Experience,* Oregon Public Broadcasting, April 9, 2007.

19. Chidester, *Salvation and Suicide,* 149.

20. Rebecca Moore, *The Jonestown Letters: Correspondence of the Moore Family, 1970–1985* (Lewiston, NY: E. Mellen Press, 1986), 286.

21. Wessinger, *How the Millennium Comes Violently,* 42; Moore, *Understanding Jonestown,* 153.

22. Moore, *Understanding Jonestown,* 75.

23. Bonnie Thielmann, *The Broken God* (Elgin, IL: David C. Cook, 1979), 85.

24. Moore, *Understanding Jonestown,* 79.

25. Ibid.

26. Ibid., 75.

27. Jim Jones, transcript from November 18, 1978, in Jonathan Z. Smith's *Imagining Religion: From Babylon to Jonestown* (Chicago: University of Chicago Press, 1988), 127–34.

28. Ibid., 132.

29. "Jonestown: The Life and Death of Peoples Temple."

30. David G. Bromley and Anson D. Shupe Jr., *Strange Gods: The Great American Cult Scare* (Boston: Beacon Press, 1981); David G. Bromley and J. Gordon Melton, eds., *Cults and Religious Violence* (Cambridge: Cambridge University Press, 2002).

31. "Nightmare in Jonestown: A Religious Colony in Guyana Turns into a Cult of Death," *Time,* December 4, 1978, 4.

32. "Messiah from the Midwest," *Time,* December 4, 1978, 5.

33. Morrow, "Lure of Doomsday," 6.

34. Moore, *Understanding Jonestown,* 5.

35. Ibid., 4.

36. John Hall, *Gone from the Promised Land: Jonestown in American Cultural History* (New Brunswick, NJ: Transaction, 1987).

37. Chidester, *Salvation and Suicide,* 137–38.

38. "Jonestown: The Life and Death of Peoples Temple." See Carter, "Murder or Suicide."

39. Tim Carter, interview by the author, August 2014.

40. "Jonestown: The Life and Death of Peoples Temple."

READING 8

The Branch Davidians

Millenarian Movements, Religious Freedom, and Privacy

Hugh B. Urban

....

W hile the case of Peoples Temple raises complex questions about how to label and make sense of new religious movements, other groups raise even more difficult questions about how law enforcement and government agencies should deal with new religions that might be violent or self-destructive. Just fifteen years after the tragedy at Jonestown, another millenarian religious movement, the Branch Davidians, became the focus not simply of media scrutiny but of a large armed raid by the Bureau of Alcohol Tobacco and Firearms (ATF) near Waco, Texas, in 1993. Acting on suspicions of weapons violations, the ATF obtained a warrant and sent heavily armed agents into the Branch Davidian compound, which in turn triggered an intense gun battle. After the ATF's failed raid, the FBI became involved and launched a fifty-one-day siege of the community, which ended with a tear gas attack and a massive fire on April 19, 1993. Although the cause of the fire remains a matter of some dispute, the flames engulfed the entire compound, killing seventy-six men, women, and children.

The tragedy at Waco has left us with a number of profound and troubling questions—not least of which is how scholars, journalists, and law enforcement should handle complex movements such as the Branch Davidians in ways that will not end in violence. On the one hand, many critics would argue that there were indeed aspects of the Branch Davidian community that were deeply problematic and warranted investigation by law enforcement. The group possessed large numbers of guns and was suspected of illegally converting semiautomatic weapons to fully automatic weapons. When combined with millenarian beliefs in a coming end of the world, it is perhaps not surprising that this alarmed many law enforcement officers. At the same time, there were allegations that the group's leader, David Koresh, had physically and sexually abused minors within the community.

On the other hand, however, the Branch Davidians argued throughout the standoff that their civil liberties had been grossly violated by law enforcement and that this religious community had been subjected to aggressive and unwarranted invasion. Many scholars have also argued that the community was unfairly targeted as a "cult" and that law enforcement was misled in its actions by ill-informed and biased anticult groups. If the ATF and FBI had listened to serious scholars of religions rather than to anticult activists, they might have had a better understanding of the Branch Davidians' millenarian religious beliefs and so avoided a violent showdown with the group.[1]

These questions of religious freedom, law enforcement, security, and surveillance have become all the more complicated in the wake of the 9/11 terrorist attacks, amid new fears of religiously motivated violence and ever more invasive forms of government surveillance. In the twenty-first century, we face not just the possibility of religious extremism and violence but also new concerns about the erosion of privacy and liberties in the name of national security. We now know that the FBI and various local police forces have been secretly monitoring mosques and other religious organizations; and with the series of revelations about the National Security Agency's secret wiretapping program in 2005 and 2013, we also know that the government has tremendous powers of surveillance over the phone and e-mail communications of ordinary citizens. All of this raises questions about how to balance the need for safety and security with the need to protect basic rights to privacy and freedom of expression, particularly for minority religious groups. Although the case of the Branch Davidians and the disaster at Waco preceded the 9/11 attacks by almost a decade, they foreshadowed many of these questions, which have only become more complex in a new age of terrorism and surveillance.

From the Millerites to the Branch Davidians

The Branch Davidians were an offshoot of an offshoot of a Christian millenarian movement whose roots go back to the first half of the nineteenth century. [...] Christian history is full of millenarian groups who hold an expectation of the imminent Second Coming of Christ, and one of the largest ever to emerge in the United States was the Millerite movement. In 1833, the group's founder, William Miller, claimed that he had calculated the date of Jesus's second coming, which he believed would occur sometime between March 21, 1843, and March 21, 1844. When Jesus failed to arrive during that period, he recalculated the date to be April 18, 1844, and then again October 22, 1844. Although Miller briefly gathered a huge number of expectant followers looking forward to the appearance of Jesus, the movement quickly fell apart by the end of 1844, leading to what became known as the Great Disappointment. Out of the collapse of the Millerites, however, a new and more successful movement emerged called the Seventh-day Adventists, founded by Ellen G. White in 1863. While the Seventh-day Adventists also look forward to the second coming of Jesus, they refrain from assigning a particular date to the event and so have become a prosperous and increasingly "mainstream" church today, with over eighteen million members worldwide.

In 1929, another group splintered off from the Seventh-day Adventists called the Davidian Seventh-Day Adventists, led by a Bulgarian immigrant named Victor Houteff. According to Houteff's interpretation of the millennium, the mission of his new church was to gather 144,000 "servants of God" mentioned in the book of Revelation in order to prepare for the coming of Christ. While the main body of Seventh-day Adventists taught that the millennium would be a spiritual phenomenon in which they would spend eternity in heaven with Christ, Houteff understood the millennium to be a literal period of divine rule on earth, and specifically in the land of Israel. The name Davidian taken by his church referred to the ideal of restoring a messianic kingdom in Palestine like that of King David. In 1935, Houteff established the headquarters of the Davidians at the Mount Carmel center near Waco, Texas.

Finally, in the 1960s, yet another group splintered off from the Davidian Adventists, led by a couple from Texas named Ben and Lois Roden.

Figure 8.1 David Koresh. Courtesy of Sipa USA.

Assuming control of the Mount Carmel property, the Rodens founded their own church called the Branch Davidians, referring to Jesus's saying that "I am the vine and you are the branches" (John 15:1–3). Like their predecessors, the Rodens believed in the imminent coming of Jesus and urged their followers to move to Israel to prepare for the final days.

In 1981, Vernon Howell (later David Koresh) joined the Branch Davidians at Mount Carmel (Figure 8.1). As a young man, Howell had two great passions—the Bible (particularly the book of Revelation) and the guitar (in fact, he recorded some of his own songs, which focused heavily on biblical prophecy and millenarian ideas). Although he had been baptized in the Seventh-day Adventist Church just two years before, Howell was attracted by the prophetic teachings of the Mount Carmel Branch Davidians and became very close to Lois Roden. However, Howell's presence soon aroused the jealousy of the Rodens' son, George Roden, who saw himself as the rightful heir to Branch Davidian leadership and Howell as a rival. Roden also accused Howell of having sex with his mother—a charge Howell did not deny.[2]

The rivalry between Howell and George Roden culminated in one of the strangest incidents in the history of the movement. In November 1987, Roden dug up the body of Anna Hughes, a Davidian who had died at the age of eighty-four and had been buried on the Mount Carmel property for twenty years. Placing the casket in the chapel, Roden challenged Koresh to a contest to see who could raise the corpse from the dead. Instead of taking the challenge, Howell went to the police to file charges of corpse abuse, but the authorities refused to investigate the claim without proof. When Howell and seven armed companions tried to break into the Branch Davidian chapel to obtain photographic evidence of the corpse, a gunfight erupted and left Roden wounded. Howell was tried for attempted murder but was released after the jury failed to reach a verdict. Meanwhile, Roden was arrested several months later for attempted murder in an unrelated incident, and Howell and his followers moved into the Mount Carmel community. After assuming leadership of the community, Howell legally changed his name to David Koresh, taken from the names King David and Koresh, the Hebrew version of the Persian King Cyrus, who was also given the title of "messiah" or "anointed one."

Like other charismatic leaders discussed in this book—such as Jim Jones and Joseph Smith—Koresh had a complicated sexual life that helped reinforce his negative image as a deviant and dangerous figure. While legally married to one wife, Rachel, he began to take multiple additional wives, many of them quite young. In 1986, he announced his marriage to Karen Doyle (age fourteen) and Michelle Jones (age twelve), and in 1987, he was married to Robyn Bunds (age seventeen), Nicole Gent (age sixteen), and Dana Okimoto (age twenty). Later in 1989, Koresh revealed a divine message called the "New Light" revelation, according to which all men in the community except himself were to remain celibate, while all women were to be his own wives. His children—both present and future—would in turn find an exalted status in the Kingdom of God, which would soon be established in Israel. According to Texas state law, Koresh clearly had sexual relations with minors and could therefore have been prosecuted with statutory rape; according to the Davidians' interpretation, however, Koresh was fulfilling the biblical role of the Lamb of God, offering his female followers the opportunity to be "sown with the light" and bear a child for Christ. As one member, Alisa Shaw, explained, "A central part of the message [of Revelation] is the marriage of the Lamb. That's the way to salvation. There are a few [women] who are worthy to be sown with the seed of God and produce children. It's considered an honor to have a baby for Christ. Not every woman is worthy of Koresh's loins."[3]

The Seven Seals and the Millennium: Koresh's Interpretation of Revelation

Much of Koresh's teachings centered on his unique interpretation of the book of Revelation and the events leading up to the Second Coming and the Last Judgment. In his words, "The servant of God will find as we continue in our searching of the scriptures that every book of the Bible meets and ends in the book of Revelation."[4] Following in the tradition of the Millerites and the Davidian Adventists, Koresh believed not only that the last days described in Revelation were coming soon but that they were intertwined with and reflected in contemporary world events. At the heart of this millennial worldview was his understanding of the "seven seals" described in the first eight chapters of Revelation. In the biblical text, St. John receives a vision in which he is taken before the throne of God; there he sees Christ, who holds a great scroll bound with seven seals. As each of the seven seals is broken open, a series of catastrophic events unfolds that heralds the dissolution of the present world and the creation of a new heaven and a new earth. Thus, when the first four seals are broken, four horsemen ride forth, bringing war, famine, plague, and death to the earth. When the fifth seal is opened, the souls who have been slain because of their testimony to the Word of God cry out, and they are each given a white robe while they wait for the rest of God's servants to be killed. When the sixth seal is broken, the entire cosmos begins to dissolve as a great earthquake shakes the ground, the sun turns black, the moon turns blood red, the stars fall from the sky, and the heavens are rolled up like a scroll. And when the seventh seal is broken, seven angels blow their trumpets, which unleash a rain of destruction as mountains are set ablaze and a third of all living creatures are slain.

Koresh understood his own role as a key figure in this narrative of the seven seals and the seven angels. Combining his interpretation of Revelation with the lineage of the Branch Davidian Church itself, Koresh saw himself as the final link in a line of prophetic figures going back to William Miller himself. Following the image of the seven angels who appear in the book of Revelation, Koresh saw Miller as fulfilling the roles of the first two angels; Ellen White, the founder of the Seventh-day Adventist Church, was the third angel; Victor Houteff was the fourth; Ben Roden and Lois Roden were the fifth and sixth; and Koresh was the seventh and final angel. As an anointed messiah, Koresh saw himself as a "suffering servant" who would help initiate Armageddon. There is some debate as to whether Koresh actually believed himself to *be* Jesus Christ or God; however, James Tabor and Eugene Gallagher make a persuasive case that Koresh never claimed to be *the* Christ but rather to be an anointed one (*christos,* like Cyrus and others) and that he understood himself to be the Lamb in Revelation who opens the scroll bearing the seven seals.[5]

Initially, Koresh believed that the role of the Branch Davidian community would be to move to Palestine and then fight on the side of Israel in an apocalyptic battle against the United Nations. However, his reading of history shifted after the 1991 Gulf War, and he concluded that this apocalyptic confrontation might in fact begin at home in Texas itself. The US federal government, in Koresh's view, represented an evil system identified in Revelation as "Babylon."[6] Preparing for a possible apocalyptic showdown in Texas, the Branch Davidians stockpiled food, weapons, and ammunition, along with a tank of propane in case of the loss of electricity.[7] Thus, when the ATF launched their raid on Mount Carmel on February 28, this seemed to Koresh to provide the ultimate fulfillment of his own reading of biblical prophecy, with the Branch Davidian community playing the role of those holy servants who are slain for the testimony to the Word of God. Ironically, the federal agents would fall right into Koresh's own prophetic narrative, playing the role of Babylon. Indeed, shortly after the raid began, Koresh announced that "We are now in the Fifth Seal," suggesting that humankind had entered that moment in the unfolding of the final days when God's loyal servants would be slain and the catastrophic events mentioned in the opening of the sixth seal would soon begin.[8]

The ATF Raid and the Fifty-One-Day Siege

Like Peoples Temple, the Branch Davidians saw themselves as a persecuted religious community that was the target of repeated attacks from the government, the media, and ex-members. In 1989, a member named Marc Breault left the community because of his concerns about Koresh's multiple wives and sexual relations with minors. After moving to Australia, Breault dedicated himself to exposing Koresh as a false prophet and warning media and law enforcement about the Davidians' dangerous beliefs. He also worked with the Australian television program *A Current Affair* to make a documentary on the group and expose Koresh as a "cruel, maniacal, child-molesting, pistol-packing religious zealot who brainwashed his devotees."[9] In 1990, Breault began to warn other former members and Texas law enforcement agents that Koresh was planning to commit child sacrifice; later in 1992, he alleged that the Davidians were planning a mass suicide that would become "another Jonestown."

In the spring of 1992, the ATF began to investigate the Branch Davidians on the suspicion of possessing and trafficking illegal weapons. The Branch Davidians did in fact run a legal arms business called the Mag Bag, which purchased and sold guns and gun parts. Together with Paul Fatta and Mike Schroeder, Koresh attended large gun shows throughout Texas and sold weapons to support the community. However, the ATF became concerned that the group was stockpiling illegal arms as well. The bureau was first alerted when a UPS driver noticed that a torn package he was delivering to the ranch contained firearms and grenade casings. In July 1992, ATF agents visited the Davidians' gun dealer and then decided to set up surveillance of the compound from a house across the street for several months prior to the siege. In addition, the ATF sent in an undercover agent named Robert Rodriguez, who claimed to be interested in studying scripture with Koresh in order to gather intelligence on the community.

The actual search warrant for the raid, however, was not justified by any proof that the community possessed illegal weapons; rather, it was based on a suspicion that they might have been converting (legally obtained) semiautomatic weapons to fully automatic weapons. It is worth noting that the "Probable Cause Affidavit" used to secure the warrant described the Branch Davidians as a dangerous "cult" and its leader as a "power-mad, manipulative leader" who abused and raped young girls.[10]

On February 27, 1993, just one day before the ATF raid, the *Waco Tribune-Herald* ran the first installment of a series on Koresh, entitled "The Sinful Messiah." The article painted a particularly unflattering portrait of Koresh, largely informed by ex-members such as Breault and anticult activists such as Rick Ross. Special attention was given to Koresh's sexual relations with multiple minors and to the Davidians' stockpile of heavy weaponry: "If you are a Branch Davidian, Christ lives on a threadbare piece of land 10 miles east of here called Mount Carmel. He has dimples, claims a ninth-grade education, married his legal wife when she was 14, enjoys a beer now and then, plays a mean guitar, reportedly packs a 9mm Glock and keeps an arsenal of military assault rifles, and willingly admits that he is a sinner without equal."[11] This was the image of Koresh that largely informed both government agencies and the national media in their coverage of Waco over the next several months.

The Botched Raid and the Siege

The ATF raid began at roughly 9:45 on the morning of Sunday, February 28. Almost from start to finish, however, virtually everything went wrong. Although the raid was supposed to be a surprise, the Davidians were alerted when a reporter for KWTX-TV was tipped off and then got lost on the way to the ranch. The reporter asked directions from a US postal carrier who happened to be Koresh's brother-in-law. Inside the compound, Koresh informed undercover agent Rodriguez that he knew a raid was coming, and the agent hurriedly left, surprised that his cover had been blown. Although the ATF knew that the Davidians had now learned of the raid, they decided to go ahead with it anyway—even though their plan depended on the community being unarmed and taken by surprise. Arriving in two cattle trailers, seventy-six heavily armed ATF agents surrounded the compound. It is unclear who fired the first shots, but heavy gunfire quickly broke out on both sides. Just minutes after the shooting began, a Branch Davidian called 911, begging them to call off the raid; nonetheless, gunfire continued for the next two hours, leaving five ATF agents and five Davidians dead and Koresh himself wounded.

After the failure of the ATF assault, the FBI took command of the siege, which dragged on in a fifty-one-day standoff. During this period, twenty-one children and fourteen adults exited the compound, while Koresh and bureau agents went back and forth on how to negotiate a peaceful resolution. At the same time, the FBI also employed a variety of extreme and at times surreal measures in the attempt to drive the Davidians out. These included inducing sleep deprivation by playing all-night recordings of loud and dissonant sounds, such as jet planes, Tibetan chanting, and even rabbits being slaughtered. Koresh, meanwhile, was outspoken in his critique of the siege, which he saw as a gross violation of his own civil liberties and an appalling assault on a religious community that posed no threat to anyone. As he put it in a conversation with FBI negotiators,

> And a lot of the things the FBI, or these generals, are doing is just kind of way beyond the scope of reason. They are not only destroying private property, they are also removing evidence. And this doesn't seem like these are moves that should be made by a government who says to a people that we're going to be able to take this up in a court of law. ...
>
> And we're also Americans, and I think that America has a patronage [heritage] ... of individual citizens who have a breaking point. The government has gotten this strong to where it can come on to something that we have worked for *hard*. ...
>
> And if this is the way our government is showing the world that its tactics are to get someone to do as they wish when realistically our rights have been infringed upon right and left.[12]

In late March and early April, two religious studies scholars named J. Phillip Arnold and James D. Tabor attempted to intervene in the siege. After learning that the FBI was planning a gas assault on the compound, Professor Arnold developed a plan to try to persuade Koresh that there were other ways of interpreting Revelation that would not necessarily lead to an apocalyptic martyrdom of the

Davidians at the hands of the US government. Arnold called the FBI and left a message explaining that he was going to present a radio broadcast that would attempt to engage Koresh in a serious discussion of the Bible, and he urged the FBI not to undertake a violent attack on the community. Thus, on April 1, Arnold and Tabor held a radio discussion of the Bible on *The Ron Engelman Show,* offering an alternative interpretation of Revelation. In their reading, the text could be taken to mean that Koresh was not intended to die at that time but rather needed a longer period during which to spread his message of God's plan for salvation to the world. An audiotape of the discussion was taken into the Mount Carmel compound three days later, and attorneys told the FBI that the Branch Davidians would come out after Passover. On April 14, Koresh sent a letter explaining that he had been told by God to write down his interpretation of the seven seals. Once his completed manuscript was in the possession of his attorney and sent to Professors Tabor and Arnold, he claimed, he would come out peacefully. In fact, Koresh did complete a portion of the manuscript before the raid—his commentary on the opening of the first seal in Revelation—and there are indications within it that he may have been planning to lead his followers out peacefully: "Should we not eagerly ourselves be ready to accept this truth and come out of our closet and be revealed to the world as those who love Christ in truth and righteousness?" he wrote, which may have indicated that he was ready to lead the Davidians out of Mount Carmel.[13]

Apparently, this information was not passed on to Attorney General Janet Reno, who instead approved a plan to gas the Branch Davidian compound. Even though Koresh had requested a battery-operated word processor to complete his manuscript and announced that he had finished his interpretation of the first seal on April 16, the FBI's plans to engage in an aggressive assault moved forward. Finally, early on the morning of April 19, the FBI sent in tanks and used grenade launchers to hurl over four hundred rounds of CS gas into the buildings. Shortly after 12:00 p.m., after tanks had begun moving into the compound and knocking down walls, a fire broke out and quickly engulfed the entire complex, killing seventy-six of the remaining Davidians (Figure 8.2).

The exact cause of the fire remains a matter of intense dispute. While the FBI claims that it was an act of suicide and a deliberate fire set by the Branch Davidians, others argue that it was more likely sparked by the CS gas grenades or by the tanks knocking over the kerosene lanterns the community was using after its power was cut off. Former US senator John C. Danforth was appointed

Figure 8.2 Mount Carmel ranch in flames. Federal Bureau of Investigation.

special counsel to investigate the incident and issued a "Final Report" on November 8, 2000. Danforth's report concluded that the FBI assault did not cause the fire and that all of the physical evidence and testimony pointed instead to the Branch Davidians setting the fire themselves. "The responsibility for the tragedy," Danforth declared, "rests with certain of the Branch Davidians and their leader."[14] However, even after the report, many critics continue to see the Waco tragedy as one of the worst law enforcement disasters in US history.[15] As such, it mirrors many of the debates surrounding the Peoples Temple murder-suicides at Jonestown. Those who want to read the fire as deliberately set tend to see the tragedy as "another Jonestown"—that is, another example of a violent "cult" committing mass suicide at the hands of a charismatic but dangerous leader. Those who want to read the fire as a result of the FBI's own aggressive assault, conversely, tend to see the tragedy as the victimization of a minority religious community on account of misunderstanding, prejudice, and unnecessary government persecution.

The repercussions of the Waco tragedy were felt for years to come and would also help inspire new forms of violence. During the siege, many defenders of the Branch Davidians arrived to show their support and voice their outrage at the federal government. Among them was Timothy McVeigh, a Gulf War veteran who had become increasingly disillusioned with the US government and suspicious of the growing power of federal agencies at the expense of the rights of ordinary citizens. While distributing progun materials and bumper stickers at the scene, McVeigh was interviewed by a student reporter. Like other defenders of gun rights, McVeigh warned that the Waco siege was only the latest example of a federal government that had become too powerful and was now squashing the freedoms of ordinary Americans: "The government is afraid of the guns people have because they have to have control of the people at all times. Once you take away the guns, you can do anything to the people. … I believe we are slowly turning into a socialist government. The government is continually growing bigger and more powerful, and the people need to prepare to defend themselves against government control."[16]

McVeigh became increasingly radicalized after the Waco siege and began distributing literature about the event, such as "Waco Shootout Evokes Memory of Warsaw '43" and "U.S. Government Initiates Open Warfare against American People." Later, he would also compose a letter addressed to the ATF, whom he denounced as "fascist" tyrants, warning that "all you tyrannical mother fuckers will swing in the wind one day for your treasonous actions against the Constitution of the United States."[17]

Exactly two years after the fire at Mount Carmel, McVeigh launched his own assault on the federal government. Together with coconspirator Terry Nichols, McVeigh constructed a massive homemade bomb consisting of five thousand pounds of ammonium nitrate and nitromethane, loaded into the back of a Ryder truck. On the morning of April 19, 1995, McVeigh drove the truck to the front of the Alfred P. Murrah Federal Building in Oklahoma City and lit a two-minute fuse. The resulting explosion destroyed the entire north half of the building and killed 168 people, including nineteen children, while wounding another 450. This was the largest act of terrorism on US soil prior to the attacks of September 11, 2001.

Key Issues and Debates: New Religions, Surveillance, and Security before and after 9/11

One of the most complex and difficult issues raised by the Branch Davidian tragedy is the delicate balance between religious freedom and public safety. How do we simultaneously respect the rights to privacy and freedom of religious expression in these communities while at the same time addressing real concerns about potential abuse, violence, and illegal activities? In the case of the Branch Davidians, were law enforcement agents justified in their handling of the allegations of sexual abuse and weapons violations? Or did they overstep their bounds and violate the rights of this religious community? These were already difficult enough questions to grapple with back in 1993, but they have only become more contested in the post-9/11 world, amid new concerns about religiously motivated violence and ever more aggressive forms of surveillance wielded by federal and local governments.

At least in the field of religious studies, most scholars agree that the Waco siege is a particularly acute example of how *not* to handle a situation like this. As Catherine Wessinger forcefully argues, the ATF and FBI completely failed to understand the Davidians' millenarian religious views and so played directly into Koresh's own prophetic narrative that his community would die as martyrs at the hands of the Babylon government: "The Branch Davidian tragedy illustrates how law enforcement agents *should not* deal with armed catastrophic millennial groups. To avoid violence, law enforcement agents have to take seriously the group's religious views and avoid acting in ways that make them appear to be agents of Satan. ... This was not done with the Branch Davidians, to a great extent because of the advice being given to law enforcement agents by anticult activists."[18] As James Tabor and Eugene Gallagher argue, the case of the Branch Davidians thus highlights in a particularly acute way the Free Exercise Clause of the First Amendment itself; and it suggests that law enforcement in this case acted in ways that fundamentally violate the Constitution: "If the purpose of the First Amendment is to protect religion from the state, rather than the state from religion, there is no constitutional basis for enlisting the power of the state in the campaign against so-called cults. ... A wholesale government crusade against 'destructive cults,' such as that championed after Waco, is illegitimate and unconstitutional."[19]

On the other hand, however, there are cases of dangerous new religious movements where one could argue that law enforcement was not aggressive *enough* in monitoring and intervening in their activities. Perhaps the best example is the Aum Shinrikyo movement in Japan, which spread sarin gas in Tokyo subways in 1995, killing thirteen people and severely injuring fifty others. In that case, many would argue that the group was able to manufacture and deploy chemical weapons in part because of the Japanese government's more hands-off policy in dealing with religious movements after World War II: "Aum Shinrikyo had free reign ... to develop weapons of mass destruction due to lack of scrutiny by law enforcement agents. In reaction to government abuses prior to and during World War II, Japanese law enforcement agents did not typically investigate religious organizations or conduct surveillance gathering by undercover work or wiretapping."[20] In this sense, the study of new religions must, in a way, steer "between Scylla and Charybdis"—between the danger of supporting government intervention at the expense of religious freedom and the danger of supporting religious freedom at the expense of security and public safety.

If this question of religious freedom versus government surveillance was already complicated after Waco, it has become far more so in the wake of the 9/11 terrorist attacks (and other subsequent attacks, such as the 2004 bombings in Madrid, the 2005 bombings in London, and the 2013 bombing in Boston). In the United States, the federal government has introduced aggressive new policies and methods of surveillance, such as the USA PATRIOT Act and the NSA's secret wiretapping program. Thus in 2002 changes were made to the Justice Department's guidelines in order to permit FBI surveillance of religious organizations. While this surveillance was initially directed primarily at Muslim organizations, it has opened the door to surveillance of many other religious groups: the FBI has also secretly monitored Quakers, Catholic peace activists, and various others who seemingly had nothing to do with terrorist activities.[21] In 2005 we learned that the NSA has been monitoring thousands—perhaps millions—of communications by US citizens, all without a warrant as required by the Foreign Intelligence Surveillance Act. And still more recently, because of the leaked information from former NSA contractor Edward Snowden in 2013, we learned that the NSA now has astonishing new powers to keep track of virtually all communications entering, leaving, or going through the country—including phone calls, text messages, e-mails, Google searches, and online activity. Indeed, Snowden's leaked documents revealed that the NSA was not only monitoring the communications of ordinary citizens but even tapping the phones of other national leaders such as German chancellor Angela Merkel. In Snowden's opinion, the NSA's staggering reach poses nothing short of "an existential threat to democracy."[22]

All of this has raised profound debates about freedom, privacy, security, and surveillance, with powerful voices on all sides of the issues. Some legal scholars have argued that an increase in security is necessary during times of national emergency, such as terrorist attacks or other violence, and that this will inevitably require some reduction in civil liberties. As Eric Posner and Adrian Vermeule suggest, this is simply the price we pay in the delicate balance between safety and freedom, and governments must be able to adjust the balance as conditions require at different moments: "There is a straightforward tradeoff between liberty and security," they write. "At the security-liberty frontier, any increase in security requires a decrease in liberty; a rational and well-functioning government will already be positioned on this frontier when the emergency strikes and will adjust its policies as the shape of the frontier changes over time. ... If increases in security are worth more than the corresponding losses in liberty, government will increase security."[23]

Other legal scholars, however, have argued that the new measures put in place after 9/11 pose serious constitutional problems. As Georgetown law professor David Cole argues, the USA PATRIOT Act contains a number of new provisions that fundamentally undermine civil liberties and should make any citizen deeply uncomfortable. Among other things, the PATRIOT Act gives the government unprecedented power to detain noncitizens indefinitely; it allows the FBI to search citizens' homes or offices and to conduct surveillance of phone and Internet use without proving probable cause; it grants authorities the power to require bookstores and libraries to list the names of all books bought or borrowed; and it gives government agencies the authority to conduct so-called "Sneak and Peek" searches—that is, to search our homes or offices without even letting us know they've been there. As Cole argues, this represents a dangerous overreaction and overreach on the part of government: "In several critical areas, Congress gave the executive branch broad new powers that went far beyond the fight against terrorism and infringed on fundamental liberties. ... The government overreacted in harmful ways, intruding on the liberties of thousands of people who had no terrorist ties whatsoever. It failed to show that many of the new powers it asserted were in fact necessary to fight terrorism."[24]

In Cole's opinion the NSA wiretapping program was even more problematic. The agency's massive data collection program, he suggests, was developed in secret and was never subjected to public scrutiny or judicial testing; as such, it "almost certainly violates the Fourth Amendment" (which prohibits unreasonable searches and seizures). Cole goes on to quote US District Judge Richard Leon, an appointee of George W. Bush, who voiced a scathing critique of the NSA program: "I cannot imagine a more 'indiscriminate' and 'arbitrary invasion' than this systematic and high-tech collection and retention of personal data on virtually every single citizen for purposes of querying and analyzing it without prior judicial approval. ... I have little doubt that the author of our Constitution, James Madison, who cautioned us to beware 'the abridgement of freedom of the people by gradual and silent encroachments by those in power,' would be aghast."[25] Others have suggested that the NSA's new powers of surveillance rival or exceed anything that George Orwell imagined in his dystopian novel *1984*. According to James Bamford—the leading expert on the history and workings of the NSA—the new wiretapping and data-mining technologies wielded by the NSA are tools that "Orwell's Thought Police would have found useful."[26]

These debates are unlikely to be resolved any time soon, as new forms of religious violence proliferate and as ever more sophisticated forms of government surveillance continue to be developed on an almost daily basis. Defenders of the government's programs will probably argue that these are necessary precisely for monitoring potentially dangerous religious groups before they become violent, in order to avoid "another Waco." Critics, however, will argue that these aggressive new measures only create new problems by further undermining civil liberties and creating even more paranoia about an invasive and authoritarian federal government. In other words, they risk breeding even more fears of a government "Babylon" ready to assault religious minorities in the name of safety and security. Negotiating these difficult questions will surely be one of the greatest challenges of the twenty-first century.

Questions for Discussion and Debate

1. Scholars such as Wessinger, Tabor, and Gallagher argue that disasters such as Waco could be avoided if law enforcement paid more attention to what serious scholars of religion have to say and less attention to journalists and anticult activists. Do you agree? Or do you think this is giving too much credit to the scholarly community? After all, scholars of religion are not trained in law enforcement or the handling of potentially dangerous situations—any more than law enforcement agents are trained in the study of religion. Are there ways in which the two communities can work productively together? If so, how?

2. Many critics argue that the ATF overreacted in its response to the Branch Davidians' possession of weapons. After all, they made a living as gun traders, and many people in Texas have large numbers of guns. However, the charges of sexual abuse of minors seem more difficult to dismiss. Would sexual abuse have provided a justification for the raid even if weapons violations did not? Or was there no justification for such a raid at all?

3. If you agree with scholars such as Tabor, Gallagher, and Wessinger that law enforcement handled the case of the Branch Davidians very badly, then how do you think they *should* have handled it? What could have been done differently that might have avoided such a protracted standoff and catastrophic outcome?

4. Was law enforcement justified in setting up surveillance across the road from Mount Carmel or in sending in an undercover agent, Robert Rodriguez, to pretend to be interested in Bible study with Koresh? Should law enforcement be able to infiltrate and surveil any religious community at any time? Or are there limits? And should religious communities be given any special exemptions or protections from government surveillance, or should they be treated in the same way as any nonreligious organization?

Suggested Classroom Activity

Imagine that you are a group of religious studies scholars whose task is to advise law enforcement agencies about how to handle a group such as the Branch Davidians today, in a post-9/11 context. How would you explain this religious group's belief system and millenarian ideas to agencies such as the ATF and FBI, and what would you recommend that they do? What sort of intervention—if any—would be appropriate? Would undercover surveillance of the sort carried out by the ATF be warranted? Would an armed raid be necessary? Or would there be other ways of addressing the questions about child abuse and illegal weapons? Do you think the situation should be handled differently today, given the new fears of terrorism and new mechanisms of surveillance possessed by the government, than it was back in 1993?

Suggested Video

"Waco: The Inside Story." *Frontline,* PBS, 1995.

Suggestions for Further Reading

Barkun, Michael. "Religion and Secrecy after September 11." *Journal of the American Academy of Religion* 74, no. 2 (2006): 275–301.

Cole, David, and James X. Dempsey. *Terrorism and the Constitution: Sacrificing Civil Liberties in the Name of National Security.* New York: New Press, 2002.

Juergensmeyer, Mark. *Terror in the Mind of God: The Global Rise of Religious Violence.* Berkeley: University of California Press, 2000.

Moore, Carol. *The Davidian Massacre: Disturbing Questions about Waco Which Must Be Answered.* Franklin, TN: Legacy Communications, 1995.

Posner, Eric, and Adrian Vermeule. *Terror in the Balance: Security, Liberty and the Courts.* New York: Oxford University Press, 2007.

Reavis, Dick J. *The Ashes of Waco: An Investigation.* New York: Simon and Schuster, 1995.

Tabor, James D., and Eugene V. Gallagher. *Why Waco? Cults and the Battle for Religious Freedom in America.* Berkeley: University of California Press, 1995.

Wessinger, Catherine. *How the Millennium Comes Violently: From Jonestown to Heaven's Gate.* New York: Seven Bridges Press, 2000.

Wright, Stuart A., ed. *Armageddon in Waco: Critical Perspectives on the Branch Davidian Conflict.* Chicago: University of Chicago Press, 1995.

Notes

1. James D. Tabor and Eugene V. Gallagher, *Why Waco? Cults and the Battle for Religious Freedom in America* (Berkeley: University of California Press, 1995); Catherine Wessinger, *How the Millennium Comes Violently: From Jonestown to Heaven's Gate* (New York: Seven Bridges Press, 2000).

2. Tabor and Gallagher, *Why Waco?,* 41.

3. David G. Bromley and Edward D. Silver, "The Davidian Tradition: From Patronal Clan to Prophetic Movement," in *Armageddon in Waco: Critical Perspectives on the Branch Davidian Conflict,* ed. Stuart A. Wright (Chicago: University of Chicago Press, 1995), 59. See also Wessinger, *How the Millennium Comes Violently,* 83.

4. David Koresh, "The Seven Seals of the Book of Revelation," in Tabor and Gallagher, *Why Waco?,* 197.

5. Tabor and Gallagher, *Why Waco?,* 205, 50–51; Wessinger, *How the Millennium Comes Violently,* 88.

6. Tabor and Gallagher, *Why Waco?*, 4, 51.

7. Bromley and Silver, "Davidian Tradition," 61, 65–66.

8. Tabor and Gallagher, *Why Waco?*, 5; Wessinger, *How the Millennium Comes Violently*, 91.

9. Marc Breault and Martin King, *Inside the Cult: A Member's Chilling Exclusive Account of Madness and Depravity in David Koresh's Compound* (New York: Signet Books, 1993), 256–57; see Wes singer, *How the Millennium Comes Violently*, 97.

10. Wessinger, *How the Millennium Comes Violently*, 62.

11. Mark England and Darlene McCormick, "The Sinful Messiah," *Waco Tribune-Herald*, February 27, 1993.

12. Wessinger, *How the Millennium Comes Violently*, 106, 108.

13. Koresh, "Seven Seals," 203; see Tabor and Gallagher, *Why Waco?*, 205–11.

14. John Danforth, "Final Report to the Deputy Attorney General Concerning the 1993 Confrontation at the Mt. Carmel Complex, Waco, Texas," November 8, 2000, http://commons.wikimedia.org/wiki/File:Danforthreport-final.pdf.

15. Eric Lichtblau, "Report Clears Feds in Death of Davidians," *Los Angeles Times*, July 22, 2000, http://articles.latimes.com/2000/jul/22/news/mn-57442.

16. Brian Morton, "The Guns of Spring," *Baltimore City Paper*, April 15, 2009, http://www2.citypaper.com/eat/story.asp?id=17888.

17. Kathryn S. Olmsted, *Real Enemies: Conspiracy Theories and American Democracy, World War I to 9/11* (New York: Oxford University Press, 2009), 197.

18. Wessinger, *How the Millennium Comes Violently*, 21.

19. Tabor and Gallagher, *Why Waco?*, 184.

20. Wessinger, *How the Millennium Comes Violently*, 150.

21. See Michael Barkun, "Religion and Secrecy after September 11," *Journal of the American Academy of Religion* 74, no. 2 (2006): 275–301; Jeff Stein, "FBI Misled Justice Department about Spying on Peace Group," *Washington Post*, September 20, 2010, http://voices.washingtonpost.com/spy-talk/2010/09/fbi_cover-up_turns_laughable_s.html.

22. Matt Smith, "NSA Leaker Comes Forward, Warns of 'Existential Threat,' " CNN, June 9, 2013, www.cnn.com/2013/06/09/politics/nsa-leak-identity/index.html; "Angela Merkel's Call to Obama," *Guardian*, October 23, 2013, www.theguardian.com/world/2013/oct/23/us-monitored-angela-merkel-german.

23. Eric Posner and Adrian Vermeule, *Terror in the Balance: Security, Liberty and the Courts* (New York: Oxford University Press, 2007), 12.

24. David Cole and James X. Dempsey, *Terrorism and the Constitution: Sacrificing Civil Liberties in the Name of National Security* (New York: New Press, 2002), 174.

25. David Cole, "The NSA on Trial," *New York Review of Books,* December 18, 2013, www.nybooks.com/blogs/nyrblog/2013/dec/18/nsa-spying-leon-ruling/.

26. James Bamford, "The New Thought Police," *Nova,* PBS, January 2009, www.pbs.org/wgbh/nova/military/nsa-police.html.

PART IV

Domestic and International Terrorist Religions

Confronting Right-Wing Extremism in the USA

The Far Right and Terrorism

George Michael

T errorism and other forms of political and social violence have long been associated with the far right. During the mid-nineteenth century, members of the reactionary Know-Nothing movement were occasionally involved in violent confrontations with Catholics and immigrants, most notably in the riot in New Orleans, Louisiana in 1858.[1] Right-wing violence in America reached its high-water mark during the Reconstruction Era Ku Klux Klan's reign of terror in the aftermath of the Civil War. The total amount of carnage that the hooded order perpetrated during that period is difficult to quantify, but it is estimated that in the state of Louisiana alone it was responsible for at least 2,000 killed, wounded or injured in the few weeks preceding the presidential election of 1868. In addition other estimates of violence for that period include seventy-five killings reported in Georgia, 109 in Alabama, and more than 150 for one single county in Georgia.[2] The primary victims were Black freedmen, "scalawags," "carpetbaggers" and Radical Republicans. The Klan's membership is estimated to have reached 555,000 during the Reconstruction period.[3] The Second Era Ku Klux Klan, which reached its zenith in the 1920s, had more than its share of violent episodes as it targeted primarily Blacks, Catholics and "morally lapsed" White Anglo-Saxon Protestants.

According to one estimate there have been 245 incidents of right-wing terrorism since 1978.[4] Although other forms of organized violence have punctuated American history, such as episodes from the political left and organized labor, right-wing violence appears to have a longer history and a more enduring quality.

Patterns of Right-Wing Terrorism

It is very difficult to quantify with precision the incidence of terrorism in the United States. The American criminal justice system treats terrorism as a crime. When caught, terrorists are tried in regular courts as there is no special classification for the crime of "terrorism." The FBI has endeavored to classify and collate terrorist incidents in America. However, much of its data on domestic terrorism are inconsistent and unreliable due to changing classifications of terrorist incidents.[5] What's more, as a 1976 government report demonstrated, the sheer number of violent incidents of a political or quasi-political nature make this effort all the more cumbersome.[6] Finally, due to the wide range in the severity of violent incidents—ranging from scuffles with police and minor injuries to bombings and homicides—it is difficult to ascertain and operationalize an overall level of seriousness or threat posed from a particular variant of political extremism in comparison to others.

According to the Israeli political scientist, Ehud Sprinzak, right-wing terrorism is characterized by a process of "split-deligitimation," in which not only the "outsider" (e.g. foreigners, ethnic and religious minorities, reds, and gays) is targeted but contemporaneously, the very state itself, which is seen as ineffective, or worse yet, under the actual sway of the outsiders. This theoretically leads to an evolution of right-wing terrorism. At first the terrorists usually avoid confrontations with authorities and their animus is directed at the "outsider." However, eventually they convince themselves that the government is not doing enough to protect the "original community" and the state also becomes a target.[7]

Significant Episodes of Right-wing Terrorism

The Greensboro Massacre

If one had to pinpoint a particular incident that really marked the genesis of the revolutionary orientation of the far right, it would be the Greensboro Massacre in 1979. On November 3 of that year, members of a neo-Nazi party, the National Socialist Party of America, and a local Ku Klux Klan organization clashed with demonstrators led by members of the Communist Workers Party in a "Death to the Klan" rally. The confrontation had been a culmination in a series of disputes between the two sides. At the demonstration a shootout between the two sides ensued, in which five members of the Communist Workers Party were fatally wounded. The Klansmen and Neo-Nazis suffered no serious casualties.

In two subsequent trials—one local and one federal—juries acquitted all of the defendants.[8] The juries were convinced by the self-defense arguments put forth by the defense counsels. This clash was significant because it was the first high-profile incident of right-wing violence since the Civil Rights era. Moreover, it demonstrated that Klansmen and neo-Nazis could cooperate. Previously, Klansmen looked askance at the foreign and un-American orientation of the neo-Nazis. Henceforth, neo-Nazism would have a significant influence on the ideology of a much broader portion of the racialist right. For many in the movement, Greensboro was seen as an event equal in symbolic significance to Lexington and Concord. This event would also be the catalyst for the creation of a progressive-oriented watchdog group, the National Anti-Klan Network, which would go on to become the Center for Democratic Renewal.

Gordon Kahl and the Posse Comitatus

The farm crisis of the mid-1980s provided a seedbed for right-wing extremism in America's heartland. One of the more prominent organizations in that area of the country was the Posse Comitatus. Despite its sometimes bombastic rhetoric, the Posse posed only a minor irritant to authorities. However, that changed on February 13, 1983, when a Posse affiliate and radical tax protestor, Gordon Kahl, got embroiled in a confrontation with federal authorities in Medina, North Dakota. A group of lawmen sought to serve Kahl a warrant for tax violations. Extremely distrustful of authorities, Kahl refused to be served and a shootout ensued in which two marshals died and four others were wounded, including Kahl's son Yorie. Amazingly, Kahl a sixty-three-year-old farmer and World War II veteran, had single-handedly caused the authorities to retreat.

Kahl evaded authorities for about four months, but on June 3, 1983, they finally caught up with him in Lawrence County, Arkansas. Still defiant, Kahl managed to mortally wound a local sheriff, who also happened to fire a fatal shot which struck Kahl in the head. Not realizing that Kahl was dead, the lawmen attempted to force Kahl outside of his bunker dwelling by pouring fuel down the chimney. The place went up in flames and sparked rumors that the FBI had summarily executed Kahl then incinerated his corpse and murdered the slain sheriff to cover up the truth.[9] As a result, Kahl entered the far right's pantheon of martyrs. His death also became the catalyst and a call to arms of an underground right-wing terrorist group, the Order.

The Order

Shortly after the death of Gordon Kahl, an annual Aryan Nations Congress was held at the compound in Hayden Lake, Idaho in the summer of 1983. At that meeting a young charismatic member of the National Alliance, Robert Jay Matthews, hatched the idea that an underground resistance group ought to be created to avenge the death of Kahl. Matthews had considerable powers of persuasion and was able to ultimately draw nearly fifty members into his clandestine terrorist group, "the Order."[10] It went on a crime spree in the early 1980s, which included several armored car heists, robberies, bombings, and at least five homicides.[11]

Matthews reportedly drew much inspiration for his organization from a novel, *The Turner Diaries*, written by his ideological mentor Dr William Pierce (under the pseudonym Andrew Macdonald), the chairman of the National Alliance, who died in 2002. Reportedly Matthews made the novel required reading for all members. It is perhaps the most widely read book in the subterranean world of the far right, and has sold approximately 350,000 copies—an amazing figure for an underground book.[12]

Like the "Organization" in *The Turner Diaries*, Robert Jay Matthews endeavored to build a clandestine resistance group. His group went on a crime spree and a terrorist campaign that gained nationwide notoriety. Its activities included counterfeiting, armored car heists, bank robberies, and four homicides. In a milieu in which terrorists often resemble more the gang that couldn't shoot straight than professional terrorists, the exploits of the Order were, in a word, electrifying. One armored car heist took in a whopping $3.6 million—which at that time in 1984 set the record for the highest amount of money ever stolen in such a robbery.

Although, the Order was racist and anti-Semitic in orientation, consistent with Sprinzak's theory of split deligitimation, it gave its highest priority to targets such as the state and other institutions. Matthews instructed Order members to avoid petty conflicts with racial minorities, as that would distract the group from its primary mission. A list of prominent enemies marked for assassination was compiled, which included the leader of the Southern Poverty Law Center, Morris Dees, the former Secretary of State, Henry Kissinger, banker David Rockefeller, television producer Norman Lear, and international financier Baron Elie de Rothschild.[13] Despite such lofty intentions, the Order settled for a Denver-based Jewish disc jockey, Alan Berg, as its first target of assassination. Berg was an acerbic talk radio host and occasionally berated far-right callers on his radio program.

The Order's exploits soon caught the attention of authorities and the FBI identified the group as the most serious domestic terrorist threat in the country.[14] Ultimately, the counterfeiting operation led to the group's demise, as one of its recruits, though not an official member, Tom Martinez, agreed to become an informant for the FBI after his arrest for passing counterfeit money that the Order had printed. He set up two of his colleagues, including Matthews, in a sting operation at a hotel. A shootout ensued, and amazingly Matthews escaped after wounding an officer.

He remained undaunted and issued a "Declaration of War" against the United States government, which he sent to several newspapers. Finally, authorities caught up with Matthews at Whidbey Island in Washington state. Matthews, however, refused to be taken alive, and a standoff which lasted a couple of days followed. He single-handedly engaged in several shootouts with SWAT teams. Eventually, the authorities lost their patience and on December 8, 1984, dropped white phosphorous illumination flares onto the roof of the house in which Matthews had barricaded himself. This set off a fire that engulfed the structure and Matthews perished in dramatic fashion. A concerted effort by federal, state, and local law enforcement agencies eventually crushed the Order, and many of its members are now serving lengthy prison sentences.

The Order's campaign caught many in the radical right by surprise. Some criticized their exploits as ineffectual and quixotic, while others lionized them as exemplary "Aryan warriors."

Although the Order tactically did not really achieve much, it was significant insofar as it marked a change in the orientation of the far right. The United States government was now seen as the enemy and the far right began to take on a more revolutionary posture. No longer did it seek to preserve the status quo. Rather it sought the overthrow of the US government, which it reasoned was now under the heel of the Zionist Occupation Government (ZOG). The Order has been lionized by the far right and its incarcerated members are regarded as POWs to others in the movement.[15]

The Covenant, Sword, and the Arm of the Lord

In the late 1970s a Christian Identity minister, Jim Ellison, founded a community in Arkansas known as the Covenant, Sword and Arm of the Lord (CSA). Over the years it took on a paramilitary orientation, as members believed that eventually their enemies would one day besiege their compound, which in a sense they did. Ellison stockpiled many weapons and trained members how to use them in a mock village called "Silhouette City."[16] Furthermore, the compound came to be seen as a safe haven for those in the far-right underground who sought to evade authorities.

The CSA was linked to several episodes of terrorism. For example, Ellison and another member, Richard Wayne Snell, firebombed a Jewish community center in Bloomington, Indiana, and a gay church in Springfield, Missouri.[17] In another incident, Snell fatally shot a pawnbroker in Texarkana, Arkansas. Finally, during a routine traffic stop, Snell opened fire on an Arkansas state trooper and fatally wounded him. The CSA also planned several other serious terrorist attacks but failed to successfully carry them out.[18]

The violence and terrorism emanating from the CSA compound eventually captured the attention of federal authorities. Once authorities had implicated the CSA in these offenses, the FBI's elite anti-terrorist unit, the Hostage Rescue Team, quickly surrounded its compound. Although the CSA demonstrated a proclivity for violence, after some negotiation, Ellison surrendered to authorities without incident. He eventually cooperated with authorities and turned state's evidence against some members of the Order in a trial at Fort Smith, Arkansas in 1988.

The Rise of "Leaderless Resistance"

After the demise of the CSA and the Order, the revolutionary right went into a period of retrenchment and did some soul-searching on the topic of revolutionary strategy. From this interlude emerged a change in the tactics of right-wing terrorists. The lessons drawn were that when a terrorist organization grew to the size of the Order, it would eventually fall prey to infiltration and eventually be crushed. The CSA demonstrated that it was not feasible for terrorist groups to congregate in a compound that could easily be identified and surrounded by authorities.[19]

The violence-prone far right now employs an approach known as "leaderless resistance," a kind of lone wolf operation in which an individual, or a very small cohesive group, engages in acts of anti-statist violence independent of any official movement, leader or network of support.[20] Inasmuch as the contemporary far right is organizationally fragmented, leaderless resistance makes a virtue out of necessity. Moreover, this notion dovetails well with the new internet technology.[21] However, a word of caution is in order. Although right-wing advocates of the leaderless approach have theorized extensively on the concept, it remains in large part a construct of academic scholars and journalists. That is to say, it is a somewhat facile way of attributing the often unorganized and sporadic nature of right-wing violence to some larger operational plan. There is anecdotal evidence which suggests that several perpetrators who appear to have employed this approach, were psychopaths with little ideological sophistication. That said, the leaderless resistance concept should not be completely dismissed as merely a topic for abnormal psychology. As one observer noted: Leaderless resistance arises in large measure because of the failure of organized right-wing terrorism.

Although a sign of desperation, the notion of leaderless resistance should not be taken lightly.[22] According to the government's own prosecution case, the most lethal act of domestic terrorism—the Oklahoma City bombing—appears to fit in the leaderless resistance category.

The Oklahoma City Bombing

On April 19, 1995, the Murrah federal building in Oklahoma City was bombed, leaving at least 168 dead and many others wounded. This attack was the most lethal act of domestic terrorism ever perpetrated on American soil. The subsequent investigation would implicate Timothy McVeigh as the chief culprit of the attack. He also had some accomplices including Terry Nichols and Michael Fortier; however, the scope of their involvement is still uncertain. In the FBI's own description, "one of its most extensive investigations" failed to turn up a significant militia connection to the bombing. McVeigh and Nichols are reported to have attended meetings of the Michigan Militia, but the group did not welcome them. To the contrary, members of the group thought they were loose cannons and should not be granted membership.[23]

Although McVeigh may not have had any formal affiliation with extremist groups, there is evidence to suggest that he was a denizen of the subterranean world of the far right. McVeigh appears to have found several reasons to carry out his attack. During the 1993 siege of the Branch Davidians, McVeigh made a pilgrimage to Mount Carmel. He was reported to have been extremely upset over how the government handled the situation. He was also angered by the government's siege at Ruby Ridge, Idaho at which federal agents shot and killed Randy Weaver's wife Vicki and their son Samuel. McVeigh had chosen the Murrah federal building in particular, because he wanted to punish the Bureau of Alcohol, Tobacco, and Firearms (BATF) and the FBI, both of which were involved in the two incidents mentioned above.[24]

In his personal letters and statements, McVeigh echoed many of the Constitutionalist themes that are popular in the Christian Patriot/Militia movement. He absorbed much of the anti-government propaganda of the Patriot movement at various gun shows that he often attended. Although he did not usually evince a visceral racism, he actively explored the propaganda of the racialist right. At one time, he obtained a trial membership of a Ku Klux Klan organization based in North Carolina. However, according to McVeigh he declined to renew his membership because he felt that the Klan was "manipulative to young people." Moreover, he felt that the government, and not racial minorities, was his enemy.[25]

The Aryan Republican Army

Around the same time of the Oklahoma City bombing, a six-man group of bandits, which called itself the "Aryan Republican Army," was making headlines in the Midwest for a series of bank robberies that confounded authorities. All totaled, the Aryan Republican Army is reported to have been responsible for robbing twenty-two banks and netting some $250,000 in cash. Although the goals of these renegades are still murky, they are alleged to have consorted with some of the more notorious figures in the far-right underground. One author goes so far as to theorize that the money stolen was used to fund the terrorist attack on the Murrah federal building in Oklahoma City.[26]

Authorities eventually closed in on the Aryan Republican Army and put an end to its campaign. Although its significance is disputable, it could presage a pattern in other countries beset by terrorism, where criminal enterprises use their ill-gotten gains to fund terrorist and revolutionary movements.

Lone Wolves

The far right is a relatively small and heavily stigmatized movement that does not enjoy broad-based support from the public. Most in the movement realize that the forces arrayed against them—the government and the watchdog organizations—are collectively vastly more powerful than they are. Consequently, there has always been a conservative majority in the far right that believed that it would be foolhardy to prematurely engage in revolutionary violence. Such an approach would almost certainly lead to organizational suicide. Thus the more conservative elements advocated a strategy that would concentrate on utilizing propaganda to build a revolutionary majority. This came to be known as the theory of mass action.[27]

A leading proponent of this approach was George Lincoln Rockwell, the founder of the American Nazi Party that was active in the 1960s. Rockwell believed that events such as racial integration, school busing, the Vietnam War, race riots and rising crime would engender urban mayhem and thus create favorable conditions for his party. He entertained the idea that his party could actually win national power by 1972. However, Rockwell fell to an assassin's bullet in 1967, and with his departure some elements of the far right became disillusioned with the conservative approach.

Joseph Tomassi, a member of Rockwell's successor organization, eventually departed and founded the National Socialist Liberation Front (NSLF), a neo-Nazi organization that patterned itself on the left-wing models of the Weathermen and the Symbionese Liberation Army. Tomassi correctly saw that in the early 1970s, the idea of creating a Nazi-style party that would win support of a majority of the population was futile. However, he believed that it was still possible to strike blows against "the system," provided that revolutionaries were prepared to act resolutely and alone. Whereas the state demonstrated over and over again that it could infiltrate and effectively neutralize any right-wing organization, it had yet to develop the capability of thwarting the actions of individuals or small groups acting alone. However, the NSLF campaign was reckless and its revolutionary arm was quickly crushed.

Like Rockwell, Tomassi was also killed by a disgruntled member. Although the organization never succeeded in striking a serious blow against "the system," according to one observer its "contribution to the leaderless resistance concept [was] incalculable."[28] Thus was born the concept of leaderless resistance in the far right. However, the approach had still not been given a name and the idea would languish for the most part among the far-right theorists until the early 1990s.

Another resistance approach occasionally used by the far right has been the cellular model. The far right's version of this approach can be traced back to an anonymous tract titled The John Franklin Letters, which was popularized by the John Birch Society in 1959.[29] The John Birch Society promoted the book as a call to resistance in the wake of a communist takeover, which the group believed was always just around the corner. Although the Birch Society organizationally patterned itself on the cellular model, it was loath to engage in any political violence.

The Minutemen also adopted the cellular structure with a centralized command structure, and some of its members were implicated in violence. Its leader, Robert DePugh, published a manual for activists, Blueprint for Victory, which gave advice on political, military, economic and psychological warfare.[30] The Minutemen tried to maintain the semblance of a centralized command structure, and discouraged individual initiative, leader less-resistance types of operation.

Despite these efforts, some members of the Minutemen ran afoul of the authorities and the organization was effectively shut down after some episodes of violence. The popularity of the cellular model reached its zenith with the campaign of the Order. The Order carried out various missions in small groups, and there were plans on splitting the organization into interlocking separate cells. Despite some spectacular moments, it was resoundingly quashed after a concerted effort by government authorities. The crushing defeat of the Order and the CSA ushered in a debate on the best strategy of "resistance" to employ in the far-right movement. Thus the concept of leaderless resistance was reexamined and updated for current conditions.

Jeffrey Kaplan observes that the movement's discourse became increasingly chiliastic by the late 1980s.[31] The mass action theories of previous generations were seen as unrealistic. The cellular model had been discredited with the demise of the Order. A period of despair and hopelessness seemed to settle over the movement. However, two events, first the ambush of Randy Weaver's home in Ruby Ridge in 1992, and second, the siege at Waco in 1993, once again galvanized a broad segment of the far right. Previously isolated voices calling for resistance found their messages being heard by a more receptive audience.

Leaderless resistance had several proponents during the 1980s, but the concept was truly crystallized and gained currency as a result of the October 1992 meeting in Estes Park, Colorado convoked by Christian Identity minister Pastor Pete Peters. This event provided a forum for the articulation of a new leaderless resistance approach. Whereas prior to the meeting the concept was only vaguely recognized by some, it was now given a name and disseminated to a much larger audience. This event, more than any other, popularized the notion in the far-right community.

Conclusion

The modus operandi of right-wing terrorists has undergone some change over the past decade or so. The primacy of leaderless resistance in the racialist right presents a challenge for authorities insofar as it is difficult to predict from where a threat may come. It is much easier to infiltrate an organization rather than a clique of a few individuals, or to read the mind of one lone wolf. It is important to keep in mind that the prominence of leaderless resistance is symptomatic of the organizational and financial weakness of right-wing terrorists. No real terrorist infrastructure as such exists in the far-right milieu. What is more, as James Adams has pointed out, the sine qua non for the development of such an infrastructure is money.[32] Generally speaking, right-wing terrorists have neither garnered support from state sponsors nor developed adequate means of self-financing.

In recent years organized groups in the Militia movement (e.g. the Montana Freemen and the Republic of Texas) have been a problem for authorities. However, the outlaws in this segment appear to concentrate their illegal activities primarily on "paper terrorism" (e.g. issuing phony checks and filing illegal liens) rather than political violence.

One obvious concern is the potentially greater lethality of instruments of terrorism. Changes in technology have enabled terrorists to inflict potentially greater damage. The Oklahoma City bombing demonstrated the potential lethality of "terrorism on the cheap" conducted by just a few individuals. Indeed, more so than the terrorists of the previous decades, contemporary terrorists appear more intent on punishing their targets.

Elements of the American far right have demonstrated on at least one previous occasion that they would not be averse to such tactics. For example, the CSA allegedly planned to poison water supplies, and recently a militia group, Southeastern States Alliance, allegedly planned on destroying a nuclear power plant. Fortunately, these examples never made it beyond the planning stages.

Another ominous trend is the targeting of vital parts of infrastructure that could potentially paralyze or do great damage to the day-to-day lives of many people. Finally, bio-terrorism, such as an anthrax attack, is one more measure that terrorists could employ.

Discussion Questions

1. What are some of the resistance movements that inspired Timothy McVeigh's bombing of the Oklahoma Federal Building?

2. Discuss the reasons why the radical right uses the approach of leaderless resistance and some of the failed approaches that preceded it.

3. Discuss some methods law enforcement might use when dealing with far-right terrorist groups and the new threats they pose.

Notes

1. See Beals, Carleton, *Brass-Knuckle Crusade: The Great Know-Nothing Conspiracy: 1820–1860* (New York: Hastings House Publishers, 1960) pp. 193–207.

2. Forster, Arnold and Benjamin R. Epstein, *Report on the Ku Klux Klan* (New York: Anti-Defamation League, 1965) p. 14.

3. Forster and Epstein, *Report on the Ku Klux Klan*, p. 14.

4. Hewitt, Chris, "Responding to Terrorism," unpublished manuscript, 2000, p. 5. According to Hewitt shootings accounted for 32 per cent of the incidents, followed by bombings (28 per cent), assaults (22 per cent) and other (18 percent).

5. For a critical examination of the FBI's data collection on domestic terrorism see Hamm, Mark S., *Terrorism, Hate Crime, and Anti-Government Violence: A Preliminary Review of the Research* (Indiana: Indiana State University, 1996).

6. In 1976 the National Advisory Committee on Criminal Justice Standards and Goals issued a Report on the Task Force on Disorders and Terrorism, which listed violent incidents of a political or quasi-political nature in the period from January 1965 to March 1976. As the report demonstrates, violent incidents were practically daily occurrences throughout much of that period. Most of the incidents appear to emanate from the political left. See National Advisory Committee on Criminal Justice Standards and Goals, *Report on the Task Force on Disorders and Terrorism* (Washington DC: National Advisory Committee on Criminal Justice Standards and Goals, 1976).

7. Sprinzak, Ehud, "The Process of Delegitimation: Towards a Linkage Theory of Political Terrorism," *Terrorism and Political Violence*, 3 (1), pp. 50–68 (1991).

8. In a civil trial however, a jury awarded approximately $400,000 for the death of one of the five slain and the injuries of two of the wounded. They found five Klansmen and Nazis, a police informant, and two police officers liable. Wheaton, *Code Name Greenkil*.

9. Coulson, Danny O. and Elaine Shannon, *No Heroes: Inside the FBI's Secret Counter-Terror Force* (New York: Pocket Books, 1999) pp. 192–3.

10. The organization used several names including "the Silent Brotherhood" and a German version of that same title, The Brüder Schweigen.

11. Aho, James, *The Politics of Righteousness: Idaho Christian Patriotism* (Seattle: University of Washington Press, 1990) p. 7.

12. Segal, David, "The Pied Piper of Racism," *Washington Post*, January 12, 2000, C1, p. 8.

13. Coulson and Elaine Shannon, *No Heroes*, p. 194.

14. This is according to the statements of Danny O. Coulson, the founder of the FBI's Hostage Rescue Team, who was involved in the Order investigation. Coulson and Shannon, *No Heroes*, p. 195. According to one estimate, the investigation is said to have involved one quarter of the total manpower resources of the FBI. Aho, *The Politics of Righteousness*, p. 61.

15. The prison addresses of the "POWs" are occasionally listed in the far-right literature, and readers are encouraged to write and provide material and moral support to them and their families.

16. Coulson and Shannon, *No Heroes*, p. 212.

17. Coulson and Shannon, *No Heroes*, p. 222.

18. Some of the alleged plots included an attempt to blow up a natural gas pipeline in Fulton, Arkansas; however, the explosive failed. Some CSA members allegedly planned to assassinate several public offices, including those of federal judges H. Franklin Waters and Jack Knox, and also US Attorney Asa Hutchinson. Ellison and Noble planned to bomb a gay church in Kansas City, Missouri, but Noble lost his nerve and failed to carry out the attack. Finally, according to Ellison and Noble, the CSA planned to use a 30 gallon drum of cyanide that it had stockpiled to poison the water supplies of New York City and Washington DC. It was hoped that this would foment urban unrest and precipitate their anticipated revolution.

19. It took the far right quite a while to learn this lesson of how vulnerable they would be if isolated in a rural setting. As Smith and Damphousse observed, the far left had widely publicized in their publications the failure of Che Guevara's similar strategy in Bolivia. Smith, Brent L. and Kelly R. Damphousse, "Two Decades of Terror," in Kushner, Harvey W. (ed.) *The Future of Terrorism: Violence in the New Millennium* (Thousand Oaks CA: Sage, 1998) p. 142.

20. As described in Kaplan, Jeffrey, "Leaderless Resistance," *Terrorism and Political Violence*, 9 (3), p. 80 (1997).

21. As an example, a website operated by an anti-abortion activist in Oregon listed the names and addresses of doctors who performed abortions. The site contained unsubtle suggestions that there should be some kind of retribution against them. See "Anti-abortion Web Site Goes on Trial," *USA Today*, January 7, 1999. http://usatoday.com/news/ndswed05.htm. This is just one example of how this notion of leaderless resistance can work. Activists with no formal organizational ties and who don't even know one another can post information on the web, and others acting independently can take these cues and commit acts of terrorism as they see fit.

22. According to James Aho, roughly one half of all right-wing homicides from the period from 1980 through 1990 can be attributed to individuals acting alone. Aho, *The Politics of Righteousness*, p. 62.

23. Stickney, Brandon M., *All-American Monster: The Unauthorized Biography of Timothy McVeigh* (Amherst, NY: Prometheus Books, 1996) pp. 97–100, 158–9. One Michigan Militia member who was present at the meeting told me that McVeigh and Nichols were not well received because of their "extreme racial feelings" and were asked to leave. Interview with Norm Olson, September 8, 2000.

24. Michel, Lou and Dan Herbeck, *American Terrorist: Timothy McVeigh and the Oklahoma City Bombing* (New York: Regan Books, 2001) pp. 167–8.

25. McVeigh claims to have joined the Klan because he thought that it was "fighting for the restoration of individual rights, especially gun rights." After more research he discovered that the Klan was "almost entirely devoted to the cause of racism." Michel and Herbeck, *American Terrorist*, pp. 88–9. His naiveté of the true nature of the Klan seems a bit disingenuous insofar as he was of above average intelligence and intellectually curious. However, it is also worth mentioning that he appears to have been a "seeker" in the truest sense of the word and was thus willing to look practically anywhere for knowledge.

26. The criminologist Mark Hamm posits the theory that the Aryan Republican Army was part of a larger conspiracy and revolutionary division of labor, in which the bandits would use their money to fund right-wing revolutionaries. He strongly suspects that members of the Aryan Republican Army were instrumental in the Oklahoma City bombing. For more on his theory see Hamm, Mark S., *In Bad Company: America's Terrorist Underground* (Boston MA: Northeastern University Press, 2001).

27. I borrow much of the analysis in this section from Kaplan's article "Leaderless Resistance," *Terrorism and Political Violence*, 9 (3), pp. 80–95 (1997).

28. Kaplan "Leaderless Resistance," pp. 81–2.

29. *The John Franklin Letters* (New York: The Bookmailer, 1959). Robert Griffin, the biographer of Dr William Pierce, believes that Revilo P. Oliver was the book's author. See Griffin, *The Fame of a Dead Man's Deeds*, p. 143.

30. DePugh, Robert B., *Blueprint for Victory*, 4th edn (Norborne MO: Salon Publishing Company, 1978).

31. By "chiliastic" Kaplan refers to several themes, including a period of tribulation in which right-wing terrorists believe that they must engage in a violent struggle before they reach victory, which will result in a period of millennial bliss. Also, there is a Manichean theme to this struggle as the right wing sees themselves as a righteous remnant while their enemies are seen as the embodiment of evil. Kaplan argues that as the far right was banished from beyond the pale of respectability it abandoned any "reformist" ambitions that it once had:

32. The state ZOG was increasingly seen as not worth claiming, and with this conclusion, the movement's dreams became increasingly chiliastic. With this too, the pattern of violence emanating from the fringes of the movement began to shift from vigilantism to anti-state terrorism. (Kaplan 1995, pp. 85–7)

33. Adams, James, *The Financing of Terrorism* (New York: Simon and Schuster, 1986) in White, Jonathan R., *Terrorism: an introduction* (Stamford CT: Wadsworth, 2002) pp. 40–42.

References

"Anti-abortion Web Site Goes on Trial," *USA Today*, January 7, 1999, http://usatoday.com/news/ndswed05.htm.

Adams, James, *The Financing of Terrorism* (New York: Simon and Schuster, 1986) in White, Jonathan R., *Terrorism: an introduction* (Stamford CT: Wadsworth, 2002) pp. 40–2.

Aho, James, *The Politics of Righteousness: Idaho Christian Patriotism* (Seattle WA: University of Washington Press, 1990).

Beals, Carleton, *Brass-Knuckle Crusade: The Great Know-Nothing Conspiracy: 1820–1860* (New York: Hastings House Publishers, 1960).

Coulson, Danny O. and Elaine Shannon, *No Heroes: Inside the FBI's Secret Counter-Terror Force* (New York: Pocket Books, 1999).

DePugh, Robert B., *Blueprint for Victory*, 4th edn (Norborne MO: Salon Publishing Company, 1978).

Forster, Arnold and Benjamin R. Epstein, *Report on the Ku Klux Klan* (New York: Anti-Defamation League, 1965).

Griffin, Robert S., *The Fame of a Dead Man's Deeds: An Up-Close Portrait of White Nationalist William Pierce* (self-published e-book, 2000).

Hamm, Mark S., *In Bad Company: America's Terrorist Underground* (Boston MA: Northeastern University Press, 2001).

Hamm, Mark S., *Terrorism, Hate Crime, and Anti-Government Violence: A Preliminary Review of the Research* (Indiana: Indiana State University, 1996).

Hewitt, Chris, "Responding to Terrorism," unpublished manuscript, 2000.

Interview with Norm Olson, September 8, 2000.

Kaplan, Jeffrey, "Leaderless Resistance," *Terrorism and Political Violence*, 9 (3), p. 80 (1997).

Michel, Lou and Dan Herbeck, *American Terrorist: Timothy McVeigh and the Oklahoma City Bombing* (New York: Regan Books, 2001).

National Advisory Committee on Criminal Justice Standards and Goals, *Report on the Task Force on Disorders and Terrorism* (Washington DC: National Advisory Committee on Criminal Justice Standards and Goals, 1976).

Segal, David, "The Pied Piper of Racism," *Washington Post*, January 12, 2000, C1, p. 8.

Smith, Brent L. and Kelly R. Damphousse, "Two Decades of Terror," in Kushner, Harvey W. (ed.) *The Future of Terrorism: Violence in the New Millennium* (Thousand Oaks CA: Sage, 1998).

Sprinzak, Ehud, "The Process of Delegitimation: Towards a Linkage Theory of Political Terrorism," *Terrorism and Political Violence*, 3 (1), pp. 50–68 (1991).

Stickney, Brandon M., *All-American Monster: The Unauthorized Biography of Timothy McVeigh* (Amherst, NY: Prometheus Books, 1996).

Wheaton, Elizabeth, *Code Name Greenkil: The 1979 Greensboro Killings* (Athens GA: University of Georgia Press, 1987).

White, Jonathan R., *Terrorism: an introduction* (Stamford CT: Wadsworth, 2002).

The Evolution of al Qaeda

Rohan Gunaratna[1]

....

The evolution of al Qaeda from an operational group of several thousand members into an ideological vanguard of the Islamic terrorist movement consisting of tens of thousands of members may be the most profound development in the international security landscape since 11 September 2001. Although al Qaeda's operational capabilities have severely diminished since 2001, the ideology of global jihad articulated by Osama bin Laden and his group has catalyzed the proliferation of jihad groups across the globe, including numerous cells in the West. Reflecting this trend, al Qaeda itself has *not* been directly responsible for most of the terrorist attacks in the past four years; rather, attacks have been *inspired* by al Qaeda but carried out by its associated groups with origins in the Middle East, East Africa, Asia, and the Caucuses.[2]

After addressing the origins of this trend, this chapter discusses the consequences of these structural changes in how al Qaeda finances terrorism. What do recent events—especially the rise of Islamic terrorism in Europe and the ongoing insurgency in Iraq—suggest about the funding and operations of the global jihadi movement into the future? What approaches are best suited to countering the financing of al Qaeda in its present form? This chapter answers these questions in four parts.

First, I describe the current structure of al Qaeda and its central place in the global jihadi movement. Today, al Qaeda has supplemented the remaining elements of the original, core organization with geographically diverse affiliated groups and ideological cells. Together with other (primarily Sunni) extremist groups, these elements constitute the global jihadi movement, which represents an even greater threat to the US and its allies and friends than earlier iterations of al Qaeda alone.

Second, I trace the evolution of al Qaeda through four phases in its life-cycle. These relate to periods during which al Qaeda based its operations in Pakistan, Sudan, and Afghanistan, and its subsequent transformation to the global jihadi movement. Throughout its evolution, al Qaeda has served not only as a source of inspiration and training, but has also provided associated groups and cells with funding and the know-how to raise and manage finances to carry out their terrorist activities. Thus, it is not surprising that during each period of transformation, al Qaeda and its affiliated cells have similarly changed methods of raising funds—most recently shifting towards self-financed criminal activities and away from donations by wealthy Arabs or business investments.

Rohan Gunaratna, "The Evolution of Al Qaeda," *Countering the Financing of Terrorism*, ed. Thomas J. Biersteker and Sue E. Eckert, pp. 47-62. Copyright © 2008 by Taylor & Francis Group. Reprinted with permission.

Third, I focus on the US intervention in Iraq, showing how it has galvanized jihadi groups world-wide to the point that the threat posed by the global jihadi movement has surpassed the terrorist threat posed by al Qaeda. The effect of the intervention has been to infuse the global jihadi movement with new human and financial resources. Through this support, and by adapting strategies to reflect the organizational learning of Islamic terrorist networks over the years since 11 September 2001, the new jihadi is even stronger and more resilient.

In conclusion, I offer some thoughts on the kinds of counter-measures—financial and otherwise—that are needed to respond to the rise of the global jihadi movement. As terrorists of global reach have shown the ability to adapt their strategy and tactics in the post-11 September period, it is critical that the international community develop responses to the changing nature of terrorist threats.

Al Qaeda Today: Group, Network, Cells, and Movement

The al Qaeda movement currently consists of three parts: (1) the al Qaeda group, founded by bin Laden and Abdullah Azzam in the late 1980s and severely weakened in the aftermath of the US invasion of Afghanistan; (2) the al Qaeda network, which is composed of the al Qaeda group and 30 to 40 associated groups located primarily in Africa, Asia, and the Middle East; and (3) ideologically affiliated cells worldwide acting in the name of or inspired by al Qaeda in pursuit of global jihad. Although the global jihadi movement embodies the ambitions of al Qaeda, global jihad is broader than the al Qaeda movement and has surpassed al Qaeda as the most significant threat to international security.

In 1988, bin Laden, the unofficial representative of the Saudi Kingdom to the anti-Soviet multina-tional Afghan jihad, and Azzam, bin Laden's Palestinian-Jordanian mentor, established the al Qaeda group. The al Qaeda group's global jihad ideology continues to hold great appeal for both associated groups waging local jihad in conflict zones and radicalized Muslim cells in the migrant and diaspora communities of the West. Also known as al Qaeda core, al Qaeda central, or al Qaeda classic, the al Qaeda group has been operationally weakened and largely depleted since the inception of Operation Enduring Freedom, but remains ideologically potent.

Operationally associated groups—the second major source of al Qaeda's support—form an umbrella of thirty to forty groups in Asia, Africa, and the Middle East known as the al Qaeda network. In Pakistan, Sudan, and Afghanistan, as well as in conflict zones such as Bosnia, Chechnya, and Mindanao, and through the internet, al Qaeda provides these groups with training, weapons, financing, and ideology. These groups hold declared or undeclared membership of the World Islamic Front for Jihad Against the Jews and the Crusaders, formed in February 1998. They include the Salafi Group for Call and Combat (GSPC), Moroccan Islamic Combatant Group (GICM), Takfir wal Hijra (TWH), Tawhid wal Jihad (al Qaeda of the Two Rivers), Lashkar-e-Taiba (LeT), Jemaah Islamiyah (JI), and Abu Sayyaff Group (ASG).

Al Qaeda's ideologically affiliated cells—the third component of al Qaeda—are operationally unconnected to al Qaeda but adhere to an ideology of a global jihad as articulated by al Qaeda. "The

Supporters of al Qaeda,"[3] the cell responsible for the bombing of the trains in Madrid on 11 March 2004, and the disrupted British cell led by Omar Khayam[4] were self-financed and independent of al Qaeda's operational control. These local jihad groups are inspired by and seek to emulate al Qaeda. The robust, post-Iraq Islamist milieu in North America, Europe, and Australasia encourages the transformation of these support cells into execution cells.

Beyond al Qaeda are primarily Sunni groups that operationally are unconnected with al Qaeda but steadfastly advocate global jihad. This category contains violent and non-violent groups. For instance, extremist groups such as Hizb-ut-Tahrir and al Mahajaroon in the UK fit into this category, as well as violent groups like Laskar Jihad and Front Pembela Islam in Indonesia. Some of these groups have even criticized bin Laden and al Qaeda, but nonetheless share the belief in global jihad and are part of the global jihad movement.

The invasion and occupation of Iraq, as well as reports of abuse at Abu Ghraib and Guantanamo, have strengthened support for like-minded associated groups and affiliated cells, as well as for Islamist groups unconnected to al Qaeda. Exploiting the suffering, resentment, and anger of Muslims, terrorist and extremist groups are now able to replenish their human losses and material costs to continue and intensify the fight. Al Qaeda thus has morphed from a group of several thousand members to a movement of several tens of thousands of members. Add to this other elements of the global jihad and the result is a robust global jihadi movement that represents an even greater threat to the US and its allies and friends than does the classic and more limited al Qaeda behind the 11 September attacks.

Phases in the Lifecycle of al Qaeda

In order to understand better how a terrorist group became a global movement, it is necessary to review the history of the various phases of al Qaeda. In doing so, I emphasize changes in the sources and methods used to finance al Qaeda operations.

Phase One: Pakistan

Al Qaeda Al Sulbha (solid base) was conceptualized by Abdullah Azzam in early 1988[5] and formally established by Osama bin Laden as an organization in Peshawar, Pakistan on 10 September 1988. Prior to its formation, however, al Qaeda existed as Maktab-il Khidamat (MAK—Afghan Service Bureau) for four years. As the premier Arab group supporting Afghan groups in their struggle against the Soviet Union, MAK received substantial financial support from the Saudi government and from Muslims living worldwide. MAK trained foreign supporters to fight against the Soviet occupation, which served to operationalize jihad as an ideology against communism.

In 1984, the Palestinian-Jordanian scholar Abdullah Azzam and his student and protégé, Osama bin Laden, established MAK with the purpose of facilitating recruitment, training, and fundraising for foreign mujahideen and chronicling the anti-Soviet multinational Afghan jihad. Both Azzam and bin Laden managed MAK, while Azzam also oversaw *Al Jihad*, a weekly magazine. As bin Laden controlled the funds, he served as the primary leader of operations while Azzam focused on ideology and popularizing the concept of jihad. Abdur Rasool Sayyaf and Gulbuddin Hekmatiyar (and his military commander Jalaludin Haqqani)—organizers of the anti-Soviet jihad with military and financial support of a multilateral coalition organized by the CIA and comprising the US, UK, Saudi Arabia, and Pakistan—were close to bin Laden, and a significant percentage of Arabs served in their groups. MAK built an infrastructure of guesthouses and training camps to support the flow of Arabs to fight against the Soviets.

MAK provided each visiting mujahideen with funds and accommodations. Mujahids would receive a Kalashnikov rifle, two hand grenades, a canteen, web gear, and ammunition. Guest houses included Beit al Ansar, Abdara Road, Peshawar; Beit al Salam, Peshawar; Beit al Quraba, Hyatabad, Peshawar; Beit al Shehada (House of Martyrs), Hyatabad, Peshawar; Miram Shah, Afghanistan–Pakistan border en route to Khost; another guesthouse in Torkhan en route from Pakistan to Afghanistan; and another guesthouse solely to house women—the wives of Arab mujahideen. Camps established beginning in 1987 included al Masada (Lions) Camp, Jaj—established by bin Laden; Areen Camp, also in Jaji; and the more specialized camps Khaled Ibn Waled and al Farooq, both in Khost.

In addition to the trainers, most of MAK's camps had a leader and a fundraiser. Sheikh Tameem Adnani, a Palestinian Jordanian who lived in the United States and raised funds internationally, oversaw finances at al Masada Camp. Although MAK did not receive support from the CIA or Western governments, MAK received support from the Saudi regime and the Muslim territorial and diaspora/migrant community, especially from the United States and the Gulf. From the MAK office in Peshawar, Abu Tariq—a Palestinian Jordanian—transported money to various camps.[6] In addition to providing false identities to the mujahideen as charity and school workers, Abdel Quddous—a US citizen—bribed Pakistani officials and provided them with Pakistani residency visas.[7]

Having played such a vital role in supporting the Afghan factions against the Soviets, Azzam and bin Laden began to focus on Israel and its steadfast supporters, especially after the first Palestinian uprising in 1987.[8] Azzam, in 1987–1988, formulated the broad outlines of what would become al Qaeda; he envisaged an organization that would channel the energies of the mujahideen into fighting on behalf of oppressed Muslims worldwide and would play the role of a pioneering vanguard of the Islamic movement. Azzam and bin Laden wanted the success against the Soviets replicated in other regions where Muslims were suffering. Upon its creation, al Qaeda inherited from MAK a fully fledged infrastructure of trainers, camps, weapons, and sources of finance. In addition to the Afghan training and operational infrastructure, al Qaeda benefited from the worldwide network created by its predecessor, with 30 offices overseas.

In 1989, bin Laden and Azzam split over disagreements regarding al Qaeda's priorities—bin Laden wanted to fund the Egyptians and Algerians, while Azzam wanted to focus on Islamizing the Afghan government. Most followers joined bin Laden, despite Azzam's assurances that following Afghanistan's

Islamization he would wage jihad starting with Tajikistan, Uzbekistan, and Chechnya.[9] Azzam took control of MAK and a building that housed the Sabalil (strong lion at night) Mosque and established Camp Khalden at Parachinar on the Afghanistan–Pakistan border. Azzam was assassinated by the members of the Egyptian Islamic Jihad in November 1989 with bin Laden's acquiescence. Following Azzam's death, MAK failed to generate "as much money,"[10] with some workers skimming money that was to be directed to support the Arab mujahideen.[11] After Abdullah Azzam's murder, MAK withered and bin Laden became the backbone and principal driving force of al Qaeda.

In this first phase of development, al Qaeda was primarily a commander–cadre organization [...]. Its operations were managed via a vertical leadership structure that provided strategic direction and tactical support to its horizontal network of compartmentalized cells or associated organizations. Separate operational committees—military, finance and business, fatwa and Islamic study, and media and publicity—were responsible for day-to-day operations.

Contributions from wealthy Arab benefactors served as al Qaeda's primary source of financing during its formative years. Initially supported by bin Laden's personal resources, al Qaeda fund-raisers increasingly approached wealthy financiers, charities, and businesses;[12] in fact, one of the key reasons al Qaeda re-established a presence in Saudi Arabia was the vast potential for recruitment and fundraising. A chart recovered from a computer in the Bosnia office of the Benevolence International Foundation on 19 March 2002 identified some of the respected individuals in Saudi Arabia, UAE, Kuwait, and Qatar who provided support. Wael Julaidan, alias Abu al Hassan al Madani, a Saudi who managed the Pakistan office of the International Islamic Relief Organization (IIRO),[13] provided funds to Asadallah al Sindi, the treasurer. Abu Ibrahim al Iraqi, a relative of an al Qaeda leader, managed the Peshawar office of the Kuwaiti Red Crescent Society, lectured about jihad, and provided funds for the mujahideen. Another Iraqi, Mamdouh Salim, alias Abu Hajir al Iraqi, managed guest-houses in Pakistan and was appointed the first head of al Qaeda's finance and investment committee. To facilitate such transactions, businesses and banks in the Gulf were used as fronts. Al Qaeda also siphoned funds from legitimate Islamic charities and infiltrated NGOs.[14]

Evidencing the keen desire of al Qaeda's leadership to monopolize the financing from Saudi Arabia, bin Laden authorized the killing of Jamil Ur Rahman, an Afghan leader. Jamil Ur Rahman reportedly had close ties to representatives of the Saudi Arabian government and "had attempted to influence wealthy Saudis not to provide money to bin Laden and his al Qaeda network."[15] Abdullah al Roomi, an al Qaeda member, killed Rahman at the behest of Muhammad Atta, alias Abu Hafs, a military leader of al Qaeda.[16]

Phase Two: Sudan

Following the Soviet withdrawal from Afghanistan, bin Laden returned to Saudi Arabia. The presence of "infidel" American troops on Saudi soil as part of Operation Desert Shield in 1990, and their continuing presence after the first Gulf War, led bin Laden to campaign against the Saudi regime. He joined the ranks of dissidents claiming those in the al Saud regime were false Muslims and that the regime needed to be replaced by a true Islamic state. Complaints that he was "financing subversive activities" in Algeria, Egypt, and Yemen, as well as his criticism of Saudi policies, caused bin Laden to fall out of favour with the Saudi government. After being warned of his impending arrest, bin Laden fled to Sudan, the headquarters of al Qaeda from April 1991 to May 1996.

Even before al Qaeda shifted its operations from Peshawar to Sudan, al Qaeda had established a small presence in Khartoum. In 1989, Azzam and bin Laden had dispatched Battan al Sudani, a trainer at Khaled Ibn Waled Camp in Afghanistan, and Abdul Halim Muhammad Dosman to Khartoum.[17] Having established an office to recruit mujahideen and begun training of the Eritrean Islamic Jihad, al Qaeda established a small organizational presence in Khartoum beginning in 1989. When the National Islamic Front (NIF) led by Hasan al Turabi came into office, al Turabi invited bin Laden to relocate to Sudan. In response, bin Laden dispatched his representatives to study the political, financial, and security environment. Bin Laden, satisfied with their findings, moved with Abu Ibrahim and Abu Hajir (also known as Mahmud Salim) to Sudan to establish a series of companies owned by al Qaeda.

Bin Laden's inherited wealth, which has been grossly exaggerated, nonetheless provided a basis to help establish businesses and diversify al Qaeda's finances while in Sudan. Al Qaeda's investments and economic ventures increased significantly and reportedly encompassed some 30 companies. These firms employed as many as 3,000 workers in Sudan in diverse fields, ranging from high-tech labs engaged in genetic research to civil engineering businesses. Al Qaeda trainer Battan al Sudani managed Taba Investments, one of bin Laden's key companies.[18] In particular, economic infrastructure and ambitious construction projects became key areas of investment. An al Qaeda camp builder, Abu Muath al Urduni, built both the Tahadi (challenge) road linking Khartoum and Port Sudan and another road linking Damazine and Koromuk.[19] Al Qaeda also cooperated directly with the government of Sudan, including co-investing to create al Hijra Construction, a firm managed by Abu Ibrahim for building roads and bridges. Bin Laden's extensive business ties with the Sudanese political and military leadership increased his stature and al Qaeda's influence. This was principally a period of consolidation for al Qaeda.

Although al Qaeda appears to have focused on its business investments from 1992 to 1996, its terrorist and militant activities continued unabated, with the economic ventures providing opportunities to further its agenda. Agricultural facilities owned by al Qaeda—the Soba and Damazaine farms—by night served as training facilities for jihadi groups. Likewise, al Qaeda transported camels from Sudan to Egypt for sale but also used the opportunity to smuggle weapons for the jihadists in Egypt. In addition to heading al Qaeda's finance and investment committee, Abu Hajir al Iraqi attempted to procure radioactive material for al Qaeda. While on a visit to Germany for such purchases in 1998, he was arrested for his alleged involvement in the African embassy bombings and extradited to the United States.[20] But, as he refused to cooperate with German and US authorities, Western nations remain in the dark about al Qaeda's financial and economic empire. There is no reliable estimate of the total value of Osama bin Laden's operations in Sudan to this point. During this period, al Qaeda also furthered its links with Islamic groups engaged in guerrilla warfare and terrorism, providing them with funds, training, and weapons.

After the 1995 failed attempt to assassinate Egyptian President Mubarak in Ethiopia attracted the attention of the intentional community, the United States used sanctions to intensify pressure on Sudan to expel bin Laden. Although bin Laden had some success in investing his personal wealth in Sudan, his enterprises ultimately lost money due to international sanctions. As his wealth evaporated, bin Laden's anger grew both against the West and against the Arab regimes that were close to the United States, notably Saudi Arabia and Egypt. By 1994–1995, Western and Israeli security and intelligence agencies identified bin Laden as a key financier of terrorism. Sudan finally bowed to international pressure in 1996 and asked the "Saudi businessman" and al Qaeda to leave.

Phase Three: Afghanistan

The relocation of al Qaeda from Sudan to Afghanistan in May 1996 hastened the transformation of bin Laden into a true international terrorist. In Sudan, bin Laden invested in huge construction projects and certainly supported terrorism although he was not directly involved. Relocating to Afghanistan, a landlocked country where Western intelligence agencies had virtually no presence, enabled al Qaeda to revive and reorganize its training and operational infrastructure. With bin Laden's expulsion from Sudan, the Western intelligence community that had previously monitored bin Laden's activities entirely lost track of his operations.

Within months after bin Laden moved to Afghanistan, the Taliban seized control of most of Afghanistan, including Kabul. Supported by Pakistan's Inter-Services Intelligence (ISI), the Taliban drew support largely from Afghan youths who had grown up in Pakistan and mujahideen leaders in Pakistan. Bin Laden quickly consolidated his ties to the Taliban leadership by financing and materially assisting the regime. Specifically, al Qaeda formed a guerrilla unit to assist the Taliban, which, while functioning as a separate organization, integrated with Taliban troops for the purpose of fighting the Northern Alliance. The Taliban regime reciprocated al Qaeda's assistance by providing sanctuary, weapons, equipment, and training facilities.[21]

Bin Laden was warmly welcomed in Afghanistan. As the most prominent Arab who fought against the Soviets, both the Afghan and the Pakistani mujahideen groups considered him a hero. Among the several thousand Arabs who had remained in Afghanistan and Pakistan, unwelcome in their home countries after the Soviet withdrawal, he found a natural following. Especially after the first World Trade Center attack in February 1993, when the United States warned Pakistan to get rid of the mujahideen or be declared a "terrorist state," most of the Arab mujahideen located in Pakistan moved to Afghanistan where al Qaeda had established a presence.

Al Qaeda's relocation to Afghanistan in 1996 created the opportunity for bin Laden to build a truly global jihad network, consolidating old relationships and building new ones. Many of the North African and East African jihad groups that al Qaeda trained in Sudan established a presence in Afghanistan. Further, bin Laden deepened the traditional links to Middle Eastern terrorist groups, particularly those from the Persian Gulf, and through partnerships with regional leaders developed closer ties with Asian groups. As an organization with a global membership, al Qaeda used Afghanistan to train, finance, and indoctrinate Islamist groups from Asia, Africa, the Middle East, and the Caucasus. Almost all the recruited Muslims came from the conflict zones of Nagorno-Karabakh, Chechnya, Tajikistan, Dagestan, Bosnia, Kosovo, Kashmir, Rohingiya Myanmar, the Philippines (Mindanao), Indonesia (Maluku and Poso), China (Xingjiang), Somalia (Ogadan), Algeria, Egypt, Jordan, and Yemen. Al Qaeda described its goal as the capacitation of a core group of fighters to alleviate the suffering of Muslims at the hands of the repressive regimes and rulers supported by the US Government and its allies.

In addition to its own training camps in Afghanistan, al Qaeda dispatched trainers to establish or serve in the training camps of affiliated groups in Asia, Africa, the Middle East, and the Caucasus. For example, beginning in 1988 and increasing after 1994, al Qaeda made efforts to embed its influence in Southeast Asia. Al Qaeda began by dispatching Muhammad Jamal Khalifa, the brother-in-law of Osama bin Laden, to establish the Manila branch of the International Islamic Relief Organization, a respectable Saudi charity, and to provide assistance to Islamist groups in the region. In 1994, Khalid Sheikh Muhammad—the mastermind of 11 September—traveled to Southeast Asia with 1993 World Trade Center bomber Ramzi Ahmed Yousef carrying plans to destroy US airliners over the Pacific. Similarly, within the Moro Islamic Liberation Front (MILF) Camp Abu Bakar complex, al Qaeda's Kuwaiti trainer Omar Al Farooq established Camp Vietnam to train Southeast Asian groups in guerrilla warfare and terrorism. Al Qaeda replicated this model worldwide from the Caucasus to North Africa.

Financing three or four thousand al Qaeda members in Afghanistan and clandestine agents overseas is estimated to have cost at least $36 million a year, on top of which the group's set-up costs—weapons, technology, infrastructure, camps, offices, vehicles—are thought to have been under $50 million, an estimate computed by examining the budgets of terrorist groups in relation to their sources of finance, geographic distribution, organizational sophistication, size, and other factors.[22] The funds came primarily from charities, businesses, and individual contributions.

Immediately following the Soviet withdrawal from Afghanistan, and for the remainder of the century, the international community ignored Afghanistan and, to some extent, Pakistan. As a result, Afghanistan and Pakistan developed throughout the 1990s as the centers for ideological and physical training of Islamist guerrilla and terrorist groups. After the Oslo Accords in the early 1990s, Afghanistan replaced the Syrian-controlled Bekkaa Valley as the principal hub of international terrorism. As the West looked the other way, Afghanistan evolved into a "Terrorist Disneyland." Together, al Qaeda and the Islamic Movement of the Taliban—the ruling party of the Islamic Emirate of Afghanistan—trained upwards of 20,000 foreign mujahideen until the US-led coalition intervened in Afghanistan in October 2001.

Phase Four: The Global Jihadi Movement

Since the 11 September attacks, al Qaeda's core strength has shrunk from about three or four thousand to a few hundred members. With the loss of Afghanistan as an operational base following the US-led intervention, and nearly 80 percent of its operational leadership and membership killed or captured, al Qaeda entered a new phase of its development. Even though al Qaeda maintains a presence in Afghanistan and Pakistan, its capacity is significantly degraded, and exercising direct control over its wide-ranging affiliated groups is increasingly difficult. Now, instead of planning and executing attacks itself, al Qaeda's greatest success has been the transfer of its operational knowledge to other groups. The most hunted terrorist group in history has evolved into an ideological vanguard, working with and through associated groups, networks, and cells, which collectively are known as the global jihad movement.

Notwithstanding the loss of its territorial sanctuary, al Qaeda successfully disseminates its ideological agenda of global jihad to its followers. Through communications from bin Laden, al Zawahiri, al Zarqawi (until recently), and others, primarily delivered via the Internet, al Qaeda provides indirect but critical ideological and strategic direction. Al Qaeda's overarching ideological goals—to expel foreign forces from the Islamic world and ultimately to create an Islamic state—facilitate the organization of regional and local groups. The World Islamic Front for Jihad Against the Jews and the Crusaders, al Qaeda's umbrella organization created in February 1998, attempts to unite its Middle Eastern, African, Caucasian, and Asian groups and provide a common agenda. Several regional groups have developed alliances similar to al Qaeda's World Islamic Front. For instance, Hambali—both an al Qaeda and a Jemaah Islamiyah leader—convened a meeting of Southeast Asian groups in Malaysia in 1999 to form the Rabitat-ul-Mujahideen (Legion of God's Warriors). After 11 September, and especially after the US-led intervention in Iraq, the international security and intelligence community has reported unprecedented unity between these groups.

The attacks in Madrid (2004) and London (2005) point towards Europe as a primary target for al Qaeda. As in Spain and Britain, the phenomenon of near-autonomous "home grown" terrorist cells carrying out attacks conforms to a well-recognized model for al Qaeda's current operations. The invasion of Iraq spurred the radicalization of alienated diaspora communities in Europe, which received ideological incitements and material support from radical preachers and networks associated with al Qaeda. In particular, some of the most significant al Qaeda-affiliated cells planning attacks in Europe have origins and links to North Africa. For example, the north London cell, discovered by authorities in January 2003 to have manufactured ricin, was originally a cell organized to support the creation of an Islamist Algerian state. Throughout Europe, Algerian terrorist support cells had generated propaganda, funds, and supplies for their campaign. Likewise, many of the terrorists involved in the Madrid train bombings in March 2004 were from Morocco or from the Moroccan diaspora. While European governments initially responded slowly to this threat, the 2004 Madrid bombings and the 2005 London bombings jarred Europeans into recognizing the necessity for action against the wider al Qaeda network, not just individual cells.

Developments in Europe call into question some of the counter-measures pursued after 11 September, especially those in the financial sector. A key component of the "global war on terror" has been the effort to cut off financial support for terrorism. Since 11 September 2001, initiatives combating the financing of terrorism have gained greater prominence as part of the international counter-terrorism effort [...]. But European Islamists who currently subscribe to al Qaeda's ideology have learned rapidly from the past mistakes of al Qaeda and its associated cells and have adapted to law enforcement initiatives targeting terrorist financing. Current dedicated operational cells of al Qaeda and its associated groups are now familiar with and can easily circumvent governmental measures, making the cells difficult to detect.

Largely as a result of national governments' efforts to cut off financial support, al Qaeda and its networks have been forced to further decentralize their financing methods. Although the core al Qaeda organization and its associated groups still raise funds and recruit members through front, cover, and sympathetic organizations—organizations used to established charities, human rights groups, humanitarian organizations, community centers, and religious associations—cells increasingly generate their own funds. Cells have adapted to the increasing pressure by becoming self-financing, primarily through criminal activities, as was demonstrated in the Madrid train bombings [...].

With most of the operations now at the local or regional level, disrupting the financing of individual cells is increasingly important. Even though the CIA interrogation of Khalid Sheik Muhammad, the 11 September mastermind, revealed that al Qaeda had no shortage of funds immediately after the US attacks, most of the subsequent terrorist attacks are believed to have been financed locally through individual terrorists or self-financed cells.

Iraq

My discussion thus far is summarized in Table 10.1. To understand the post-11 September phase in the evolution of al Qaeda, however, it is necessary to focus on the Islamist response to the US-led invasion of Iraq in 2003. The Iraq war has provided a substantial impetus to al Qaeda and other jihadi groups, breathing new life into the movement and providing it with a base to recruit, train, and fight. As the major focal point for terrorist activity, Iraq has attracted "foreign fighters" from Islamic communities across the globe, serving as an experiential "training ground" of jihad, much as Afghanistan, Bosnia, and Chechnya inculcated generations of mujahideen into the terrorist lifestyle throughout the 1980s and 1990s.

Muslim public support for jihad depends on the ability of al Qaeda and like-minded groups to inculcate the belief that Islam is under threat by the United States and its allies. The Iraq war, the Abu Ghraib photographs, reports of prisoner abuse at Guantanamo, and Muslim loss of life in Iraq serve to encourage even moderate Muslims to support jihadi groups. Today, extremist and terrorist groups ably exploit Muslim suffering, resentment, and anger. In that process, several new "al Qaedas" have

Table 10.1 The Phases of al Qaeda and Its Financing

Phase	Financial Source(s)	Organizational Structure
Phase 1: Pakistan (1984–1991)	Solicitations of wealthy Middle Eastern benefactors, charities	MAK infrastructure under bin Laden and Azzam
Phase 2: Sudan (1991–1996)	Business fronts, Osama bin Laden's personal wealth	Hierarchical structure in consultation with Sudanese government, plus extended network
Phase 3: Afghanistan (1996–2001)	Taliban sanctuary, charity diversion, smuggling, solicitations	Hierarchical structure with extensive training camps, networks, and partnerships, including with the Taliban
Phase 4: Post–11 September	Self-financing of cells through petty crime	Weakened hierarchy providing inspiration and ideological justification to regional associates

been created. Just as the Madrid bombers called their group "The Supporters of al Qaeda," jihadists now independently conduct al Qaeda-style coordinated simultaneous suicide and non-suicide attacks.

Underscoring the centrality of the war in Iraq to al Qaeda's current objectives and the global jihadi movement, Osama bin Laden endorsed Jordanian-born terrorist leader Abu Musab al Zarqawi as an al Qaeda affiliate and leader of operations in Iraq. Bin Laden characterized Iraq as a "golden and unique opportunity" to defeat the United States, and as the central battleground in a "Third World War, which the Crusader Zionist coalition began against the Islamic nation."[23] Zarqawi was responsible for coordinating the largest number of suicide and non-suicide attacks in Iraq, working with a dozen groups to amplify the threat. Although he trained with al Qaeda in the Heart Camp and even lost a leg in combat, he worked not only with al Qaeda but also with al Ansar al Islami in Iraq and al Tawhid in Europe. Bin Laden has encouraged Islamic elements in Iraq to work with other insurgent groups such as the Baathists.

Within Iraq, this network supports itself through many of the finance mechanisms used by al Qaeda, including:

> [F]unds provided by charities, Iraqi expatriates, and other donors, primarily in the Gulf, but also in Syria, Lebanon, Jordan, Iran, and Europe, and criminal activities such as kidnapping for ransom ... narcotics trafficking, robbery, theft, extortion, smuggling, and counterfeiting (goods and currency).[24]

Many of the funds that come from external sources are smuggled into Iraq using cash couriers. This is the most convenient and preferred method of moving funds by virtue of the availability of smuggling routes across porous borders and the difficulty of tracing cash payments of US dollars in the primarily cash economy of today's Iraq. In addition to Syria's serving as such a conduit, the US Government maintains that Iranian-backed proxy groups transfer into southern Iraq funds and materiel provided directly by Iran.[25]

Al Qaeda has ideologically incited local and regional Islamist groups to fight what they perceive to be not only corrupt Muslim regimes and false Muslim rulers such as those in Algeria, Egypt, Jordan, Saudi Arabia, Morocco, Kuwait, Indonesia, and Pakistan but also those governments' patrons, the United States and its allies. This strategy has achieved a number of significant objectives. First, despite enhanced counter-terrorism law enforcement and detection initiatives in the worldwide hunt for members and supporters of al Qaeda, incidents of terrorism have increased. Second, although the ability of al Qaeda and other terrorist groups to mount attacks, especially against well-defended facilities or hard targets such as diplomatic missions, military bases, and other government targets, has diminished, terrorists remain intent to attack. One of the unforeseen consequences of the West's counter-terrorism policies has been a shift from hard targets to soft ones, such as commercial infrastructure, tourist resorts, and population centers. Such vulnerable targets are too numerous to protect, making mass fatalities and casualties inevitable. Considering the sustained terrorist drive to attack, the West is not likely to stop suffering periodic terrorist attacks any time soon.

In short, the Iraq conflict has provided al Qaeda with an infusion of new human and tactical resources. For the foreseeable future, Iraq and to a lesser extent Afghanistan (and possibly Chechnya) will remain the primary fronts of the global jihadi movement.

Conclusion: Countering al Qaeda and the Global Jihadi Movement

Since its emergence in the 1980s, al Qaeda has evolved from a core group of radicals determined to execute and facilitate acts of terrorism to an ideological vanguard inspiring a global jihadi movement. Al Qaeda as an organization has demonstrated its proficiency at adapting its structure and strategy in response to counter-terrorism measures taken by the international community since the 11 September attacks. To evade technical methods of monitoring, al Qaeda has developed greater discipline and operational security. Having lost its training and operational infrastructure in Afghanistan, al Qaeda has increasingly relied on and operated through associated groups.

As al Qaeda has evolved, its methods for raising and moving funds have varied. In response, Western governments have adopted a wide range of measures to suppress al Qaeda's operational and financial capability. However, while the threat of al Qaeda has evolved, to a large extent, the conception of al Qaeda utilized by security and intelligence services in the West has not. The unfortunate consequence is that our responses to the threat of al Qaeda today are designed to counter the al Qaeda of 2001, not the fragmented global jihadi movement of 2005. This is an important deficiency.

Therefore, we must ensure that our policies change to accurately reflect our understanding of the current threat, just as al Qaeda has changed in response to our efforts to suppress terrorism. If al Qaeda is truly atomized into self-financing cells, then our efforts must match this new understanding. Unfortunately, the US focus on Iraq and on eliminating the al Qaeda leadership has limited the ability of US officials to understand and respond to the changing threat. Equally pressing are the many gaps in our knowledge about the structure of today's al Qaeda. In these cases, recognizing our blind spots and holes in our understanding will serve to spur caution and further inquiry that may make a substantial difference in future attempts to disrupt al Qaeda and its affiliates.

In light of al Qaeda's evolution, counter-measures against the global jihadi movement should go beyond the tactical targeting of terrorist cells. Critically, we must act strategically to prevent the creation of terrorists. Strategies for fighting terrorism must include countering the appeal of abstract and hate-based ideology of jihad against the West, especially the United States, its allies, and friends. It is also necessary to send the message that al Qaeda and its associated groups are not Koranic organizations and that they are presenting a corrupt version of Islam by misinterpreting and misrepresenting the Koran and other texts. The jihadi movement uses Islam as a tool of mass mobilization through the manipulation of prophetic truths from the Koran. The West should work with the Muslim elite to confront and stop these jihadists from preaching and conducting violence and to create space and a platform for the moderate Muslims. Muslim leaders must get the *ulemas* (Muslim scholars) and *ustaz* (religious teachers) to preach that Islam is a religion of peace, not terror. Islam must be portrayed as tolerant of other faiths, as Muslim scholars in history have proudly asserted. It is also incumbent upon the international community to work together to roll back the threat of radical Islamism by helping the Muslim community recover from the current ideological crisis. Furthermore, conditions must be created under which Muslims can achieve a balance between personal piety, peace, freedom, and prosperity.

Overall, the key to defeating al Qaeda and reducing the terrorist threat is to develop a multi-agency, multi-juristic, and multinational strategy to combat the organization's ideology. Such a strategy will necessarily concentrate on combating regeneration—terrorist ability to replenish human losses and material costs. As strategies target the recruitment ability of such an organization and the impetus for any individual to attach his or herself to such an agenda, the group will start to decay over a period of time. Counter-strategies should seek to address grievances and aspirations. Such a perspective will discredit the ideology of al Qaeda, limit their activities, and undermine their ability to incite and enact violence. Therefore a both preventative and proactive strategy, in concert with continued law enforcement and financial measures, should be employed through all new policy initiatives.

Notes

1. I wish to express my gratitude to Peter Romaniuk, Sue E. Eckert, Arabinda Acharya, and Jaime Sarah Burnell for their assistance in writing this chapter.

2. Al Qaeda itself has conducted an average of only one terrorist attack per year since the 11 September attacks. Four times that number, or an average of one attack every three months, has been mounted by al Qaeda-associated groups.

3. Briefing by CNI, the Spanish Intelligence Service, December 2004.

4. Briefing on Operation Crevice, SO 13, New Scotland Yard, December 2004.

5. R. Paz, Personal Communication, December 2001. Dr. Paz, a former head of research of the Internal Security Agency (Shin bet) of Israel, was the first to bring to the attention of the operational and the academic community the founding charter of al Qaeda. The charter authored by Azzam was published in *Al Jihad*, the principal journal of the Arab Mujahideen in Peshawar, 1988.

6. Al Qaeda detainee commenting on Tareekh Osama, Folder 56, Document 136, recovered from Benevolence International Foundation's Bosnia Office, 19 March 2002, p. 9.

7. Ibid.

8. A. al Zawahiri, "The Knights under the Prophet's Banner," unpublished manuscript, December 2001.

9. Al Qaeda detainee commenting on Tareekh, Al Musadat, 86, 87, 88, Folder 8, Documents 301–347, recovered from Benevolence International Foundation's Bosnia Office, 19 March 2002, p. 5.

10. Ibid.

11. Ibid.

12. Considerable speculation has taken place as to Osama bin Laden's personal wealth. Bin Laden was alleged to have inherited upwards of $300 million when his father died, funds thought to have formed the basis for al Qaeda financing in Sudan and Afghanistan. Such exaggerations have been discredited, and his personal wealth has been estimated to be closer to $30–40 million—about a million dollars per year from about 1970–1994 according to the 9/11 Commission's *Monograph on Terrorist Financing*. In 1994, the Saudi government forced the bin Laden family to sell Osama's share of the family company and to freeze the proceeds, thereby depriving him of what could have been a $300 million fortune. J. Roth, D. Greenberg, and S. Wille, *Monograph on Terrorist Financing* (Staff Report to the Commission), National Commission on Terrorist Attacks Upon the United States, 2004. Online. Available HTTP: <http:// www.9–11commission.gov/staff_statements/911_TerrFin_Monograph.pdf#search=%229%2F11%20 commission%20monograph%22>

13. IIRO functioned under Rabita al Islami, also known as MWLKA.

14. For a more detailed description of al Qaeda's financial network, see R. Gunaratna, *Inside al Qaeda: Global Network of Terror*, New York: Columbia University Press, 2002.

15. Al Qaeda detainee commenting on Tareekh, Al Musadat, 86, 87, 88, Folder 8, Documents 301–347, recovered from Benevolence International Foundation's Bosnia Office, 19 March 2002.

16. "Posing as a journalist Al Roomi visited with Jamil Ur Rahman and while interviewing him about his relationship with the Saudi government pulled out a small handgun and killed him. Al Roomi was killed by Jamil Ur Rahman's bodyguard. Jamil Ur Rahman was killed after Abdullah Azzam, the ideological father of al Qaeda was killed, also by al Qaeda." Ibid.

17. Ibid.

18. Ibid.

19. Al Qaeda detainee commenting on Tareekh Osama, Folder 56, Document 136, recovered from Benevolence International Foundation's Bosnia Office, 19 March 2002, p. 7.

20. Al Iraqi attempted to procure a uranium canister for $1.5 million, but al Qaeda was duped. The canister had been irradiated from outside and sold. While in detention, al Iraqi used a sharpened comb to stab a US corrections officer in his eye.

21. Gunaratna, *Inside Al Qaeda*, p. 54.

22. Gunaratna, "The Lifeblood of Terrorist Organisations: Evolving Terrorist Financing Strategies," in Alex Schmid (ed.) *Countering Terrorism Through International Cooperation*, International Scientific and Professional Advisory Council of the UN Cooperation and the UN Terrorism Prevention Branch, 2001, pp. 180–205. R. Gunaratna, *Inside al Qaeda: Global Network of Terror*, New York, Columbia University Press, 2002, p. 61.

23. Bin Laden audio tape released 27 December 2004, Foreign Broadcast Information Service (FBIS) Report FEA20041227000762, 27 December 2004.

24. D. L. Glaser, "Who Pays the Iraqi Insurgents?" testimony of Daniel L. Glaser, Acting Assistant Secretary for the Office of Terrorist Financing and Financial Crimes, US Department of the Treasury before the House Financial Services Subcommittee on Oversight and Investigations and the House Armed Services Subcommittee on Terrorism, 28 July 2005. Online. Available HTTP:<http://financialservices.house.gov/media/pdf/072805dg.pdf> (accessed 21 October 2005).

25. Ibid.

PART V

Satanism

The Church of Satan and the Temple of Set

Religious Parody and Satanic Panic

Hugh B. Urban

O n April 30, 1966—the night of Walpurgisnacht, or the traditional European spring festival—an American occultist named Anton Szandor LaVey shaved his head and proclaimed the formation of the Church of Satan (CoS). Declaring this "Year One, Anno Satanis," LaVey quickly generated a great deal of media attention by performing the first Satanic wedding in 1967 and then enacting the first modern "black masses" in the basement of his Victorian San Francisco home, called the Black House. With LaVey draped in a mock devil outfit, complete with billowing black robes, clerical collar, and horned skullcap, surrounded by masked figures and a naked woman serving as the altar, these early black masses were clearly as much burlesque parody as religious ritual. Throughout his writings (such as *The Satanic Bible*) and his colorful ritual performances, LaVey often walked a fine line between serious religion and comical satire, exploiting the power of performance art as much as the power of occult philosophy and magic. Yet he did help give birth to modern Satanism as a new religious movement that has had a widespread influence not just on American spiritual life but on popular culture, music, and film.

Today, the Church of Satan is the best-known Satanic movement in the United States, and it has certainly been the focus of the most media attention and sensationalism. However, there are now numerous other Satanic groups operating throughout the United States, England, and Europe, many of them more "serious" and less parodic than LaVey's church. In this chapter we will also look at two movements that emerged out of the Church of Satan and moved in a more radical direction, usually called the "Left Hand Path": the Temple of Set (ToS), founded by Michael Aquino in 1975, and the Setian Liberation Movement, founded by LaVey's daughter Zeena and her husband Nikolas Schreck.

However, perhaps the greatest influence of modern Satanism has been not on contemporary American spirituality but on music, particularly hard rock and heavy metal. Since the late 1960s, a variety of folk and rock bands such as the American group Coven had begun making serious use of Satanic imagery and lyrics; by the 1970s, bands such as Black Sabbath (while not particularly "Satanic" themselves) helped popularize Satanic themes, combined with down-tuned guitars and dissonant,

Hugh B. Urban, "The Church of Satan and the Temple of Set: Religious Parody and Satanic Panic," *New Age, Neopagan, and New Religious Movements: Alternative Spirituality in Contemporary America*, pp. 179-200. Copyright © 2015 by University of California Press. Reprinted with permission.

minor, and atonal chords. By the 1980s and 1990s, a huge variety of new genres had emerged, such as black metal, death metal, doom, and others, that made extensive use of Satanic themes and often Satanic performances on stage.

Not surprisingly, the emergence of new Satanic movements such as CoS and ToS, combined with the growing influence of Satanic themes in popular music, helped give rise to a widespread paranoia throughout the American media in the 1980s, often called the Satanic Panic. The panic was in turn part of a broader anticult paranoia in the United States that dates back to at least the 1960s and that rapidly intensified after the Charles Manson murder spree in 1968 and then after the Peoples Temple suicides in 1978 [...]. While most of the charges later proved to be imaginary, a powerful narrative spread throughout the mainstream media that Satanic groups were whisking children away to be sexually abused and subjected to all manner of bizarre ritual perversions. Ironically, the Satanic Panic and the hysteria about "Satanic ritual abuse" probably only encouraged the black metal bands and other groups to employ Satanic imagery, since it lent even more power, fear, and awe to the idea of Satanic ritual and its threat to mainstream society.

The Secret Life of a Satanist: Anton Lavey and the Birth of The Church of Satan

Neither the concept of Satan nor the idea of a black mass was new in the late 1960s, of course. When Anton LaVey began his new church and performed his first Satanic rituals, he was drawing upon a very long tradition of belief, folklore, superstition, literature, and popular imagination surrounding the devil and devil worship in Western history. With a few notable exceptions, however, virtually all of the stories about Satanic worship and black masses from the last 2,000 years have been imaginary—largely the product of cultural hysteria, paranoia, and fantasies of a "world turned upside down." Virtually every group that was labeled as heretical by the mainstream Christian Church was accused of black magic, devil worship, and usually obscene rituals. From early Christian heresies such as Gnosticism down to medieval sects such as the Cathars and military orders such as the Knights Templar, marginal religious groups were commonly accused of engaging in corrupt, inverted, and perverted rituals and worship of dark forces. These fantasies culminated in the late Middle Ages and the early modern period with the witch trials and the execution of thousands of people—particularly women—on suspicion that they were engaged in witches' sabbaths, interactions with demons, and other evil rites.[1]

Documented cases of actual black masses being performed prior to the twentieth century are few and far between. Perhaps the most famous was the case of the so-called Guiborg Masses at the court of French King Louis XIV in the seventeenth century. The priest performing the rites was Abbé Étienne Guiborg (1610–86), a Catholic priest and occultist who became involved with the king's mistress, Madame de Montespan. Fearing that the king was losing affection for her, Madame de Montespan first sought out a witch known as La Voisin, who performed a series of rites that involved calling upon the devil and killing and taking the blood from a newborn infant. In 1666, Montespan went still further by enjoining the Abbé Guiborg to perform a black mass over her nude body in a ritual that also involved an infant sacrifice. While it is unclear how many of these black rites actually took place and how many were imagined, they would become a central part of the larger narrative of the black mass in modern times. In the late nineteenth century, French novelists such as J. K. Huysmans would help popularize the idea of the black mass in widely read works such as *Là-bas* (Down there; 1891), which explores the occult underworld and culminates in a sensational account of a secret black mass in Paris.[2]

When he formed his own new Church of Satan in the late 1960s, Anton LaVey drew upon all of these historical and imaginary narratives of the black mass. But he also creatively reworked them in the new context of modern America, amid the new circumstances of the sexual revolution and the rise of a wide range of alternative spiritual movements.

Like the biographies of other new religious leaders, LaVey's life story is a complex mixture of history, embellishment, and sometimes fantastic elaboration (Figure 11.1). Most of what we know of LaVey's life is derived from his own personal accounts from Blanche Barton's "official" biography, *The Secret Life of a Satanist* (1990), but the details in these official narratives are often at odds with the findings of more skeptical journalists and scholars, and even LaVey's own daughter Zeena would later denounce much of his biography as "a catalogue of lies" and "self-serving bullshit."[3]

According to the legendary narrative as told by Blanche Barton, the story goes something like this: LaVey was born in Chicago in 1930 of French, Alsatian, Russian, and Romanian descent, though he also claimed to possess gypsy blood and to have learned about vampires from his grandmother. Brought up in San Francisco, LaVey was the proverbial boy who ran off to join the circus, leaving his family and school at age sixteen to work in amusement parks, first as a roustabout and then as a cage boy with big cats. He also worked as a musician, playing calliope and organ, performing for both the provocative carnival dancers and the Christian tent revivals—an experience that, he claimed, proved to him the hypocrisy of Christianity and the deeper reality of carnal desire: "On Saturday night I would see men lusting after half naked girls dancing at the carnival and on Sunday morning when I was playing at the other end of the carnival lot I would see these same men sitting in the pews with their wives and children asking God to forgive them. ... I knew then that the Christian Church thrives on hypocrisy and that man's carnal nature will out!"[4]

Figure 11.1 Anton LaVey. Photo by Nick Bougas. Courtesy of the Church of Satan.

Another formative experience in his early life, LaVey claimed, was his time working as a criminal photographer for the San Francisco Police Department, where he regularly saw examples of horrible cruelty and bloodshed. If his organist days proved to him the reality of carnal desire and the hypocrisy of religion, his time as a police photographer proved to him the violence of human nature and the nonexistence of God.

During the 1950s and '60s, LaVey developed an interest in the occult and parapsychology, investigating reports of ghosts, UFOs, and other unusual phenomena. Eventually he would begin holding classes on esoteric subjects, attracting a number of people interested in occultism, spirituality, and the supernatural, including science fiction author Forrest Ackerman and filmmaker Kenneth Anger. LaVey also read widely in Western philosophy, particularly the works of the German philosopher Friedrich Nietzsche and the Russian-born American author Ayn Rand, which helped form the basis of his highly individualist and anti-Christian ideology. During the late 1960s, LaVey made his headquarters in an old house on California Street in San Francisco, which became known as the Black House because he had painted it entirely black. This became the home for his new Church of Satan, formally announced in 1966 at the dawn of his new Anno Satanis, the Age of Satan. As LaVey later recalled, the late 1960s in America was exactly the right time to launch a new Satanic movement: "The Satanic Age started in 1966. That's when God was proclaimed dead, the Sexual Freedom League came into prominence, and the hippies developed the sex culture."[5]

Many of the details of Barton's biography have been challenged by later authors and journalists. For example, LaVey's claim to have worked for the San Francisco Police Department has been found to be completely unsubstantiated; he also claimed to have had an affair with the young Marilyn Monroe while playing the organ at burlesque houses in Los Angeles, and this also appears to have been imaginary. Yet regardless of the truth of his official biography, LaVey's reputation as the high priest and "Black Pope" for a new age of sensual religion spread rapidly. In 1967, a year after the founding of the Church of Satan, LaVey began to attract tremendous media attention, first by performing a Satanic wedding for radical journalist John Raymonds and New York socialite Judith Case and then by performing the first Satanic baptism for his daughter Zeena. Also in 1967 Ira Levin published his popular Satanic horror novel *Rosemary's Baby*. When director Roman Polanski decided to turn the novel into a film, LaVey seemed a natural choice to serve as the technical adviser and even to appear as the devil in the film's surreal impregnation scene. By 1969, LaVey had published his *Satanic Bible,* and his reputation as the devil's spokesman was well established.

Lavey's Satanic Philosophy

LaVey's Satanic worldview is founded on a complete rejection of all existing religious and moral systems, which are in his view bankrupt, hypocritical, and irrelevant. His own new creed is based on the fundamental acceptance that all religions are human creations, that all moral codes are relative, and that we may as well create a new religion that we can enjoy rather than feel guilty about: "No creed must be accepted upon authority of a 'divine' nature. ... No moral dogma must be taken for granted—no standard of measure deified. There is nothing inherently sacred about moral codes. Like the wooden idols of long ago, they are the work of human hands, and what man has made man can destroy."[6]

LaVey's philosophy is perhaps best described as a kind of radical materialism and hedonistic individualism that celebrates the human body, ego, and sensual pleasure. It is, in sum, "a system based on rational self-interest, sensual indulgence, and the constructive use of alienation."[7] While LaVey's writings greatly resemble those of earlier authors such as Aleister Crowley, Nietzsche, and Rand, LaVey clearly marketed his philosophy for a new generation of sexual freedom and individualism in 1960s' America. The main point for LaVey is that Satanism does *not* mean the worship of some actual deity named Satan who is the opposite of some imagined God. Rather, it is the rejection of *all* gods altogether and the worship of one's own individual self. Here Satan—literally "the adversary"—is merely the symbol of the individual human ego, with all its desires and passions, which should be embraced, not repressed.

LaVey made no secret of his disgust for Christianity, which he saw as a religion of weakness, repression, guilt, and hatred of the body. Christianity, in his view, is largely the root of our present misery, since it has taught us to repress and deny our true physical desires rather than to embrace and celebrate them. Yet he was no less harsh in his criticism of the various forms of neopaganism and feminist witchcraft that had become so popular in the wake of Gardner's Wiccan revival. All of that nature worship and naked dancing in circles was merely so much "namby-pamby ethicalism" mingled with "sanctimonious fraud" and "exoteric gibberish."[8]

What humankind needed today, LaVey argued, was a religion based not on hypocrisy or sentimental morality but rather on the worship of the individual human being as a carnal beast with desires that need to be fulfilled. As he put it in an interview in 1970,

> Well, it had occurred to me for many, many years that ... no religion had ever been based on man's carnal needs or his fleshly pursuits. All religions are based on abstinence rather than indulgence, and all religions therefore have to be based on fear. Well, we don't feel that fear is necessary to base a religion on. The fact that religions for thousands of years have been telling people what they should do or shouldn't do according to the basic whims of the person who might be running the show is very understandable. We're realists, we Satanists. But we also feel that a person has to be good to themselves before they can be good to other people. So we feel that the greatest sin is self-deceit. This is a very selfish religion. We believe in greed, we believe in selfishness, we believe in all of the lustful thoughts that motivate man, because this is man's natural feeling. This is based on what man would naturally do.[9]

This "carnal" philosophy is embodied in the "Nine Satanic Statements" that constitute LaVey's response to the Jewish and Christian Ten Commandments. Deliberately turning the latter on its head, LaVey proudly declares,

1. Satan represents indulgence instead of abstinence!

2. Satan represents vital existence instead of spiritual pipe dreams! ...

3. Satan represents vengeance instead of turning the other cheek! ...

4. Satan represents all of the so-called sins, as they all lead to physical, mental or emotional gratification![10]

In many ways, LaVey's Church of Satan could be said to represent the dark side of the 1960s, the sexual revolution, and the American counterculture. The church emerged at the epicenter of the counterculture—in San Francisco in the late 1960s—and it embraced many elements of the counterculture, such as individualism, opposition to religious and political establishments, freethinking, and sexual liberation. But LaVey also openly despised many aspects of the hippie movement and drug culture blossoming all around him in San Francisco during the 1960s. "I found the hippie movement distasteful on a personal level," he recalled. "Suddenly the ingestion of lysergic acid made every man a king. It made nincompoops self-assured ... and my beloved San Francisco became engulfed by the movement."[11] Perhaps more than anything, LaVey rejected the new forms of feminism that emerged in the 1960s, along with the more androgynous style of dress and hair adopted by both men and women. For LaVey—a self-described "misogynist"—women should look "like women" (i.e., curvy and feminine) and men should look "like men" (strong, aggressive, masculine), and the hippie blending of gender roles was a disaster. On August 8, 1969, LaVey even held a special ceremony called the Rising Forth in which he launched a terrible curse on the hippie movement: "Beware you psychedelic vermin! Your smug pomposity with its thin disguise of tolerance will serve you no longer! ... Our steeds await and their eyes are ablaze with the fires of Hell!"[12]

Satanic Ritual: Ceremony, Magic, and Dramatic Performance

Though LaVey rejected the idea of Satan as an actual being existing outside the individual, he did believe in the power of ritual, and he developed a wide repertoire of rites and ceremonies for the church. As he put it in an interview, dramatic performance is as important to Satanism as it is to the Catholic mass: "Drama and melodrama are very meaningful. Bombast has its place in Satanism—in some ways, Satanism takes up where Catholicism leaves off."[13] Shortly after forming the Church of Satan, LaVey began to attract widespread media attention for performing the first Satanic wedding and then the first Satanic baptism (of his daughter Zeena). In 1972, LaVey published a collection of practical techniques entitled *The Satanic Rituals,* which also explains the philosophy behind the seemingly paradoxical idea of performing rituals for a being who does not exist outside oneself. As LaVey explains, the rituals of other religions are designed primarily to control and subdue followers, but the rituals of Satanism are designed to liberate the individual and empower him or her to accomplish real goals in the world: "The religious rites of Satanism differ from those of other faiths in that fantasy is not employed to control the practitioners of the rites. The ingredients of Satanic ritual are not designed to hold the celebrant in thrall but rather to achieve his goals. Thus, fantasy is utilized as a magic weapon by the individual rather than by the system."[14] Despite not believing in an external deity, LaVey believes in the power of magic, which can have real effects in the world by generating emotional intensity and directing that toward some desired end.

The most infamous of LaVey's rituals was the black mass, first performed in San Francisco in the late 1960s. Although LaVey would downplay the importance of black masses, they did help solidify his reputation as the "Black Pope." One of them was recorded in 1968, and many of its elements became standard format for performances of the rite throughout America and Europe. LaVey's early black mass ritual was performed with an almost absurdly demonic drama. It opened with dramatic chords from an organ and the appearance of LaVey, wearing a horned cap and a long cape, and surrounded by black-robed worshippers; on the wall was the Sigil of Baphomet (a goat's head superimposed onto an inverted pentagram), and beneath it was a naked female body serving as the ritual altar. Extending a long sword in the four directions, LaVey invoked Satan, Lucifer, Belial, and Leviathan and then passed around a chalice (according to LaVey's *Satanic Rituals,* the chalice should be filled not with wine but with some other beverage of one's choice, such as bourbon).

The text of LaVey's black mass is a mixture of a Latin parody of the Catholic mass and English and French prayers to Satan. Several paragraphs of the text are drawn directly from Huysmans's famous literary account of the of the black mass in his novel *Là-bas,* including the following ironic Satanic prayer to Jesus: "Thou, thou whom, in my quality of Priest, I force, whether thou wilt or no, to descend into this host, to incarnate thyself into this bread, Jesus, artisan of hoaxes, bandit of homages, robber of affection, hear! Since the day when thou didst issue from the complaisant bowels of a virgin, thou hast failed all thy engagements, belied all thy promises. Centuries have wept, awaiting thee, fugitive god, mute god!"[15]

LaVey's mass also contains various instructions for the desecration of the ritual and the sacred Host by means of bodily fluids and sacrilegious acts. For example, the nun lifts her habit and urinates into the font, after which a ritual implement analogous to one used in Catholic services to sprinkle holy water is dipped into the urine and shaken in the four directions. The wafer, which is to be made of turnip or coarse black bread, is placed between the exposed breasts of the woman who serves as the altar, then touched to her vaginal area, and finally trampled by the priest, deacon, or subdeacon.

Clearly, much of this ritual is aimed at an explicit, exaggerated, even ridiculous inversion of the Catholic mass. LaVey himself more or less acknowledged as much, suggesting that the early Church of Satan had to use such extreme displays of Christian inversion in order to awaken the American public and make itself known to the world: "Any ceremony considered a black mass must effectively shock and outrage, as this seems to be the measure of its success."[16] Once the original shock had worn off, however, these theatrical performances of the black mass would no longer be necessary, and Satanists could move on to attacking other "sacred cows."

Other Satanic and Left-Hand Movements: Temple of Set, Werewolf Order, and Sethian Liberation Movement

While the Church of Satan is the most famous modern Satanic group, it is by no means the only one. Just a few years after LaVey founded his church, a variety of other Satanic groups, such as the Cathedral of the Fallen Angel and the Church of the Satanic Brotherhood, spread across the United States, the United Kingdom, and Europe. By the mid-1970s, LaVey's own church had also begun to develop internal tensions and finally splintered into a variety of new groups. Among other things, many members were unhappy with LaVey's increasing focus on money and finances rather than the philosophy and practice of Satanism. In 1975, LaVey began marketing the degrees of initiation within the church; higher degrees could now be obtained by contributions in cash, real estate, or valuable pieces of art. As LaVey himself acknowledged, he never had any illusions that the Church of Satan was somehow above the practice of business and the need to make money: "Satanism as mass culture is great. ... There's a great advantage in mainstreaming and I'd be a hypocrite to dislike it."[17]

Many of his early supporters saw this as a sign that LaVey had allowed a blatant commercialism to creep into and undermine the church. One of the most prominent figures to leave the CoS at this time was Michael Aquino, a former high-ranking officer in US military intelligence, who held a PhD in political science and had served in Vietnam. Aquino joined the church in 1969 but already by the mid-1970s was beginning to feel that LaVey's movement was attracting the wrong sort of crowd. It had become, in his view, "a carnival of freaks," composed of "sexual inadequates ogling the naked altar, social misfits looking for an identity, intellectual poseurs." The leadership had meanwhile fragmented into "petty squabbles over titles, ranks and privileges."[18] However, Aquino was even more appalled by LaVey's policy of selling degrees, which he saw as the same sort of hypocrisy that Satanists had been attacking in the mainstream Christian churches: "If there had been a single factor that had brought us to Satanism, it was the church's stand against hypocrisy. So when we learned of this policy, our reaction to it was that LaVey was ... betraying everything that he had worked for for so many years."[19]

In 1975, Aquino broke from the church and founded his own new order, the Temple of Set. During the summer solstice of June 21–22, 1975, in Santa Barbara, California, Aquino undertook a "Greater Black Magical Working," which resulted in a text called *The Book of Coming Forth by Night*. Aquino presented the text as an inspired work, generated by some power other than his own hand but working through him. The title is a reference to and an inversion of the famous Egyptian Book of the Dead, which is also known as the Book of Coming Forth by Day. In the text, the Egyptian god Set declares himself to be the ancient and powerful deity called Satan by the Hebrews, now revealing himself for a new age following the decline of LaVey's Church of Satan:

> The Equinox has succumbed to my Solstice, and I, Set, am revealed in my majesty. The time of the Purification is past. …
>
> I am the ageless Intelligence of this Universe. … All other gods of all other times and nations have been created by men. This you know from the first Part of my Word, and from my Manifest semblance, which alone is not of Earth. Known as the Hebrew Satan, I chose to bring forth a Magus, according to the fashion of my Word. He was charged to form a Church of Satan, that I might easily touch the minds of men in this image they had cast for me. In the fifth year of the Church of Satan, I gave to this Magus my Diabolicon, that he might know the truth of my ancient Gift to mankind, clothed though it might be in the myths of the Hebrews.[20]

Just as LaVey before him had announced the new Age of Satan, Aquino announced the dawn of a new era, the Aeon of Set.

For ToS, Set is the god who always opposes the status quo and conformity, the god who slays conventional social norms and patterns of thought just as he slew Osiris in Egyptian mythology. Ultimately, Set points the way for human beings to become "gods" themselves, to achieve an immortal and all-powerful state of divinity. As a former high priest of the temple, Don Webb, explains,

> Set, the Egyptian god of Darkness, is the Divine origin of the Word. Set's name ultimately means the "Separator" or "Isolator." His chief enemies are the gods of Stasis and Mindlessness. The first of these is Osiris, Death himself. Set's slaying of Osiris has a twofold significance. … Firstly this represents the slaying of old thought patterns; the dethroning of those internal gods that we have received from society. On a second level this was the act by which Set, alone of all the gods of ancient Egypt, became deathless. The Left Hand Path is a quest to Become an immortal, potent and powerful Essence.[21]

The key word used to convey Setian philosophy is the Egyptian verb *Xeper* (pronounced "Khefer"), meaning "I have come into being." As Webb explains, *Xeper* refers to the experience of an individual becoming aware of his or her own existence and deciding to develop that existence through his or her own actions. It represents the freedom and possibility that we have to move forward into a divine state, into godhood—"an immortal, potent and powerful Essence." Setian practice is thus a "Left Hand

Path," set in contrast to the "Right Hand Path" of most traditional religions. While the "Right Hand" is a path of submission and denial (submission to an external deity or denial of physical desire), the "Left Hand" is the path of *self-deification* achieved through the *embrace* of the desires, pleasures, and pains of existence. Its goal is, in short, that of "becoming a god while still alive": "The tradition of spiritual dissent in the West has been called Satanism, but more universally the Left Hand Path is a rationally intuited spiritual technology for the purpose of self-deification. We choose as our role model the ancient Egyptian god Set. ... As part of our practice we each seek the deconstruction of the socially constructed mind, so we begin in rebellion. ... We do not worship Set—worshiping instead only our own potential."[22] The verb *Xeper* thus captures the Setian idea of both eternal being and eternal becoming—that is, "being" an eternal part of the cosmos forever and "becoming" in the sense of an ever-changing process of evolving and self-refining.

A second and even more extreme current within modern Satanism evolved out of LaVey's church through the work of his daughter Zeena LaVey and her husband Nikolas Schreck. Zeena served as the high priestess of the Church of Satan from 1985 to 1990 and had actually been the church's chief spokesperson against allegations of Satanic ritual abuse. In 1990, however, she and Schreck left her father's church and began to explore other, more radical forms of Satanism.

The first of these was the Werewolf Order, a movement based on the idea that mythical figures such as werewolves and vampires are actually archetypal models for the next step in human evolution, toward higher, superhuman existence. A flyer for the Werewolf Order describes this as "the frontline of the demonic revolution" aiming to "unleash the beast in man," and features a figure wearing a pointed hood with an image of a snarling werewolf behind him presiding over a congregation of hooded figures. The flyer goes on to proclaim the werewolf uprising against Judeo-Christian society and the return to a pagan heritage: "We are the shock troops of a youth uprising against the Judeo-Christian tyranny; the focus of a return to the ancient pagan/satanic tradition that is the birthright of Western European men and women. Like Faust, we have made our pact with the mighty powers of darkness. No boundary can halt our quest for dominion."[23]

Schreck has been particularly controversial (probably deliberately so) because of his open admiration for some of history's greatest villains, including Hitler, Nazi SS commander Heinrich Himmler, and serial killer Charles Manson. In 1989, Schreck released a documentary film entitled *Charles Manson Superstar,* which presents Manson as the victim of demonization by a sensationalist media, and in 2011 he published a book entitled *The Manson File: Myth and Reality of an Outlaw Shaman.* In the mid-1980s Schreck's band Radio Werewolf, which combined dark, violent music with experimental performance art, generated criticism for songs that focused on serial killer John Wayne Gacy and an imagined former Nazi commander and employed imagery of vampirism and necrophilia.

In addition to the Werewolf Order, Zeena and Nikolas formed a Satanic group called the Sethian Liberation Movement (SLM) when, after briefly joining Aquino's Temple of Seth, they left it over religious and organizational differences. The SLM, also a "Left Hand Path" group, draws heavily not

Interview with Don Webb

Don Webb served as the high priest in the Temple of Set from 1993 to 2002 and is still extremely active in the Setian movement. He is also the author of several books on magic and the occult, such as Mysteries of the Temple of Set *and* Aleister Crowley: The Fire and the Force, *as well as numerous mystery, fantasy, and science fiction novels. Here he recounts how he first came to be involved in the Temple of Set, his views on "Satanism," and the connection between his magical practice and his fictional writings.*

In 1988 I was commissioned to write a short story about the Salem witch trials. … I worked a little chart for my reference about how the hysteria spread—suspicions about child care, spectral evidence, et cetera. I took a break from my work and flipped on the television. There was the Geraldo Rivera special on Satanism in America. What a circus. I listened to the "experts" talk. After a few minutes I picked up my chart and started crossing off the schema I'd just written. Human superstition was alive and well. I noticed this Vulcan-looking guy representing Satanism. Jeez, another freak. After one of the "experts" claimed to have huge files on Satanic crime, the Vulcan said, "Well then, why don't you arrest them?" I actually cheered. This was the first logical statement made in the show. The next night I mentioned to a few friends that I wish I could send that "Aquino guy" a fan letter. One of my friends kept eyeing me strangely. She pulled me aside and said that if I wished I could give the letter to her because she was seeing Aquino next week at the international Conclave of the Temple of Set.

I had been attracted to the occult and the mysterious all my life, but I had always found occultists a few tacos short of a combination plate. They are overwhelmed by the symbol systems they seek to manipulate. Yet here was a college-educated middle-class person with a real job who held a senior position in a cult. Not what I was expecting.

I sent a letter off to Dr. Aquino praising his coolness on the show but telling him that I had serious doubts that a group could work toward individuality. I threw in a couple of remarks about Set in history so I would look smart. He wrote back and said that folks in the Temple didn't know why it worked either and that maybe I should join and explain it to them.

I researched the group. I read all of the negative press. I read the scant information I could find on the group. I talked to my friend's husband, Dr. Stephen Flowers. The mixture of anti-nomianism and Neoplatonism appealed to me, so in 1989 I joined. Maybe I could explain it to them. Seven years later I was high priest and began writing books on Setian practice.

Fiction is magic. Magic is the art of changing the subjective universe so that a proportional change occurs in the objective universe according to the desire and precision of the magician. Fiction guides the reader through changes in her subjective universe. Is anyone the same after reading *To Kill a Mockingbird, One Hundred Years of Solitude,* or "The Call of Cthulhu"?

(continued)

Human imagination is the "place" where imagination takes place. The Temple has a couple of full-time (i.e., more successful than me) fiction writers in it.

Now this does not mean that I use my fiction to further the Temple's goals, other than in the broadest sense of increasing Mystery in the world. Fiction written for initiation often falls very flat. Magic lies in enchanting your audience, whether in a ritual chamber or not—it does not lie in preaching to them. In fiction one willingly applies one's imagination, for the sake of pleasure. Fiction is the opposite of conventional religion.

"Satanism" is a label for spiritual rebellion in a host culture ruled by the Abrahamic faiths. For self-change to occur, the self must first be isolated. Then after luminal experiences (magic), the self must reintegrate into the world. I feel that "Satanism" fails in the third step of the process. The Temple has moved beyond that label—let's face it, real antinomianism lies in acting against media-constructed reality. Satan lost a lot of his power when he became a way to sell music. *Left Hand Path*—the process of self-deification through a mixture of antinomianism and experience of the direct and mysterious effect of the psyche on the world—is a better term. We are the Western version of certain [Hindu] Shaivists—however, we value the aspect of reintegration more highly than carrying our skull cups and smearing ourselves with ashes. ...

The "Satanic Panic" of the '80s led to Setians adopting the term *Satanist* more dearly. Like the early Christians taking on the derogatory term *Catholic,* or homosexuals have embraced the term *queer.* One of the ways to work your will on society is to use their dark side to your advantage.

only on Egyptian mythology but also on ritual and magical techniques drawn from India, such as Hindu and Buddhist Tantra. In their book *Demons of the Flesh,* Nikolas and Zeena describe their Left Hand Path in deliberately transgressive and provocative terms, as a path that unveils the secrets of "Sadomasochism, Orgies, Taboo-breaking, Fetishism, Orgasm prolongation, Sexual vampirism, Ritual intercourse with divine and demonic entities, Awakening the Feminine Daemonic."[24] Here we see that, even after parting ways with LaVey's Church of Satan, they have continued his goal of attacking all existing sacred cows through the power of shock, transgression, and the overstepping of all conventional boundaries.

Satanism and Popular Culture: The Devil in Film and Music

While Satanism's influence on modern American religious life has been limited, its influence on modern popular culture has been significantly greater. In the American film industry, Satanic themes had appeared in Hollywood since its origin, beginning with *The Devil's Darling* in 1915 and *The Devil's Assistant* two years later. The same director who had made the influential American film *The Birth of a Nation* in 1915 also highlighted John Milton's romantic figure of Lucifer in his 1925 film

The Sorrows of Satan. In the 1930s and '40s, Satanic themes entered the emerging genre of horror film in movies such as *The Black Cat* in 1934, starring Boris Karloff, and *The Seventh Victim* in 1943, which tells the story of a devil-worshipping conspiracy on the loose in Greenwich Village.

However, it was really in the late 1960s—in the larger atmosphere of the counterculture, the sexual revolution, and cult paranoia—that Satanic film really began to flourish. One of the classics of this genre is the 1968 British film *The Devil Rides Out,* which was based on a popular occult novel of the same name by Dennis Wheatley. The story features a diabolical Satanic priest named Mocata, who is loosely based on the infamous British occultist Aleister Crowley and his circle of devil worshippers. The climax of the film is a "sabbat" held in the English countryside that culminates in the invocation of Satan himself and a kind of bacchanalian drunken orgy among the congregants.

That same year, director Roman Polanski would make what is arguably the greatest Satanic film of all time, *Rosemary's Baby.* Based on a 1967 novel by Ira Levin, the film is the story of a young couple who move into a New York City apartment building that happens to be inhabited by a group of Satanists. The young wife, Rosemary (played by Mia Farrow), is drugged by the Satanists while at a dinner party and falls into a dream state filled with bizarre and frightening psychedelic images. Under the influence of the drug, she is raped by the devil himself—played by none other than Anton LaVey. At the end of the film, she learns that the baby's father is not her husband but Satan, and she is urged to join the cult.

While *Rosemary's Baby* may be arguably the finest example of Satanic horror in film, it was surely not the last. Other Hollywood blockbusters quickly followed, playing upon Satanic themes, such as *The Exorcist* in 1973, *The Omen* in 1976, and many others. In 1999, Polanksi returned to the Satanic horror genre with the apocalyptic thriller *The Seventh Gate,* starring Johnny Depp, which revisited many of the earlier Antichrist themes explored in *Rosemary's Baby.*

Satanism and Rock 'N' Roll

Even greater than Satanism's influence in film has been its influence—both real and imaginary—in music, where it has inspired artists working in genres from folk to hard rock and of course various forms of heavy metal. Ironically, many of the bands most often associated with and accused of Satanism—such as Black Sabbath, Blue Oyster Cult, and AC/DC—had little or no real Satanic influence, while some of the most important and serious Satanic bands received little attention in the popular media.

One of the first and most dedicated early Satanic groups was the American folk band Coven. Today Coven is best remembered for their recording of the popular antiwar song "One Tin Soldier," which was also featured in the soundtrack of the film *Billy Jack.* However, in addition to their lighter pop recordings, Coven recorded a number of explicitly Satanic albums, beginning with their first record in 1969, *Witchcraft Destroys Minds & Reaps Souls.* Featuring a thirteen-minute track of prayers and chanting entitled "Satanic Mass," the album also included a black mass poster with the members of the group making the sign of the horns as they surround the body of a naked woman on an altar. In fact, this is the first photographed use of the horned salute, which would later become a ubiquitous feature of heavy metal from the 1980s onward. Interestingly enough, although Coven recorded their "Satanic Mass" at roughly the same time as LaVey performed his own black mass, the two appear to have developed independently and suggest the existence of a wider underground Satanic subculture during the late 1960s.

The imagery of Satanism and the black mass was widely popularized in the 1970s through early heavy metal bands such as Black Sabbath. In their first self-titled album, Black Sabbath used the imagery of a Satanic mass to cultivate an atmosphere of horror, fear, and dread (though certainly not worship or reverence), a theme that was continued on their 1973 album *Sabbath Bloody Sabbath*. But the band also included many pro-Christian songs and never really embraced Satanism as anything more than a powerful and provocative trope.

Satanism did not really enter the heavy metal genre until the 1980s and 1990s, particularly in England and Europe. With the rise of new trends such as black metal, death metal, and doom metal, many bands began to explore far more explicitly anti-Christian, aggressive and violent themes, along with a far more open embrace of Satanism as a philosophy. The first wave of black metal began with British bands such as Venom and European bands such as Bathory, Hellhammer, and Celtic Frost; and by the 1990s a second, even more aggressively Satanic wave had spread particularly in Norway through bands such as Mayhem, Darkthrone, and myriad others. Featuring very fast rhythms, aggressive double bass drumming, heavily distorted guitars, and raspy snarling vocals, black metal embraced the anti-Christian, nonconformist, and radically individualistic ideology of Satanism, sometimes adding elements of racism and anti-Semitism.

Although a huge number of black metal bands emerged from Norway and other parts of northern Europe in the 1990s, one of the most influential and controversial is Gorgoroth. Taking its name from the realm of darkness and evil in the land of Mordor as imagined in Tolkien's *Lord of the Rings,* Gorgoroth is best known for its aggressive mixture of dark fantasy, explicit Satanism, and extremely fast, dissonant, and distorted music. Much like LaVey's Church of Satan and its burlesque performance of the black mass, Gorgoroth is very much a performative act that takes the themes of devil worship and Satanic violence to their most exaggerated extremes. From its demo first recording, "A Sorcery Written in Blood," and first studio album, *Pentagram* (1993), to its most recent *Instinctus Bestialis* (2012), Gorgoroth has been at the forefront of a vast pack of bands vying to outdo one another in their use of violent, demonic, and aggressively anti-Christian themes, both in studio recordings and on stage, in highly dramatic Satanic live shows.

One of the best examples of this performative aspect of black metal was Gorgoroth's 2004 concert in Krakow, Poland. The event featured a massive bloodbath of eighty liters of sheep's blood, an array of sheep's heads spitted on stakes, and three naked models covered in blood and arrayed on crucifixes across the stage. Adorned in bloody corpse makeup, inverted crosses, and armbands bristling with nails, the band launched into its opening song, entitled—appropriately enough—"Procreating Satan," an explicit call to rise up and greet the Dark Lord:

> I awake
> The raging blasphemy
> Rise all to hell
> Procreating Satan
> Satan!
> Whenever demons fornicate
> Shout the purified beliefs
> Sacrificial lambs
> Procreating Satan
> Our master is coming
> The one wants to return
> Take place up high
> Throne of god
> Our masters return
> Praise Satan, Praise Satan.[25]

As a result of this hugely controversial event, the band was investigated for religious offense and cruelty to animals, and the concert organizer received a large fine. Ironically, however, the publicity from the event only catapulted Gorgoroth into international celebrity, making the band far more popular than ever before, and the footage from the infamous concert was released as a DVD entitled *Black Mass in Krakow, 2004.*

Between 1992 and 1996, the Norwegian black metal subculture also gained international attention from a series of over fifty church burnings carried out by fans and musicians. The cover of the band Burzum's album *Aske* (Ashes) even featured a photo of a church after its destruction, and the band's leader, Varg Vikernes, was suspected of being behind the arson. In 1994, Vikernes was found guilty in the burning of three other churches and in the murder of fellow black metal musician Euronymous, for which he was sentenced to twenty-one years. While some musicians in the black metal scene condemned the church burnings as attention-seeking acts by misguided fans, others praised them. One of the most outspoken and controversial figures during this period was Gaahl, lead singer of Gorgoroth, who publicly embraced Satanism in interviews and defended the need for this attack (or in his view, counterattack) on Christianity. When asked what were the primary ideas that fueled Gorgoroth's music, he answered simply, "Satan," who in his view embodied "freedom." When asked about the church burnings, he replied quite frankly: "Church burnings and all these things are, of course, things that I support 100 percent and it should have been done much more and will be done much more in the future. We have to remove every trace from what Christianity and its Semitic roots have to offer this world."[26]

In the American heavy metal scene, Satanism typically entered in a more eclectic and less violent way. Perhaps the most famous artist to speak publicly about the influence of LaVey in his work is Marilyn Manson, another artist who is well known for his highly dramatic, often over-the-top performances and open embrace of Satanic themes, particularly in his 1996 album *Antichrist Superstar.* The back cover of the album, for example, features a red symbol consisting of a downward-pointing lightning bolt surrounded by a circle and Hebrew letters spelling "Leviathan," drawn directly from the Church of Satan's goat-head pentagram symbol. In interviews, Manson has been quite frank about the fact that the Church of Satan is one—though only one—of many influences on his thinking and music. As he put it in an interview in 1997, "Over the years I've spent a lot of time interested in religion, and I've read into all different dimensions, whether it was Judaism or … Christianity. And Satanism is one that particularly appealed to me. So I struck up a friendship with Anton LaVey. … But Satanism is really just, in my view, a philosophy, not unlike Nietzsche or Darwin, an idea of man and his self-preservation, man being his own God. And the word Satan, which tends to scare a lot of people, represents the ultimate rebellion against the mainstream."[27] But Manson was also quick to cite the many other influences on his thought, including Jesus Christ. Of course, this would not prevent many religious leaders and politicians for blaming Manson for tragedies such as the 1999 Columbine school shootings, which were carried out by two students who were fans of his music.

Like Gorgoroth, Marilyn Manson has often played upon the most outlandishly dramatic and performative aspects of Satanism. In his live shows during the 2001 Guns, God and Government tour, for example, Manson appeared behind a prop that seemed to be a cross between a political podium and a priest's lectern, which was adorned with a cross made of a rifle and two guns. Manson's outfit, meanwhile, was a mixture of Nazi and sadomasochistic imagery, with a black SS-style hat and a leather corset and garter belts.[28] Much like LaVey himself, Manson appeared in these shows to be enacting an exaggerated, even absurd, parodic inversion of dominant symbols and ideals; in this case, however, Manson's performance was an inversion and satire not only of Christianity but also of the American political system, now mocked on stage with authoritarian chants, crosses made of guns, and Nazi imagery.

"Far Beyond Teenage Obsession": The Satanic Panic of the 1980s

By the 1980s, Satanism came to be seen as far more than a small fringe group of alternative religious movements such as CoS and ToS. Indeed, throughout the American popular media, tabloid newspapers, and daytime TV shows, it began to be imagined as a vast underground secret conspiracy linked to child abuse, human sacrifice, bizarre pornography, and various other atrocities. Thus, on May 16, 1985, the popular news show *20/20* aired a program called "The Devil Worshipers" that claimed to reveal a host of "perverse, hideous acts that defy belief," including "suicides, murders, and ritualistic slaughter of animals and children," often accompanied by cannibalism, eating of human hearts, and drinking of urine, feces, and blood.[29] Although virtually all of these claims turned out to be completely imaginary, they helped create a widespread Satanic paranoia throughout the United States and a broader fear of new religious groups in general that continues to have lingering implications today.

The reasons for the rapid spread of the Satanic Panic in 1980s America are multiple and complex. In many ways, this was a continuation of the cult paranoia and the anticult movement that had already been growing in the United States since the 1960s, following the rapid growth and spread of new religions, particularly among young people. Particularly after the grisly murders carried out by Charles Manson's quasi-religious group the Family in 1968, and then after the mass suicides of over nine hundred members of Peoples Temple in 1978, there were widespread fears that deviant cults might be brainwashing young people and manipulating them into carrying out other heinous acts.

A second reason was the rise of new forms of socially and politically conservative Christianity during the 1970s and '80s through groups such as the Christian Coalition, the Moral Majority, and Focus on the Family. Reacting against the liberalism and permissiveness of the 1960s, these groups warned of America's loss of a moral compass and saw the alleged spread of Satanism as a telling example of that dangerous trend.

Finally, a third reason was the spread of numerous stories of children involved in abusive and often bizarre Satanic rituals, allegedly uncovered by social workers during child protection investigations. The most famous reports began with Kee MacFarlane, who joined a network of child protection workers in Los Angeles and claimed to have uncovered vast numbers of abuses, perversions, and "bizarre rituals involving violence to animals, scatological behavior," and black magic among the children she examined.[30] Although these allegations later proved to be fabrications generated by coercive and leading interviewing techniques, they had a huge impact on popular awareness and even inspired Congress to double its budget for child protection programs. They also helped popularize the idea that adults might suddenly uncover repressed memories of childhood ritual abuse. As the rumors of Satanic abuse began to spread wildly, some individuals in therapy sessions began to claim that they had unlocked buried memories from their early years, often in outlandish detail.

One of the first and most influential accounts of Satanic ritual abuse appeared in the book *Michelle Remembers* in 1980. Based on a long series of therapy sessions between Michelle Smith and psychiatrist Lawrence Pazder, MD, the book claims to uncover and present the childhood memories of forced involvement in a secret Satanic organization and its violent, sexual, and abusive rituals. With her doctor's help, Michelle claimed to have dredged up memories beginning from age five when she was forced to participate in a Satanic cult, which involved being smeared with the blood of slaughtered babies, being buried in a grave as part of a "rebirth into evil," and participating in an eighty-one-day black mass called the Feast of the Beast. Michelle also recalled seeing Satan himself, whom she described as a huge, hideous figure made of shifting, fiery blackness: "His face is more like fire. You think you see it, and by the time you look hard, it's already changed. … His legs are long, and he has funny toenails. There's lots of hair on his legs. … Sometimes all you see are huge legs, and then a minute later you can just see a clawlike hand. And other times, he's just a dark space with glistening eyes. You never see him all at once—he's always distorted and not quite substantial, more like a vapor."[31] Those who have seen *Rosemary's Baby* will probably notice that this description sounds very similar to the dreamlike rape scene in Polanski's movie, where the devil appears only in fragmentary, shifting images, with glistening eyes and hairy, clawed hands.

By the late 1980s, accounts of Satanic abuse had begun to appear in truly outlandish and sensational ways in the American popular media. One of the most infamous examples is an episode of Geraldo Rivera's talk show that aired on October 22, 1988, entitled "Devil Worship: Exposing Satan's Underground." Mixing all the most sensational tropes of sexual perversion, drug abuse, and heavy metal, Geraldo described this as nothing less than a "nationwide network of Satanists" working secretly underground to prey upon vulnerable teenagers and entice them into violent and depraved rituals:

> Satanism is more than a hodge-podge of mysticism and fantasy, more than a Halloween motif. It's a violent impulse, it preys upon the emotionally vulnerable, often teenagers, alone and lost. … It attracts the angry and the powerless … possessed by an obsessive fascination with sex and drugs and, yes, heavy metal rock and roll. … Satanism goes far beyond teenage obsession. Today there are cults that worship the devil, engage in secret ceremonies, believe in ancient or bizarre theologies, all of it constitutionally protected, as long as no laws are broken. … The other face of adult Satanism is violent and fiendish, centered on sexual ritual and too frequently descending into the vilest crime of all, sexual abuse of children.[32]

Members of the actual Church of Satan, however, did not remain silent on the issue. In their view, the Church of Satan represented a legitimate religious movement that had been grossly misrepresented by an irresponsible media and thus wrongfully associated with these fanciful narratives of Satanic ritual abuse. At the time, Zeena LaVey was still serving as the public spokesperson for CoS. Delivering a scathing critique of sensationalistic television journalism such as Geraldo Rivera and *20/20*, Zeena argued that religious minorities such as CoS had been made an easy and convenient scapegoat for other social anxieties:

> The average person these days looks to the television for comfort. And we liken the television to the new god. … The media now is that comfort source for the more

ignorant of our society. And what Satanists are experiencing now is the result of that ignorance and what that god has created. ... We are the last scapegoat, we're the last minority, we're the last religion that always requires somebody to define what we are. ... We're the only thing that the media can toss our name around ... indiscriminately with no regard for whose lives it affects. And the fact of it is that many Satanists' lives and their families have been completely destroyed, and it's because of this ignorance.[33]

In sum, the Satanic Panic of the 1980s adds a new twist to the theme of performance and spectacle that runs through modern Satanism from the late 1960s onward. While the early Church of Satan had made a point of performing shocking and provocative ritual spectacles such as the black mass, the American media of the 1980s made a spectacle of their own, by sensationalizing and exaggerating the power of Satanism in the modern world.

In the twenty-first century, Satanism seems far less sensational as either a religious movement or a popular spectacle, since today all kinds of religious extremism, terrorism, and violence can draw the mainstream media's attention. However, the questions that it raises concerning religious performance, social and moral transgression, and religious violence remain central ones that we continue to grapple with to this day.

Questions for Discussion and Debate

1. Can a movement that involves a strong element of religious parody and inversion—as we see in the early black mass and LaVey's deliberately silly costumes, complete with devil's horns, cape, and tail—be taken seriously as "religion"? Or should it be viewed more as theater, performance art, or satire? And what is the point of this sort of religious satire? Is it just an ironic game, or is there a more serious philosophical and spiritual point behind it?

2. Why do you think the Satanic Panic was such a powerful and widespread phenomenon during the 1980s? What other social, cultural, historical, and religious forces might have helped give rise to the remarkable paranoia that gripped the United States, with widespread fears of Satanic ritual abuse, animal and human sacrifice, the influence of Satanic themes in rock and heavy metal music, and so on?

3. How would you approach a case such as that of Michelle Smith and her claims to recall elaborate details of Satanic abuse? Can she be dismissed as simply an attention seeker or possibly mentally ill? Or does she reflect in more complex ways the larger social, cultural, and religious context of the United States during this period?

4. Defenders of the Church of Satan such as Zeena Schreck argued that this religious minority had been made a convenient scapegoat for the mainstream media, which is interested more in

titillating sensationalism than serious information. Yet at the same time, the work of LaVey and others does seem to have helped inspire acts such as the string of church burnings in Norway during the 1990s. So is CoS completely innocent in these cases of serious criminal activity? Or should we hold it accountable in some sense for the violent acts that some individuals have carried out in its name?

Suggested Classroom Activity

Critically examine an example of a Satanic "performance," such as LaVey's black mass in San Francisco or Gorgoroth's musical drama in Krakow. How would you analyze these performances in terms of their sociological function, their psychological impact, and their religious significance? Is it possible for a radically iconoclastic and rebellious performance like this also to be a "religious ritual," filled with sacred meaning and value for its participants? How would you compare these performances to more mainstream religious performances, such as a Christian "passion play" about the trial and death of Jesus, or a Hindu drama about the life and activities of Krishna (among myriad other examples)? Does the "Satanic" nature of this performance make it fundamentally different from other examples of religious drama, or is it just another example of people using dramatic forms to enact larger religious ideas?

Suggested Film

Laurent, Ray (director). *Satanis: The Devil's Mass.* Something Weird Video, 2003.

Suggestions for Further Reading

Aquino, Michael. *The Temple of Set.* San Francisco, 1975. https://xeper.org//maquino/nm/TOS.pdf.

Baddeley, Gavin. *Lucifer Rising: Sin, Devil Worship and Rock 'n' Roll.* London: Plexus, 1999.

Barton, Blanche. *The Secret Life of a Satanist: The Authorized Biography of Anton LaVey.* Los Angeles: Feral House, 1990.

Drury, Nevill. *The History of Magic in the Modern Age.* New York: Carroll and Graf, 2000.

Frankfurter, David. *Evil Incarnate: Rumors of Demonic Conspiracy and Satanic Abuse in History.* Princeton, NJ: Princeton University Press, 2006.

LaVey, Anton. *The Satanic Bible.* New York: Avon, 1969.

———. *The Satanic Rituals.* New York: Avon, 1972.

———. *The Satanic Witch.* Los Angeles: Feral House, 1989.

Schreck, Nikolas, and Zeena Schreck. *Demons of the Flesh: The Complete Guide to Left-Hand Magic.* New York: Creation Books, 2002.

Smith, Michelle, and Lawrence Pazder, MD. *Michelle Remembers.* New York: Congdon and Lattes, 1980.

Urban, Hugh B. *Magia Sexualis: Sex, Magic, and Liberation in Modern Western Esotericism.* Berkeley: University of California Press, 2005.

Victor, Jeffrey. *Satanic Panic: The Creation of a Contemporary Legend.* Chicago: Open Court, 1993.

Webb, Don. *The Seven Faces of Darkness: Practical Typhonian Magic.* Smithville, TX: Runa-Raven Press, 1996.

———. *Uncle Setnakt's Essential Guide to the Left Hand Path* (Smithville, TX: Runa-Raven Press, 1999.

Wright, Lawrence. "Sympathy for the Devil: It's Not Easy Being Evil in a World That's Gone to Hell," *Rolling Stone,* September 5, 1991.

Notes

1. See Hugh B. Urban, *Magia Sexualis: Sex, Magic, and Liberation in Modern Western Esotericism* (Berkeley: University of California Press, 2005), chap. 1.

2. See ibid., chap. 7.

3. Zeena Schreck to Michael Aquino, December 30, 1990, quoted in Urban, *Magia Sexualis,* 201.

4. Blanche Barton, *The Secret Life of a Satanist: The Authorized Biography of Anton LaVey* (Los Angeles: Feral House, 1990), 39–40.

5. Anton LaVey quoted in Urban, *Magia Sexualis,* 201.

6. Anton LaVey, *The Satanic Bible* (New York: Avon, 1969), 31.

7. Blanche Barton, "About the Author," in Anton LaVey, *The Satanic Witch* (Los Angeles: Feral House, 1989), n.p.

8. LaVey, *Satanic Bible,* 21.

9. Anton LaVey, interview in *Satanis: The Devil's Mass,* dir. Ray Laurent (Something Weird Video, 2003).

10. LaVey, *Satanic Bible,* 25.

11. Anton LaVey, interview by Gavin Baddeley, in Baddeley's *Lucifer Rising: Sin, Devil Worship and Rock 'n' Roll* (London: Plexus, 1999), 66.

12. Ibid., 67.

13. Ibid., 76.

14. Anton LaVey, *The Satanic Rituals* (New York: Avon, 1972), 15.

15. Ibid., 49.

16. LaVey, *Satanic Bible,* 101.

17. LaVey, interview by Baddeley, in Baddeley, *Lucifer Rising,* 133.

18. Michael Aquino, interview by Gavin Baddeley, in Baddeley, *Lucifer Rising,* 100.

19. Michael Aquino, quoted in Nevill Drury, *The History of Magic in the Modern Age* (New York: Carroll and Graf, 2000), 196.

20. Michael Aquino, "The Book of Coming Forth by Night," n.d., http://cd.textfiles.com/thegreatunsorted/texts/txtfiles_misc/TEMP/BOCFBY.TXT.

21. Don Webb, "Xeper: The Eternal Word of Set," 2012, Xeper.org, https://xeper.org//pub/pub_dw_xeper.html.

22. Don Webb, *Uncle Setnakt's Essential Guide to the Left Hand Path* (Smithville, TX: Runa-Raven Press, 1999), 105–6, and *The Seven Faces of Darkness: Practical Typhonian Magic* (Smithville, TX: Runa-Raven Press, 1996), 5.

23. Ministry of Propaganda and Public Enlightenment, "Werewolf Order: To Unleash the Beast in Man," flyer, Los Angeles, n.d.

24. Nikolas Schreck and Zeena Schreck, *Demons of the Flesh: The Complete Guide to Left-Hand Magic* (New York: Creation Books, 2002), back cover advertisement.

25. Gorgoroth, "Procreating Satan," from *Twilight of the Idols* (Nuclear Blast, 2003). See also Gorgoroth, *Black Mass in Krakow, 2004* (Metal Mind, 2008).

26. Gaahl, interview, in *Metal: A Headbanger's Journey,* dir. Sam Dunn (Seville Productions, 2005).

27. Marilyn Manson, interview, CMJ Music Marathon, New York, 1997, www.mansonwiki.com/wiki/Interview:1997_CMJ.

28. Marilyn Manson, *Guns, God and Government,* DVD (Eagle Rock Entertainment, 2002).

29. "The Devil Worshipers," *20/20*, ABC News, May 16, 1985.

30. David Frankfurter, *Evil Incarnate: Rumors of Demonic Conspiracy and Satanic Abuse in History* (Princeton, NJ: Princeton University Press, 2006), 57.

31. Michelle Smith and Lawrence Pazder, MD, *Michelle Remembers* (New York: Congdon and Lattes, 1980), 201.

32. "Devil Worship: Exposing Satan's Underground," *The Geraldo Rivera Show,* October 22, 1988.

33. Zeena LaVey, interview on KJTV, 1990, www.youtube.com/watch?v=cDNwdcKdboQ.

PART VI

Vampirism and the Goth Movement

READING 12

Spirituality Bites

Xers and the Gothic Cult/ure

Julia Winden Fey

....

Monique is rather typical of the Goths I have encountered. I had arranged to meet her at a coffeehouse in San Francisco's Haight-Ashbury district, and although we had never met before, I identified her as soon as she walked through the door. At three o'clock on a sunny afternoon, this tall, extremely pale-skinned, raven-haired woman was dressed entirely in black—hat, shirt, vest, skirt, tights, and shoes. Her fingernails too were coated with glossy black polish, and her eyes were heavily lined with kohl. The starkness of her appearance was relieved only by her blood-red lips and the large quantity of silver jewelry that adorned her hands, ears, and neck. She was a striking figure, even in a neighborhood where unusual garb is the norm.

Monique had responded to my posting on the Internet newsgroup alt.gothic, in which I asked for subjects willing to discuss their involvement in the Gothic subculture. As we talked over hot cider, she told me that she was twenty-five, and a student in the Bay Area. A self-described army brat, she had spent much of her childhood in Europe, and had only returned to San Francisco in the late 1980s. Although aware of the Gothic subculture as a child, she says that her involvement in the movement only developed after her move back to California. Since then, her participation in San Francisco's Gothic community has provided her with a way of hooking up with others who share her love of Gothic literature, architecture, music, and costume.

When I asked Monique about her religious background, she said she had attended church up until the age of five, when her parents divorced. From that point on, she was raised primarily by her father, a nonpracticing Presbyterian, who "thought that it would be more fun to see the castles [of Europe] than to go to church." Consequently, she and her father often spent weekends touring through French and German castles, as well as cathedrals and art museums. While these excursions may have removed structured religion from her life, they did instill in her an ongoing fascination with medieval architecture, art, and cultures—interests that continue to influence her perception of life and its meaning. Although she describes herself as having no strong religious ties, Monique has nevertheless developed a belief system of her own out of the hodgepodge of religious and secular ideas she has encountered over the years. Identifying herself as "spiritual" rather than "religious," she says, "I'm interested in religions from around the world, but for me, spirituality is more of a personal sense of connection with the universe. It's more of a personal development of my own morals or ethics." She builds her "personal sense of connection" by selecting from among the beliefs of the various faiths she has experienced or at least read about, ultimately creating her own, unique spiritual collage. Importantly, she recognizes Gothic as a central, even unifying part of that collage. She notes that being part of the Gothic world has become an integral aspect of her worldview and her own identity. "Gothic" interests and "Gothic" values delimit the outlines of her passions and provide a context for her ongoing self-development. Being Gothic for her is an important part of "becoming who I am," as it enables her to do so within a community in which she feels free to explore her ideas and indulge her interests.

I have heard Monique's views on the spiritual nature of the Gothic world echoed by other Goths, former Goths, and even outside observers. Based on these perceptions, I offer the following discussion of the Gothic underworld as an introduction to one form of Generation X spirituality. After considering in some detail various aspects of the Gothic scene and its history, I will explore the manners in which this particular subculture provides its inhabitants with a unique, if loosely defined, worldview that is rich in spiritual resources, and perhaps typically Generation X in form. This discussion is drawn from one-on-one interviews, questionnaires, and observations conducted primarily in San Francisco and Los Angeles in the mid- to late 1990s. Although the Goths quoted below are real individuals, I have changed their names so as not to "out" anyone. Ultimately, based on these interviews and observations, I have come to think of the Gothic world as a *cult/ure,* a term I use in order to speak of Gothic as something existing somewhere between, or perhaps beyond, the traditional concepts of subculture and cult. As a cult/ure, Gothic can be understood as one more example of Xers' refusal to fit into predetermined categories or to trod solely on an already beaten path. Gothic Xers, while mostly rejecting traditional means and modes of spirituality, nevertheless seek out and seem to find spiritual elements within the shadowy realms of Gothicdom. As such, an exploration of those realms is in order.

Gothic Club Culture

For many Goths, the hub of the Gothic world is located in the various late-night clubs primarily scattered across the United States, the United Kingdom, and Germany. With names like the Bat Cave, Vampire's Kiss, and Helter Skelter, these clubs are found mostly, if not exclusively, in metropolitan areas, where the concentration of Goths, or at least the Gothicly inclined, is high enough to support a weekly nightclub. Like contemporary dance clubs in general, Gothic clubs tend to come and go with the popularity of the music—or, more precisely, with club owners' perceptions of the music's popularity. Today music fashions change rapidly, and so do their venues. However, while Gothic rock first made its appearance in the early 1980s, it has remained—or perhaps is again—trendy, keeping newer clubs, as well as older ones open.

Although the clubs differ in appearance and size, the experience they offer tends to be similar, with dim lighting, loud, droning music, and plenty of clove cigarettes. Now approaching its twentieth year in operation, Los Angeles' Helter Skelter is typical of such clubs. Located in a warehouse in a slightly run-down business section of the city, it is unmarked except for the street number over the door. The surest way of locating it is to wait until eleven o'clock on a Wednesday night, after which the line of people dressed in black, and the two or three hearses parked out front, serve as reliable guideposts. Before entering, you must present proper identification and pass through a security inspection. Although the guards are looking for concealed weapons, they are quick to admit that Goth Night at Helter Skelter generally involves fewer fights or problems than any other night. Goths, they have told me, tend to be introspective and nonviolent.

Having passed through security, those over the legal drinking age are given a plastic bracelet. Once inside, you face a long dark hallway filled with cigarette smoke, with a desk where each person signs a membership book and pays the cover charge. The hall ends with a long stairwell leading to a balcony overlooking the dance floor. From here, you might watch people on the dance floor swaying to the sonorous drone of an early David Bowie song. Video screens on the side walls will flash black-and-white images of people in various sexual positions, including several stills of women in bondage chains. You might also be able to discern fifty or so people scattered about the edges of the dance floor, standing in the gloom with drinks and cigarettes in hand, watching those dancing or, occasionally, trying to make conversation above the din. By midnight, the room fills with another three hundred people or more, and the smell of clove cigarettes becomes suffocating. On the dance floor, people sway in the serpentine, self-absorbed manner that characterizes Gothic dance, and the noise level becomes deafening. In the nearly nonexistent light, made even dimmer by the smoke, it is difficult to distinguish one body from another. The room is reduced to a crush of black velvet dresses, satin skirts, lacy shirts, shiny polyvinyl chloride pants, fishnet stockings, combat boots, and black high heels, all topped by beautifully eerie faces, with uniformly kohl-rimmed eyes, blood-red mouths, and white faces.

Central to the Goth club experience is the music, known as Gothic rock. The term *Gothic* in reference to a genre of music was first used by the manager of the band Joy Division. In a 1978 BBC interview he described Joy Division as "Gothic compared with the pop mainstream" (Wake 1994). Although Gothic aficionados generally do not include Joy Division in the Gothic category, the term was quickly picked up by the U.K. music media, and "they applied it in a nasty sort of pigeonholing way to a number of bands that were around in the early 80s." Bands such as Bauhaus, Siouxsie and the Banshees, the (Southern Death) Cult, the Cure, and the Sisters of Mercy eventually became leading representatives of this new genre, acquiring the Gothic tag in part for the style and mood of their music and lyrics, but also because of their look, most dressing solely in black.

Despite its disparaging origins, the term *Gothic* has now been embraced by bands, record companies, and fans alike. The typically Gothic sound, if one exists, is similar to its punk roots, yet darker in both tone and content. Retaining some of punk's anger and its expressive driving beat, Gothic emphasizes bass guitar and deep vocals. One online Goth lists the following as technical earmarks of Gothic music: "At least one layer of thickly distorted, chorused, flanged, or otherwise heavy and ethereal electric rhythm guitar. ... Musical construction suggesting a blend of gregorian chant, baroque minuets, and [heavy] metal on morphine. Melodies produced by old world instruments, be they real or synthesized, such as harpsichord, viola, cello, pipes, and ESPECIALLY cathedral organ. And vocals which are thick, smooth, ephemeral, and riddled with angst" (Couchman 1995).

The overall effect is dark, sensuous, and eerie. Fans of Gothic often mention the emotional reaction they have to this music as the reason for its appeal. Another online Goth says he sometimes likes industrial music, which has a hard, mechanical sound, but at other times prefers Gothic because it "speaks more to the heart" (Neely 1995). Club dwellers at Helter Skelter also point to the emotional tones or mood of Gothic music as a primary source of its appeal. One woman summarized her attraction to Gothic music by saying, "It puts me into a deep, dreamy, contemplative state. I consider myself a very thoughtful, introverted person, so I identify with the lush sounds." Another clubber said he liked Gothic music, "because it is the most beautiful music anywhere. The songs have more meaning relating to our lives and the way most of us feel in the Gothic scene. I like the music's down tone and depressing feeling which is more true to life." An online Goth perhaps best summarizes the overall emotional effect of Gothic music as consisting of three words: "MELANCHOLY, MELANCHOLY, MELANCHOLY," and then suggests that while at first Gothic music can be frightening, its melancholic tone becomes comforting with familiarity (Couchman 1995).

As is suggested above, sound is only one aspect of Gothic music. For many, lyrical content is equally important in distinguishing Gothic from other genres of rock music. As with punk, much of the music produced by Gothic bands has been "angst ridden but all the hatred is turned inwards and the music is typified by introspective lyrics" (Gothic FAQ 1994). Where punk deals with anger, Gothic lyrics tend toward absorption in the singer's quieter or more internalized emotions and personal desires, and frequently concern loss, sadness, and death. Because of its occasional use of vampiric imagery and themes, and because of many musicians' vampiric appearance, it is also sometimes referred to as "Vampire music." The band Bauhaus's 1979 release "Bela Lugosi's Dead" is probably the most famous of the early Gothic songs dealing with death and vampires. Its fame is in large part due to the movie *The Hunger,* in which this song accompanied the opening shots of a very gaunt, pale, and literally vampiric David Bowie. However, its monotonous lyrics, while fitting the stereotypical content of Gothic, do little justice to the greater lyrical depth of later Gothic songs. The refrain of the Bauhaus song, which actually constitutes most of the song and is sung in a low drone, accompanied by a steady, driving beat, is as follows: "Alone in a darkened room, the Count. Bela Lugosi's dead. Bela Lugosi's dead. Bela Lugosi's dead. Undead, undead, undead. Undead, undead, undead." In comparison, songs from contemporary bands, such as Los Angeles' London after Midnight (LAM), more poetically incorporate the standard Gothic themes of death, pain, and suffering: "Is this life this degradation—this pointless game, humiliation. Born to die, we're born to lose—and not one choice we make we choose. And when this life is at an end we find that Death's our only friend. Must we suffer through your games, oh Lord? Can God really be so bored?" (London after Midnight, 1998). Themes such as these abound in Gothic songs. Even the names of bands pick up this dark focus, as in Black Tape for a Blue Girl, Love Spirals Downwards, Thanatos, and Bleak.

Although Gothic music is often equated with punk, heavy metal, and industrial, it should be seen as occupying its own niche within the music world. Punk has traditionally been seen as an expression of youthful anger and frustration over social conditions, while heavy metal has been regarded as an effort to evoke raw power in order to empower its listeners (Walser 1993). In similar fashion, industrial music's cacophony of sound has been understood as an attempt to represent its creators' (and audience's) sense of chaos and meaninglessness in the world. Departing slightly from these other genres, Gothic rock encourages its listeners to address and embrace the darker aspects of their inner selves and of life. Indeed, many Goths believe that this embracing of "the dark as well as the light" is what Gothic and Gothic music is, finally, about. Carlos, whom I interviewed, explains this by saying,

> To me, personally, it means being ... I don't know, like I guess enjoying the darker sides of life, you know? Like, when you think about it, there's happiness, there's sadness, there's life, there's death, there's joy, there's agony, you know? It's like everybody usually tries to go out in this happy little world or whatever. I'm not saying that it's bad. I like to be happy. But the way I see it, we try to, in order to get a better experience in life, it's kind of best to see both the light and the dark. You know, the happiness and the sadness. Life and death. Just try to experience both of them in order to maybe appreciate the other one.

Serving as a conduit to life's darker side, Gothic music thereby seeks to uplift its listeners rather than depress them, as many non-Goths, or "Casuals," might think. Echoing findings about the cathartic nature of heavy metal for alienated young people. Gothic music's affirmation of death and darkness serves to reinforce Goths' own beliefs about the value of all aspects of life, providing both reassurance and comfort to its listeners (Arnett 1995).

Gothic music, however, is not all there is to Gothic club culture, for the music does not exist in a vacuum. Gothic is as much an experience, a look, and a way of life as it is a genre of music. It is produced by, and in turn produces, an international community of people who share an interest in the music, the look, and the lifestyle. For most, the music remains the hub of this culture, yet it does not constitute its entirety. The bands and their music, the bands' promoters, the clubs that play Gothic music, the record companies and distributors who make it accessible, the online "Net Goths" who keep up a running conversation about the merits of the music and the culture, and the many fringe retail operations—Gothic clothing stores, catalogs, art and paraphernalia vendors—all exist in a complex relationship that results in what my interviewees call "the scene." The Gothic sensibility that is explored in and promoted by the music manifests itself throughout this scene that also overlaps and is sometimes Indistinguishable from the industrial crowd, as well as S/M culture, vampire culture, the tattoo and piercing worlds, and many more.

The scene, referring primarily now to those who frequent the clubs and keep up with the newest bands, had its beginnings in a London nightclub called the Bat Cave in 1981. After its initial popularity faded in the U.K., the Gothic craze moved to the United States, primarily to Los Angeles and San Francisco, although Gothic clubs and bands have a strong presence in New York and Seattle and can even be found in places like Atlanta and Cleveland, as well as many smaller urban areas. Almost two decades after Bauhaus's release of "Bela Lugosi's Dead" and the early Siouxsie and the Banshees albums, Gothic rock continues to thrive in the United States, the U.K., and Germany, a survival directly attributable to the development of the larger scene. As Deena Weinstein notes in her study of heavy metal music, while most musical genres tend to follow a process of formation, crystallization, and decay, some, like heavy metal, and here I would include Gothic, have "persisted in large part because of the development of a supportive subculture." This subculture not only provides a venue for music to be played (the clubs) and a group of consumers to buy the music but creates a fertile breeding ground for the emergence of new groups and new fans. Additionally, in the early 1980s, and again in the late 1990s, this subculture has provided a base population from which fashion designers, fiction writers, and others have been able to commercialize and popularize "the Gothic look" and attitude within the broader culture. The explosion of interest in vampires and vampire fiction, as well as the promotion of Gothic designs in 1990s fashion and cosmetics, while temporarily making Gothicdom "in and trendy," much to the disgust of those who consider themselves "real" Goths, nevertheless must be credited with assisting in the continuation of the Gothic scene. Clubs only remain open as long as there are sufficient numbers of patrons crossing their thresholds, and marketers of Gothic items have greatly increased the number of people looking for somewhere to go wearing their new Gothic fashions.

Gothic Online

There is another aspect of the scene that is not as visible as the fans, the bands, the music and retail industries, and the clubs, but which also contributes to the vitality of the Gothic world. Coexisting with the real world, Gothic culture is a flourishing virtual community. Many are introduced to the Gothic culture by the Net Goths who post on the Internet newsgroup alt.gothic. With messages being sent from countries worldwide, this online site averages almost one thousand postings per week. Topics of conversation on this site include postings from people who "delurk" (post) for the first time to ask. What's really Gothic? and lamentations by rural Goths over their isolation from real Gothic culture, which generally means clubs and clothing or music stores. Responses to these lonely Gothic teenagers, stranded in the wilds of Arkansas or Minnesota, with no other Goths in sight, generally include welcomes, but also a lot of warnings not to fall prey to the "Goth police," or any other semiauthorities, such as some of the slicker Gothic magazines who might pretend to define what is Gothic and what is not Gothic. Gothic, the newcomer is told, is *whatever you feel it is.* End of discussion.

While such threads reappear on alt.gothic with reliable frequency, other topics that regularly show up include discussions of new and old bands, favorite songs, characteristics that make a song Gothic, club openings and closings, and Anally, discussions about why someone feels Gothic. Questions about where to find a new black hair dye or a clothing or record catalog also appear frequently, although some of these are shunted to alt.gothic-fashion. And then there are the endless lists of the best Gothic albums, and movies, and numerous jokes—the latter invariably poking fun at stereotypes of Gothic dress and attitudes. For example:

> *What do you store your heavy velvet cape in for the summer?*
> Goth balls.

> *Why is it so hard for Goths to get work?*
> Because all they can do is mope the floors and depress the buttons.

In spite of their reputation for moroseness, Goths, or at least Net Goths, seem to have a sense of humor.

Perhaps surprising to many outside the Gothic world, these Goths also reveal a social conscience. Despite the results of my survey, which showed that less than half of the respondents vote regularly, and even fewer are registered with a specific party, the online discussions generally entail a few threads concerning current social and political issues. For example, during one particular week in June 1997, alt.gothic contained discussions of various efforts in the United States to ban handguns, as well as calls for a counterboycott of Southern Baptist-owned businesses in retaliation for their boycott of the Disney Corporation and its same-sex-partner-friendly policies. Discussion of these issues was lively and well informed. Past threads have also touched upon feminism and sexism—both within Gothicdom and the larger culture—and issues surrounding sexuality and sexual identity.

Not limited to the alt.gothic newsgroup, this active online community also cross-posts to many other newsgroups—such as alt.vampyre, and alt.AnneRice—and also creates and maintains a staggering number of websites or home pages dealing with everything Gothic, or even remotely Gothic. The elaborate designs of personal Gothic home pages by persons with names such as "Cryptie" and "Vulture Miranda" often include advanced graphics such as flames licking around the edge of the screen, or blood dripping down the screen as you scroll through the site. Such pages often contain lists of the favorite songs and lyrics, poetry, and photographs (sometimes sexually explicit) of the page's webmaster. These webmasters are obviously technologically adept; it is not surprising that almost all of the Net Goths who responded to my survey claimed to spend more than five hours per week online, many even indicating that their web surfing time usually exceeds fifteen hours each week.

Gothic Style

The third aspect of the Gothic scene to be considered, and generally the first one most people notice, is the appearance and attire of many Goths. The Gothic look, while admittedly open to variation, tends toward a pale, preferably gaunt face, with heavily lined eyes and red or black lips, and, of course, black clothing. Although I have been assured that one can be Goth without dressing the part, Gothic garb seems to play a key role for many in feeling Gothic.

According to Generation X scholar Tom Beaudoin, this emphasis on clothing and appearance clearly marks Goths as members of their generation. In his book *Virtual Faith: The Irreverent Spiritual Quest of Generation X* (1998), Beaudoin notes that Xers have used fashion as a means of expression ever since they were old enough to determine their own style. He suggests that clothing is an important means by which members of Generation X have been able to work through their experiences of hardship and suffering. Among the earliest fashion trends to be created and adopted by this generation were the military look and grunge, both styles expressive of what Beaudoin calls an "emerging bunker mentality among Xers." He further suggests that grunge, with its unkempt and ragged look, expresses much about Xers' feelings of neglect and need. Reputedly survivors of parental and social disregard, and sometimes abuse, the teens and twenty-somethings of the 1980s and '90s, he says, have hid their bodies and spirits within the protective camouflage of oversize flannel shirts and ripped jeans.

Beaudoin notes, however, that it is another such fashion trend, found particularly within metropolitan areas, that is the quintessential expression of Xer suffering, loneliness, and need. In its emphasis on death, decay, and darkness, Gothic, he says, is the starkest expression of Xer suffering. Whether dressed in the traditional, romantic Gothic look of black velvet, flowing white lace, and rich brocade, or in the more contemporary look of black leather, glossy polyvinyl chloride (PVC), and chains that shares much with industrial fashion, Gothic attire always has intimations of suffering, pain, and death. Within their elaborate costumes and makeup, Goths give tangible form to Xer experiences of separation and aloneness through an irreverent mimicking of death: "The gothic style is excessively funereal. Survival, it seems, is only possible by hyperbolizing death, by making an entire wardrobe out of bleakness" (Beaudoin 1998, 104). In appropriating a deathlike wardrobe and mask, Goths attempt to overcome what seems so daunting. Their social, emotional, and physical suffering is cathartically faced, allowing Goths to empower themselves to move beyond feelings of loneliness, repression, and unimportance.

Beaudoin's observations certainly provide an important insight into Gothic fashions, but my interactions with Goths suggest that there is more to their garb than simply catharsis. From their perspective, their attire and makeup more importantly serve as means for creating and then communicating who and what they are. For many, adopting Gothic clothing enables them to feel comfortable with themselves by allowing them more fully to reveal their inner selves. As one twenty-four-year-old woman writes, "I see black as absorbing all color, all emotions. It is a metaphor or symbol for the vast universe and the unknown. It is also quiet and contemplative at times. Also, I have a deep love of travel and exploring unusual cultures (compared to my own mainstream [Mormon] culture). I always felt like a minority in personality, and now I choose to be comfortable with my unusual tastes [rather] than die trying to conform. Expressing myself with clothing and jewelry feels *freeing* and natural [emphasis hers]." Another woman comments that Gothic attire "makes me feel real. It makes me feel like myself." Finally, one Gothic man says, "It makes me feel good. I wear it almost every day because it says something about me to everyone."

For these and others, Gothic fashion both liberates and validates. Indeed, one woman announces, "It doesn't make me feel anything to be dressed in the goth garb. However, it makes me feel plain SILLY to be dressed in anything else. I can't stand to wear colours anymore; they slide off me like an oil slick. It would drive me insane." For this woman and many others, the black garb becomes essential for expressing and affirming identity. In fact, some Goths even have two separate wardrobes, one for work and one for comfort. Kyla, who works as a special education instructional aide, says that while her daily wear is "totally black," her work wardrobe, unfortunately, "has color." Still, she limits the color of her work clothes to darker tones such as navy blue, often accessorizing with black shoes and nylons.

Beyond the clothing, however, Kyla also points out another aspect of her preferred self-presentation that work requires her to do without—the elaborate makeup so cherished by most Goths, male and female. Generally involving white face powder, black or blood-red lipstick and nail polish, and a dark kohl eyeliner. Gothic makeup, like Gothic garb, becomes a defining element in many Goths' appearance and self-perception. Without it, they feel lost and exposed. Kyla, whose daily look includes what she terms "Cleopatra eyes," notes that the first thing she does after work is to remove her work clothes and reapply her makeup.

> I come home, and I actually have to go "bbbllllll" and take [my work clothes] off. Run to my bathroom, and scrape my makeup on, and go "aaaahhh." Seriously, I feel like that's who I am. That's who I am. … I need to put all my black on, and I need to get out of here and go to school. When I go to school, to my college, when I've just got off of work, I feel so weird. I'm like so, I'm like so totally self-conscious, because I don't wear makeup to this other thing, and it drives me nuts. It's still taking a bunch of my friends to convince me, "You look OK without your makeup. You're still a pretty girl." I'm like NO. I can't stand it.

Other Goths relate similar sentiments regarding the role and importance of makeup in their lives. One woman says she wears makeup because her "gypsyesque alter-ego" loves captivating faces and drama. Another said she uses it "as another way to be creative and express my inside on the surface, though I'm sure I hide behind it also the same as many other things." For men, too, elaborate makeup and dress serves the dual purpose of hiding and revealing their inner selves. Michael, who showed me Polaroid photographs of himself in full makeup and wearing an evening gown, alluded to the ways in which the wearing of makeup reflects the way the Gothic culture encourages both men and women to get in touch with their emotions: "I think a lot of Gothic men are more in touch with themselves because they are able to express their emotions. They're able to get in touch with the other side of life [the 'feminine'], while a macho jock would be too afraid to put on lipstick."

In addition to makeup and dark clothing, the Gothic look increasingly involves accessories such as colored contact lenses, fangs, piercings, and tattoos. The newest of these fads—the colored or even cat's-eye contact lenses—is largely a product of Hollywood. Contact lenses in vivid red, green, and yellow have been used by characters in recent shows ranging from the television production *Babylon 5* to the wildly popular (among many Goths) syndicated vampire detective show *Forever Knight* and the screen adaptation of Anne Rice's *Interview with the Vampire*. In each of these, nonhumans, including and especially vampires, are shown to have senses and abilities superior to that of humans, as suggested by the catlike shape or dramatic color of their eyes.

Hollywood is also responsible, at least in part, for the growing number of Goths with altered orthodontics. While always popular with Gothic's vampire-loving crowd, fangs have become increasingly so with the development and availability of professionally designed incisors. Initially created for use in movies, these are a far cry from the plastic teeth popular among children at Halloween. Often custom-made, these fangs can be either temporarily or permanently adhered to one's real teeth, much like a corrective cap. When someone wearing these smiles, the fangs produce an eerie and highly realistic effect.

Finally, in addition to these more temporary artifices, the Gothic look today increasingly involves more permanent markings, primarily tattoos and piercings. Like other Xers, Goths appear to be infatuated with this evergrowing trend of "body modification." Although cost again is often cited as prohibitive, especially for tattooing, many Goths sport intricate designs as well as rather imaginatively placed piercings. Of those who responded to my survey, nearly 80 percent of the women and a third of the men have piercings, while half of the women and a third of the men are tattooed. In response to the questions of whether or not they have tattoos or piercings, here is a sampling of the replies I received from women:

> Yes, [I have] two tattoos. One is an arm band and the other [is] on my ass, and [I have] seventeen piercings: my septum, earlobes, labrette, lip, two traguses, two stretched earlobes, navel, two clit piercings, tongue, five in my ears.
>
> Two [piercings] in my nose (left side); two in my tongue; eight in my left ear; two in my outer labia; a tattoo of a winged horse on the back of my right shoulder; [and I am] planning more of both.

and from men:

I have four holes in my left ear, two in the right, and both nipples pierced. I have a tattoo of Giger's alien on the back of my right shoulder and a tattoo of a large rose on the left side of my chest.

When asked to explain why they adorn their bodies in these ways, most talk about finding meaning through controlling, pleasuring, and/or beautifying themselves. The man mentioned above writes that

The piercings were purely ornamental, although the nipples were also for the sensation (which is exquisite) and have made them more sensitive than before. The tattoos have meaning: the alien played a large part in my life and Giger's work is just wonderful. The Rose is a reminder of the pain I went through when I separated from my wife and my family. It's to remind [me] never to allow myself to get into that situation again.

A woman with five piercings in her right ear, one in her left nipple, and a navel pierce replies,

I feel that piercings help me to regain a sense of reality through pain. When I've completely lost control of my life, or when things seem to get out of control, it is quite therapeutic to get a needle shoved into your flesh. It's like, if you can handle having a thick needle shoved into your body, and watch it and not flinch, then you could take on [anything] anytime. For me, piercings are not for show, but for personal gratification and emotional stability.

And finally, another woman, who is in the process of "starting an industrial project (big bars through my ear cartiledge [sic])," argues,

I think the least you can do to liven up your short lifetime is to make your sort of beauty wherever you can, starting with yourself (unless you find something better to do), and I find little bits of metal and dermal pictures to be nice additions to the strange body I've picked up.

For this woman, and other Goths, tattoos and piercings, in much the same manner as Gothic clothing and makeup, are a means of establishing control over the only thing many Xers feel they can control—their own bodies—while also being a conduit for self-exploration and expression. Through these external accoutrements Goths, and Xers in general, are able to develop themselves into a self that is uniquely their own, reclaiming and delineating their own physical and spiritual boundaries.

Gothic Vampires

Finally, no discussion about Gothicdom is complete without direct mention of the figure whose spectral image lurks beneath much of Gothic music, fashion, literature, and art. Beloved by the majority of Goths I have encountered, the vampire makes its haunting presence known throughout most elements of Gothic culture. In hundreds of novels, comic books, films, and poems, all avidly read and sometimes written by Goths, these dark kin of humankind skulk and suffer their way through time. In the plush velvets and elegant laces of high Gothic fashion, they receive homage from adoring fans who are eager to emulate their antiquated (and obviously wealthy) style. Particularly notable members of this undead race have had songs written about them, and some even have their own fan clubs. In Gothicdom, it is good to be undead.

Gothic admiration of these creatures is significant, as it marks a notable departure in Western attitudes toward the vampire. Europeans in the Middle Ages spoke fearfully of these creatures, whom they saw as putrefied, corpselike monsters, able to return from the grave to suck the blood of the living. Nineteenth-century audiences shuddered in horror as vampires moved up the social ladder and drained polite society of its females, one by one. Even certain types of contemporary treatments of the vampire, especially low-budget horror flicks, continue to represent the undead as fiends. Like their many predecessors, these films suggest that the only good vampire is a truly dead one. Goths, however, seem to disagree. Where others have seen only a horrifying beast, they see a tragic hero. Instead of a monster who brings death, they see the promise of eternal life. Rather than the bearer of a curse, Goths perceive vampires as beings who are immensely powerful and highly erotic. But why this shift?

According to several scholars of popular culture (Auerbach 1995; Dresser 1989; Gelder 1994), vampires have always served as mirrors capable of reflecting their society's particular fears and desires. Nineteenth-century vampires, like their human counterparts, existed in a sex-segregated world. In this context, vampires were creatures who formed "special friendships" with individuals, and then drained the life out of them. In Bram Stoker's notorious work, written in 1897 as the Western world saw women increasingly entering the public domain, Dracula threatens to vampirize (read: sexualize) Mina and destroy the harmony of the Harker home. Now, as this millennium comes to a close, vampires have become powerful, rich, sexy, and of course eternally young. They have attained the American dream. Or have they? In the midst of their success, it seems they have begun to doubt the dream. They have begun to question the meaning of it all.

The vampires whose charisma and angst most pervade Gothic culture are undoubtedly the brood created by Anne Rice in *Interview with the Vampire*. Led by her beloved Lestat, these children of the night have come to define the late twentieth-century image of the vampire, much as Stoker's Dracula did for earlier generations. However, whereas Stoker portrayed his vampire as a cold, ruthless, and nonhuman character, driven solely by bloodthirst, Rice has indelibly stamped contemporary vampires as creatures possessing sarcastic wit, devilish good looks, and most interesting, spiritual burdens that could be said to make Judas Iscariot look carefree. The movie version of *Interview,* featuring a blond Tom Cruise as Lestat and Brad Pitt as the angst-ridden protagonist, Louis, only serves to reinforce these characteristics. Unlike the older image of the cool, aloof vampire, Lestat and Louis struggle with the guilt and extravagances of possessing an eternal life that is based on repeated killing and the consumption of blood. They spend centuries in search of the answers to their questions on the origins and meaning of their undead existence. Endlessly searching for the truth of their existence, and even for God, these millennial vampires have reached a spiritual crisis, one perhaps matched only by that of their fans.

Gothic as a Religion?

Although a "spiritual crisis" might seem too harsh a description of the current status of religion in Western culture, few observers of the religious scene will deny that significant changes that have occurred in the twentieth-century religious landscape pose new dilemmas and difficulties for the study of contemporary religion. A complete discussion of these issues and their relevance to Gothicdom is beyond the scope of this particular work, but in brief, several scholars of the baby-boom generation have described boomers as "religious seekers," noting that members of this generation frequently seek out their religiosity within a variety of traditional and nontraditional venues (Roof 1993). Often choosing self-guided exploration over inherited dogma, boomers have created a climate in which faith involves actively selecting beliefs and practices from among an array of sources. As children of boomer parents, Xers are now following the older generation's lead, perceiving "spirituality"—as they more often call it—as something to be shaped and practiced however and wherever one chooses. Significantly, this distinction between *spirituality* and *religion* is more than mere semantics, for it reveals a distinction among both boomers and Xers between established, organized religion and what many perceive to be a more genuine or more "real" faith. Religious subjectivism, like subjectivism in general, is key with members of Generation X.

Of the Goths I have contacted, the majority tell me they were raised in a religious tradition, but only a few describe themselves or their parents as having been very involved with a religious group during their childhood. When asked if they consider themselves to be religious or spiritual now, more than half say yes, but few affiliate themselves solely with mainstream Protestant, Catholic, or Jewish denominations. Instead, they identify their spirituality as consisting of beliefs and practices drawn from Christianity, Judaism, and a variety of other faiths, including Buddhism, neopaganism, Taoism, Santeria, and Scientology. Even those who continue to identify with their parents' religious tradition say they are very selective as to which elements of this tradition they continue to observe. Others, believing that no religious tradition offers them anything of value, define themselves as not religious or spiritual, or they take the approach of a woman who says, "I worship me, and now I'm much happier."

When I have asked Goths if they see Gothic as a religion, the most common response is a laugh and a quick no. A few have said yes, it is for them religious, but for most, Catholicism and Judaism are religions, while Gothic is just Gothic. Upon further consideration, though, many have conceded that Gothic, while not a religion, certainly has spiritual aspects. Building upon such comments, I offer the following exploration of Gothicdom's potentially spiritual elements. To do so, I have utilized Joachim Wach's three forms of religious expression—theoretical, practical, and sociological—as a framework for teasing out and examining these religious, or at least spiritual, aspects of the Gothic world.

Wach argues that it is human nature to give expression to that which we experience, and says that religions traditionally enable us to do so in three specific ways (Wach 1958; Ellwood 1999). The first of these is the theoretical, which concerns the ideas and theories we develop about our experiences, and how we then convey these through the use of words, pictures, statues, or symbols. For most religions, this aspect seeks to communicate information about our encounters with the sacred, our experiences of reality, and our interactions with one another. From my observations, Goths do not share any explicit notions about God or the sacred. Some speak of God, others do not. They do, however, often share a specific understanding of the world, one that portrays the cosmos as consisting of complementary forces that must be kept in balance. Some will even mention the Taoist concepts of yin and yang in their discussions of these forces. It is typically thought among these Goths that Western culture has failed to obtain or even to seek such a balance, instead focusing on attaining happiness while desperately avoiding or denying pain, suffering, and death. As Carlos explains above, while not disparaging the pursuit of happiness, Goths perceive the importance of contemplating life's bleaker aspects. As a result, they devote what some consider to be an inordinate amount of attention to the darker things in life. Their poetry, literature, and songs become purposeful celebrations of the fearsome, the dark, and even death. "Life and death," says Carlos, "just try to experience both of them in order to maybe appreciate the other one."

I believe this is the aspect of Gothic culture that accounts for Goths' avid fascination with the vampire. As portrayed by Rice and others, the vampire is no longer merely loathsome or frightening. Instead, it has gained a humanity that brings nobility and pathos to its struggle with its own nature. When Louis denounces Lestat's viciousness in killing, asking if there is not more to vampire nature, the reader's sympathies no longer lie solely with the victims.

> "Why did you become a vampire?" I blurted out. "And why such a vampire as you are! Vengeful and delighting in taking human life even when you have no need." … He shook his head. "Louis!" he said. "You are in love with your mortal nature! You chase after the phantoms of your former self." … I objected to this at once. "My vampire nature has been for me the greatest adventure of my life; all that went before it was confused, clouded; I went through mortal life like a

blind man groping from solid object to solid object. It was only when I became a vampire that I respected for the first time all of life. I never saw a living, pulsing human being until I was a vampire; I never knew what life was until it ran out in a red gush over my lips, my hands!" (Rice 1976)

Suddenly, there is an eerie similarity between the plight of the vampire and that of humanity. In the vampire, late twentieth-century human concerns and fears become visible. It rails against its own kind and God in search of meaning. It experiences life's pleasures, while also tasting its bitterness. It recognizes that it is caught in a web of ceaseless violence. In this being, then, coexist the same darkness and light, or good and evil, found in humanity. For Gothic Xers, such vampires have become archetypes of their own experiences of the world.

Beyond such theological and cosmic concerns, the theoretical expression of Gothicdom also includes issues surrounding individuals' interactions with one another. As in nearly all religious traditions, the Gothic scene has its ethical codes, proscribing some behaviors while encouraging others. When asked about these, Goths generally point to two injunctions: respect for the rights of all persons, and tolerance for individual creativity and diverse lifestyles. Monique and others say that most people in the movement emphatically denounce sexist, heterosexist, or racist behavior and try to make the clubs a "safe" environment, one in which women and sexual or racial minorities will not be harassed, segregated, or oppressed. Any degrading treatment of others, they say, is "un-Goth."

This focus on respect and care for others can often be found in the lyrics of Gothic songs. Themes dealing with the lack of, or loss of, love in a world dominated by violence and oppression run throughout the music. For example, in "The Ghost in You," Siouxsie and the Banshees lament over the tragedy of events such as occurred in China's Tiananmen Square. Love, Siouxsie sings, is not only forgotten in such instances but is destroyed and betrayed. Using their music to comment on the frequent and often overpowering immorality of the world in this way, Gothic musicians express their frustration and outrage with the world, while also acting as conduits of Gothic mores.

In addition to such illustrations of support for basic human rights, Gothic music and culture also emphatically embrace individuals' rights to develop and express themselves, particularly through explorations of their identity and sexuality, and encourage people to accept—even appreciate—others who are doing the same. Vampire scholar J. Gordon Melton suggests that Gothicdom, in taking an "explicit nonconformist stance vis-a-vis the dominant establishment," is similar to other countercultural forms in its advocation of androgyny and experimental forms of sex play (Melton 1994). The tangible effects of this nonconformist attitude within Gothic culture include experiments with anything from makeup and dress to same-sex sex and S/M. As long as no one is physically or emotionally endangered, such searches are considered enriching. Indeed, the majority of women I have encountered in Gothicdom describe themselves as bisexual, or at least as "bicurious." Some say they understood themselves in this way prior to their involvement with Gothic, but for others, it is the Gothic culture that has made them more open to the possibility of a relationship with another woman. Even Goths who identify as straight are mostly supportive of same-sex relationships.

Most Goths also see other so-called deviant sexual practices, especially S/M and blood drinking, as acceptable avenues of sexual exploration, again with the stipulation that all parties must be fully consenting. One man summarizes this requirement by saying that, while S/M is personally not his cup of tea, "If all parts are in, then why not!" Of those who engage in S/M, most say they use such practices only occasionally, as a form of "spicing up" their sex life. One woman compares S/M to action movies, arguing that a nice romantic movie is good, but sometimes she likes something a little more exciting. While much less common than S/M among Goths, blood drinking is also generally tolerated, if not encouraged. Many express concern over the obvious risk involved in this behavior, in light of the AIDS epidemic, but among those who regularly, or even occasionally, drink a partner's blood, all I have spoken to say they are careful to practice "safe sex." Ultimately, Gothic sexual ethics, like the Gothic worldview, encourage individuals to embrace the darker pleasures of sex, but to do so in full awareness of the dangers involved.

The second form of religious expression that Wach discusses is the practical, or what is more commonly understood as the ritual aspect of religious traditions. The most notable rituals found within the Gothic club culture are the rituals of dance and costuming. While the music itself is central to the club experience, it is the act of dancing that connects the dancer with, or better yet, involves the dancer in the music. Swaying in a serpentine manner, Goths unite their bodies with the keening, mournful sounds of the music. While yet part of the larger crowd, dancers in Gothic clubs generally dance alone. Their movements, sometimes "voguelike," vacillate between the contemplative and the ecstatic. As they move around the floor, their bodies seem to give silent testimony to things intoned by the music but otherwise inexpressible.

In addition to the dancing itself, it is important to recognize the role played by the dancers' costumes. Costuming performs a key part in creating the proper ambience within a club. Without the sea of black, the scene would lose its mysterious, mesmerizing aura. Without the clothing and the painted faces, and the fangs and piercings, the appropriate spirits and beings are not present for the ritual gathering. In order to experience the world as a Goth, one must "feel" Gothic, and while this can be done without the garb, it is often facilitated by Gothic accoutrements and the rituals involved in donning them. As in the act of putting on religious vestments or wearing one's "Sunday best," applying makeup, or even putting on a black skirt or a leather collar, can alter one's self-perception and sense of time and space. As Kyla comments above, putting on the garb and makeup is an experience of "aaahhh"—of reentering the realm of Gothic.

Although speaking about piercings, rather than Gothic attire, Elias Farajaje'-Jones has argued that various forms of "body modification" can also be redemptive (1995). He suggests that such things constitute an "act of de-colonizing our bodies" from a culture that is erotophobic and heteronormative, by enabling us to bring the spiritual and the erotic together once again. These alterations serve as reminders to the one pierced of his or her erotic nature, both at the time of piercing and each time a piece of fabric, a hand, a tongue, or a stranger's gaze touches the hoop or stud embedded within them. I would extend his argument to the acts of costuming and applying Gothic makeup. Each time a Goth sees a Casual look at her on the street and do a double take, or each time he is admired in his long black skirt, a Goth has her or his self-perception of being someone mysterious and dark confirmed. The makeup and fashion along with piercings and tattoos become a means to transcending the world of the Casuals and their mores for Goths who have chosen to demarcate themselves from the ordinary world through their bodies.

Finally, Wach's third form of expression concerns the ways in which a movement expresses itself through social structures and organization. The obvious beginning point for such an analysis of Gothic is the club scene, for it is in the clubs that Gothic originated, and it is there that the Gothic world most clearly becomes visible to observers and participants alike. One of the first things to note about the Gothic world is that it provides its members with something sought through most religious traditions: community. As Monique says earlier, in the club scene and its various extensions, she readily finds others with whom to associate who share her interests. In Gothicdom, she and others find a group in which wearing black lipstick, for both women and men, is not only not strange, it is the norm. They find people who have read all of Anne Rice's works, including those she wrote under her various pseudonyms. They even meet others to whom it is generally acceptable to introduce your same-sex partner. Because of these things, many people who have not been able to fit in elsewhere find a haven. They find somewhere they actually belong.

As for the particular groups that give structure to Gothicdom, as indicated above, the heart of Gothic culture is found in the bands who perform at the clubs and record the albums, and the fans who attend the clubs and buy the albums. However, as also noted, the Gothic scene is a much more complex structure than this implies, with record producers, club owners and promoters, publishers, authors, and vendors of various items each playing their part in creating the scene. To further complicate things, the Gothic world also exists within the murky territory of the Internet, as well as within the private lives of Goths themselves. Determining where Gothic begins and ends, therefore, is nearly impossible. It has its visible and invisible social structures, as well as its quasiclergy, its laity, and its many supporting groups and industries. As already discussed, it also has its beliefs and practices.

In the end, I think it is clear that Gothic has spiritual elements. However, it is less clear how we should categorize and label this world. How, exactly, do we define this movement? Is it a religion, or merely one more youth subculture? One man I interviewed, who had been in the Los Angeles Gothic scene since its beginnings, said that originally many people he knew understood being Gothic as being opposed to traditional religions, and as such, it was almost an "'anti-religion' religion." For this Goth, like others, it appears that Gothic, if not a religion per se, nevertheless functions as a religion, or at least an "anti-religion." But what does this mean? Is an "anti-religion" a religion?

Merely conceptualizing Gothic as a youth subculture, where *subculture* refers to "the blueprint for behavior of a smaller group within the society" (Sebald 1968) is, I think, inadequate. Gothic, as a blueprint, includes much more than just its adherents' behavior. But is it a religion? Ultimately, I think to affirm that Gothic is an established or organized religion would be to go too far, particularly as most of its members do not themselves perceive it as such. But if it is not a religion, yet functions in religious ways for many Goths, how might we best describe it? The sociology of religion offers the construct of a cult, with which I think Gothic has much in common. Conventionally understood, a cult is a group disenchanted with common religious forms (as many Goths claim to be), that tends to be urban in nature (which Gothic is, except on the Internet), centered around a charismatic figure or figures (such as the musicians), which develops its own terms and symbols to describe reality—in this case, the use of vampire imagery (Johnston 1983). Usually more concerned with the needs of the individual rather than the collective, this form of religious group also tends to be loosely organized (Dawson 1997). One difficulty that arises in applying this term to Gothicdom, however, is that cults, like subcultures, have generally been perceived as being geographically located and institutionally distinct. The Gothic realm is not located within one geographical area, nor does it follow one leader or even an identifiable hierarchy of leaders. Recent discussions within the sociology of religion, however, have begun to expand the cult typology in an effort to reflect the more fluid, unstructured nature of many contemporary groups. Such endeavors have resulted in the generation of new cult types, such as "audience" cults and "client" cults (Stark 1985; Dawson 1997), as well as the introduction of new constructs, such as "correspondence religion" (Deitrick 1997). Although none of these yet describe Gothic adequately, I believe that this recognition of the increasing fluidity and creativity of form occurring within the modern religious realm opens the door for considering movements such as Gothic religious.

Ultimately, I have concluded that I will have to be satisfied with describing the Gothic world as a movement existing somewhere between, or maybe beyond, a subculture and a cult—something I have dubbed a "cult/ure" for my own purposes. As a cult/ure, Gothic, like many other current movements, points to the increasing difficulties of separating religion from other aspects of contemporary and popular culture, and of defining exactly what is meant by the term *religion*. Members of Generation X, like their boom generation parents, are breaking the old rules and seeking meaning far beyond the confines of churches and synagogues. While admittedly not typical of a large number of their peers in certain respects, members of the Gothic cult/ure clearly exemplify a yen within their generation for meaning and community, as well as a willingness to seek—or even a preference for seeking—these in nontraditional venues. I believe that Goths, like most of their peers, are searching for an environment that supports creativity and difference, as well as a perspective from which to make sense of a fast-paced, enjoyment-based, homogenizing, and potentially isolating world. For Gothic Xers, an affirming community and a tenable worldview are found within the clubs, myths, music, and makeup of Gothicdom. In demarcating themselves from those of us who generally favor the day over the night, or the light over shadows, Goths create and sustain a haven and a worldview that is uniquely theirs. One particularly poetic and insightful Net Goth succinctly captures these aspects of the cult/ure in describing her own understanding of Gothic: "To me, 'Gothic' is rather an aesthetic and sometimes, a collective worldview. A lot of people sharing the same tint on their glasses realized each other and said, 'Hey, y'know we could have some fun with this sad world, or at least on it, before we shuffle off,' and we could do it our way.'"

Her message is signed, "A completely anonymous, utterly guessable soul."

References

Arnett, Jeffrey Jensen. 1995. *Metalheads: Heavy Metal Music and Adolescent Alienation.* Boulder, Colo.: Westview Press.

Auerbach, Nina. 1995. *Our Vampires, Ourselves.* Chicago: University of Chicago Press.

Bauhaus. 1986. "Bela Lugosi's Dead." *Bauhaus, 1979–1983.* Atlantic Recording Corporation.

Beaudoin, Tom, 1998. *Virtual Faith: The Irreverent Spiritual Quest of Generation X.* San Francisco: Jossey-Bass.

Couchman, Stephen, 1995. "What Makes a Song Gothic?" Online posting, January 25. Retrieved from alt. gothic December 30, 1998.

Dawson, Lorne L. 1997. "Creating 'Cult' Typologies: Some Strategic Considerations." *Journal of Contemporary Religion* 12, no. 3.

Deitrick, James E. 1997. "Who Needs Church when You Have a Mailbox? Correspondence Religion and the New Spirituality." Paper presented at the Society for the Scientific Study of Religion Annual Meeting, San Diego, Calif., November.

Dresser, Norine. 1989. *American Vampires: Fans, Victims, Practitioners.* New York: Vintage Books.

Ellwood, Robert S., and Barbara A. McGraw. 1999. *Many Peoples, Many Faiths: Women and Men in the World Religions.* 6th rev. ed. Englewood Cliffs, N.J.: Prentice Hall.

Farajaje'-Jones, Elias. 1995. "Piercing Analysis or in-to Body Travel." Paper presented at the American Academy of Religion Annual Meeting, Philadelphia, Penn., November.

Gelder, Ken. 1994. *Reading the Vampire.* London: Routledge.

Johnston, Ronald L. 1983. *Religion in Society: A Sociology of Religion.* 2d rev. ed. Englewood Cliffs, N.J.: Prentice Hall.

London after Midnight. 1998. "A Letter to God." *Psycho Magnet.* Available from London after Midnight, P.O. Box 1377, Hollywood, CA 90078–1377.

Melton, J. Gordon. 1994. *The Vampire Book: The Encyclopedia of the Undead.* Detroit: Visible Ink Press.

Neely, Neil. 1995. "Gothic Music." Online posting, November 28. Retrieved from alt.gothic November 1995.

Rice, Anne. 1976. *Interview with the Vampire: Book 1 of the Vampire Chronicles.* New York: Ballantine Books.

Roof, Wade Clark. 1993. *A Generation of Seekers: Baby Boomers and the Quest for Spiritual Style.* New York: HarperCollins.

Sebald, Hans. 1968. *Adolescence. A Sociological Analysis*. New York: Appleton-Century-Crofts.

Siouxsie and the Banshees. 1991. "The Ghost in You." *Superstition*. Geffen Records.

Stark, Rodney, and William Sims Bainbridge. 1985. *The Future of Religion: Secularization, Revival, and Cult Formation*. Berkeley and Los Angeles: University of California Press.

Wach, Joachim. 1958. *The Comparative Study of Religions*. Edited with an Introduction by Joseph M. Kitagawa. New York: Columbia University Press.

Wake, Peter, comp. 1994. "Gothic FAQ." Online posting, May 31, Retrieved from alt.gothic September 14, 1995.

Walser, Robert. 1995. *Running with the Devil: Power, Gender, and Madness in Heavy Metal Music*. Hanover, N.H.: University Press of New England.

Weinstein Deena 1991. *Heavy Metal: A Cultural Sociology*. New York: Lexington Books.

PART VII

Syncretistic Religions, Wicca and Neo-Paganism

Palo Monte Mayombe

Nathaniel Samuel Murrell

....

Regla de Ochaö (Lucumi/Santeria) is the most well known and investigated Afro-Cuban religion, locally and internationally, but its correlatives—Abakua, of the Efik-Ibibio; Regla Arara, from Ewe-Fon Dahomey (the modern People's Republic of Benin); and Regla de Palo Monte, of the Bakongo and Bantu-speaking peoples—are perhaps equally important to the practice and study of Afro-Caribbean religions. [...] The Bakongo and Bantu culture of Central Africa (especially in the Congo, Cameroon, and Angola) resonates in Cuban religions, Brazilian Candomble de Angola and Candomble de Congo, Haitian Vodou, and to a lesser extent, Jamaican Kumina and Obeah. During her decades of research in Cuba, art historian Judith Bettelheim found that practitioners of "Palo Monte Mayombe ... refer to their homeland as Ngola (Ngola a Kilunje, 'the land between the lower Kwanza and the Dande'), from which derives the Europeanized 'Angola.'"[1] The cadre of names used for Palo Monte (see the section that follows) suggests that the religion encompasses other subsets of Kongo traditions, of which little might be known. Palo Monte is said to have spread among Afro-Latinos in the Dominican Republic, the United States, Venezuela, Colombia, and Puerto Rico (said to have more than five thousand followers),[2] a claim not corroborated herein.

Although Paulo Monte plays an important role in the religious culture of Afro-Cubans, it is still not well known or studied by many people outside of Cuba. Some religion researchers[3] correctly charge that recent upsurges of interest in Afro-Cuban religions among anthropologists, religionists (like myself), and other ethnographers focuses much too narrowly on the Yoruba-based Lucumi at the expense and neglect of other creole religions like Arara, Ifa, Abakua, and Palo Monte.[4] Unfortunately, space and cost constraints prevent coverage of all Afro-Cuban religions in this work. This brief survey on Palo Monte is written as a complement to some of the important recent ethnographic works published on the religion by Lydia Cabrera (1979, 1986, and 2000), Stephen Palmie (1995 and 2002), Arturo Lindsay (1996), Judith Bettelheim (2001), Miguel Barnet (2001), Fernandez Olmos and Paravisini-Gebert (2003), David Brown (2003), Jesus Fuentes Guerra and Armin Schwegler (2005), and Erica Moret (2008) in the hope of inspiring further examination.

Delimitation and Origination

Palo Monte is one of the leading Afro-Caribbean creole religions of the largest Spanish-speaking Antilles. It took its language, beliefs, and most of its ritual practices from the Bkango and Bantu culture of Central West Africa and decoded them in the multiethnic, multilingual, and diverse religious environment of colonial Cuba. The religion operates in concord with nature and the environment and places strong emphasis on the individual's relationship to ancestral and nature spirits. Its practitioners specialize in infusing natural objects with spiritual entities to aid or empower humans to negotiate the problems and challenges of life. Palo Monte is referred to often as Reglas Congas ("Kongo religions"), and has accrued more symbolic names than one wishes to countenance: Palo Monte Mayombe, Congas Reglas, Regla de Palo, Regla de Conga, Regla de Palo Monte, Las Reglas de Conga, Palo Kimbisa, and Santo Cristo Buen Viaje (or locally Palo, Kongo, Bantu, and Conga Regla), among others. These locutions share a common accent; they are creole (African-Spanish) historical significations of an African spirituality.

Palo and *monte* ("sticks of the forest") are creole-Cuban creations. Onlookers probably labeled the religion "palo monte" facetiously, because followers used numerous wooden sticks to prepare their artistically designed imposing sacred altars for the spirits, perhaps near the forest. Palo and Mayombe also are said to have a distinct connection to the religious import of trees for the Bakongo people; *palo* is a Portuguese word for "tree" while Mayombe is a deep-forest area in the Central African region. Fu Kiau Bunseki is recorded as saying that, in the Kongo, most judgments and "courts are held under trees, and debate, marriage, and initiation, are done under a tree. The tree is seen as the symbol, the pipe through which the *miela* comes to us."[5] Palo Monte (hereafter, Palo) also points to the reputation of Kango people in rural Cuba as being as resilient and intrepid as the spirits of their religion.[6] Worthy of note is the fact that Afro-Spanish designations define Palo (Regla de Conga) practitioners as *paleros, ngangeros,* and *nganguleros,* terms that augur the religion's dual Kongo and Cuban reality.

Provenance of Palo

Although the actual dating of Palo's advent remains imprecise, Bantu-speaking people from central Africa were taken to Cuba starting with the sixteenth century.[7] Palo began with the Kongo religious traditions among Afro-Cubans (the *bozales* and *esclavos, or* "newly arrived" and "enslaved"; the *gente de color,* or "free population of color"; and the *Ladinos,* or African-born Spanish-speaking Cubans[8]) around the eighteenth century. In more modern times, it is preserved and embraced by Cubans of mixed ethnicity who often identify themselves as being of Yoruba, Carabali, Kongo, or other ethnic nations; Palo's adherents are "a fusion of not only very mixed African background, but also Spanish, Asian, and Amerindian"[9] peoples. *Criollos* ("creole")—Cuban-born Africans, Europeans, and Asians—now constitute its primary supporters.

A recent etymological study of the language and vocabulary used in Palo, by Jesus Fuentas Guerra and Armin Schwegler, claims that much of the religion's cultural content, ritual language, and tradition are traceable, lexically and unambiguously, to one location in Africa, the area of western Congo called Mayombe. The study argues that a significant number of Africans sold into slavery in Cuba originated from that narrow region (circa fifty kilometers in width), from which they preserved a "lingua sacra" for Palo. Guerra and Schwegler conclude that "the esoteric vocabulary of this religious tradition (as exemplified by the names of its divinities) is derived in its entirety from a single Central African language, Kikongo."[10] This, as Kenneth Bilby argues, "contradicts previous scholarship, most of which represent the ritual vocabulary of Palo Monte as a diverse amalgam of terms from a ... variety of Bantu languages."[11] Bantu languages, cultures, and peoples are still common throughout the huge expanse of Central Africa, not just within a region in Angola. As W. van Wetering and H.U.E. Thoden van Velzen argue, the so-called lingua sacra may not account for cultural turbulence and historic demographic dislocations in the area. Hawks of the Atlantic slave trade and their agents scavenged deep into the interior of West Central to Southern Africa to forage for their desired quantity of human cargo. "It seems improbable that Mayombe would have remained exempt from these tribulations," and thus one should not take the isolation of the region for granted.[12]

The work of Guerra, Armin, and Schwegler is very fascinating. However, scholars observe that "Kikango-derived ritual vocabulary of Palo Monte in Cienfuegos" is inseparable "from [the] broader Afro-Caribbean cultural matrix with which it is enmeshed, as evidenced by the complex semantic associations its practitioners perceive between their own terminologies and concepts, and those of other forms of Cuban religions such as Santeria and Catholicism."[13] Given the widespread presence of Bantu culture in Central Africa, it may be difficult to prove, with any certainty, that Palo represents cultural traditions from only one Angolan or Kongo region rather than from the broader Bakongo and Bantu geographical reach. Although Palo is indebted to Kongo for its conceptual language and may "boast a ritual vocabulary that seems to be derived exclusively from Kikongo," Bilby asserts, "it appears to have emerged and taken on many of its fundamental and distinctive meanings in relation to other locally developed religious systems, with which it now shares a certain broad cultural 'logic'"[14] in Cuba.

The Kongo peoples of Cuba originated from many ethnic communities, each with its own culture, dialect, and concept of religious reality. Names of local Congo, Cameroon, and Angolan communities still identify groups in Cuba. Barnet suggests that "the names Briyumba, Kimbisa, and Mayombe are recognized as three sources of culture and religion. These have become the principal terms for the Kongo religious cults of Bantu origin, at least in the western part of the island";[15] Benguela, Musundi, Kunalungo, Loanga, Ngola, Kabinde, Basongo, Quimbanda, and Bukumba nations show imprecise places of origin, but they constitute African "signifiers" of Palo. Partially for this reason, the religion became a melting pot of "Conga" spiritual traditions from the Bantu and Central Africa. The Bantu, a large linguistic group of people, and the "Bakongo inhabit a broad area of sub-Saharan Africa stretching from the southern part of Cameroon through northern Angola" and running diagonally "to Mozambique in the southeastern coast of Africa."[16] J. Lorand Matory observes that Central and Southern African cultures of Bantu-speaking peoples, "including the BaKango, are the products of a demographic and cultural expansion within Africa that dwarfs the transoceanic influence of the Yoruba's ancestors. By the eighth century A.D., the Bantu languages had spread from a small nucleus in what is now Nigeria to Zanzibar, off the coast of East Africa."[17] Among the close to one million Africans taken from about forty-five different ethnic groups and inserted into Cuban plantation slavery, many embarked at depots in West Central Africa.[18]

In captivity in Cuba, the Bakango-Bantu peoples held on to their cultural traditions—perhaps as strongly as their Yoruba counterparts did[19]—as a resource for mitigating their harsh life conditions in the Americas. No evidence exists of a nineteenth-century Afro-Cuban return to the Congo or Angola to reauthenticate a "pure" Palo religion, as the female founders of Candomble did, reexperiencing the religion in West Africa in the 1800s, and as Orisha avatars in Trinidad and Tobago did in the late 1900s for the same purpose. Slavery, however, was not abolished in Spanish Cuba before the last decades of the nineteenth century: the last officially recorded slave ship was said to disembark in Cuba in 1873,[20] or more likely in 1886,[21] and many new arrivals from the Kango and Bantu regions kept the religion alive. Because of Cuba's commerce with Africa in the very late nineteenth century and the fact that Palo does not emphasize a pantheon of divinities as Lucumi does, the stamp of Catholicism on the religion is not as indelible as it is in Vodou, Santeria, Candomble, and Trinidad and Tobago Orisha. The African traditional religions (ATRs), however, morphed into different creole forms as Africans struggled to preserve their traditions in a hostile foreign land.

Symbiotic Creole Filaments

Historically, Palo was influenced more by Lucumi practices than by external traditions. However, it is more open to the outside, and accommodating of other beliefs, than its counterpart, resulting in some of its African beliefs and practices becoming somewhat attenuated. This could be due also to the fact that, through political and ecclesiastical actions, Kongo people lost some of their traditional religious knowledge between their forced transition into slavery and the period following the deterioration of the cabildos. Barnet suggests that "the flexibility of the religious beliefs, together with their remote and imprecise origins, awakened an imagination that is less dogmatic, more fanciful and creative than that of the Yoruba."[22] Practitioners of Palo are not reticent in identifying their own divinities or spirits with those of the Yoruba and the sainthood of Catholicism,[23] although they do not have a pantheon of divinities to shadow the Catholic saints. They even chant to the spirits using the names of Bantu, Yoruba, and Catholic origination, and employ terms used in Santeria to identify some ritual activities and religious titles. Both Lucumi and Palo leaders, for example, use the affectionate title *tata*, the category *bozales*, and the initiation term *fundamentos*. Stephen Palmie reasons that "ocha and palo stand to each other like religion and magic, expressive and instrumental forms of human-divine interaction."[24] Palmie's preference for Lucumi, as religion, to Palo, as "magic," reflects his cultural preconception against a religion that exist sui generis, whose practices he sees as "morally ambivalent and potentially malignant."[25] The cultural borrowing between Palo and Lucumi is as common as it is in other African religions of resistance in Haiti, Jamaica, Brazil, and Trinidad.

Altars and sacred objects carrying African names (nganga, nkisi) and Spanish names (el caldero, la prenda) have become visual symbols of Palo. The religion comprises a diversity of practices, passed down in what might be termed *fragments of bone* (the term is borrowed from Bellegarde-Smith, 2005[26]), that have been redefined as its newer elements continue to merge with the remaining knowledge of ATRs and culture. It is argued that one should speak of Kongo religions in Cuba because several strands are "subsumed under the general rubric of 'Regla de Palo Monte Mayombe"; this includes also "Regla Biyumba, Regla Musunde, Regla de Quirimbaya, Regla Vrillumba, and Regla Kimbisa del Santo Cristo del Buen Viaje ('of the Holy Christ of the Good Journey')."[27] How these strands differ one from the other, whether each one still constitutes a religion sui generis, and how much of these filaments are incorporated in Palo rituals make for an intriguing further study. Religions of African originations, as Matory notes, adopted "new contrasting moral valences" that are unique to their Caribbean setting. Yoruba-related Lucumi practices and those of West Central Africa identified with Palo, "draw their primary meaning not only from their respective African cultural precedents, but from the moral contrasts between them as they are perceived in Cuba."[28] Palo was facilitated by the memory of Kongo languages, conceptions, and cultures.

Palo may constitute a putatively unique religion, but it operates in a geographical space and in multireligious communities with many competing cultural traditions. This allows some Cuban devotees of Palo to expand their religious appetite. David Brown explains the eclectic phenomenon this way: since the beginning of the twentieth century, one could make the saints through the rite of initiation into Santeria. One could also become a priest (tata nkisi) of Palo, "worship Arara deities of Ewe-Fon (Dahomey) origin, become an *abonekue* (member) of the Abakua society, the sacred brotherhood of Old Calabar origin, as well as rise through the ranks of the Masons, rely on Rosicrucian geomancy, and take communion in the Catholic church."[29] The dual induction into Palo and Santeria would entail one being initiated into Palo first, and later into Santeria; the opposite is usually not allowed, because of the jealousy of the orishas. This religious envy could be likened to the vigilance in the Catholic Church over its ministry. If one is ordained a Catholic priest, it is easier for him to be an adept in the rituals of ATRs simultaneously than the other way around. A clear exception is early nineteenth-century Haiti, where Vodou *oungans* served freely as priests in abandoned Catholic parishes in the wake of the revolution.

While seeking spiritual guidance through the use of both Palo and Santeria services, initiates generally keep the Palo spirits at a great distance from the orishas, because it is believed that the ancestral and nature spirits are fierce; they are considered fearless and unruly entities of the forest. As Brown notes, in pictures with Palo insignias, "the Warriors' rustic and fierce iconography of war, hunting, and the countryside is made up of implements analogous to those carried by their forest counterparts in the 'strong' Palo Monte religion (hooked staffs ... knives, machetes, and 'charged' animal horns ...)."[30] Because it is a stronger earth energy, for example, the prenda or nganga receptacle is kept outside in a shed, in a cellar, or close to nature, whereas the orisha is kept largely in the house, probably in the bedroom. It is not unusual for a palero (leader) to follow both Palo and Santeria, utilizing the myths and implements of each faith as complements in his practice.[31] How much intermixing is allowed between the two groups depends completely on who is involved as well as their personal interpretation of what is correct or appropriate.

As its practitioners cross the religious lines, Palo incorporates concepts, terms, names, practices, and devotees of Santeria. Maria Teresa Velez's in formant, Felipe Garcia Villamil, whose father strictly practiced Palo, said, "My father didn't believe in Santeria, he only believed in the pot (prenda or nganga) and nothing else. And I made santo [became an initiate of Santeria] quite late because of him."[32] The relation between Santeria and Palo in a devotee is therefore dynamic; some avatars freely mix the two in a religious eclecticism typically shared by Palo followers. Cuban curator Gerardo Mosquera puts it this way: in Cuba, along with one's own religious tradition, "every *santero* considers himself also a Catholic, and in addition he may be a palero, an Abakua, and a Freemason, without contradictions, in a system of coexisting fragments."[33] These eclectic fragments are important features of multiethnic Palo.

Instances such as these, where one person finds harmony by blending the two Afro-Cuban traditions whereas another strictly forbids it, are representative of the reality present in the acephalous structure of each faith. Neither Palo nor Santeria has a central authority who controls what is accepted and what is not. The only notion of hierarchy rests inside a single temple, with the priest, and not among the following as a whole. This is another reason why such great diversity exists within the religion. As these intricacies have intensified over the years, it is not surprising to find people (such as Velez's Felipe) with a heterogeneous mixture of backgrounds who still remain loyal to their religion and traditions in their own eclectic way. With the clear spirit of individuality at the heart of Palo, the diversity within its defining features continued to expand as assimilation between Kongo groups became more widespread. Likewise, within local Cuban communities, borrowing from the many groups surrounding the religion's practitioners added to the complexity of the groups' beliefs and ritual traditions.

Marshaling Spirits of Fragments

During the period of Atlantic slavery and ensuing colonialism, enslaved Africans from the Bantu-Kongo region were able to bond, in various ethnic enclaves, to form survival and cultural groups within Cuba. Although they hybridized in what Fernando Oritz calls an *ajiaco,*[34] a "rich soup of varied ingredients," some of their traditions remained somewhat distinct, and different ethnic "nations" blended with those who had original traditions and languages most closely resembling their own from Africa. As with Santeria, the first large organized groups of a general nature, the cabildos, allowed Africans of Kongo and other ancestry to collaborate in celebrating their cultural traditions and addressing social concerns. This cooperation afforded them an opportunity to express themselves publicly through ritual, music, and dance, with the reluctant blessings of the Catholic Church and the Spanish Government; the latter became increasingly more disinclined than the church in the later colonial period. Afro-Cubans were able to perform initiation rites, wakes, and other ceremonies[35] that, in the hostile Cuban plantation environment, kept their religion alive through cultural appreciation. This was often done secretly but, more often than not, under the umbrella of church-state initiated or endorsed brotherhoods or cabildos. Barnet observes that throughout the colonial period and "for sometime afterwards, there were numerous *cabildos* of all nations in Havana, the smaller towns and provincial capitals. Among these were: the Congas which comprised: Basongo, Mumbona, Bateke, Mundemba, Bakongo, Musabela, Kabinda, Bayaka, Benguela, Mondongo, Myombe, Ngola and so forth."[36] The African Kongo connection in this multitude of ethnic names is unmistakable.

Accommodation and Organization

Cabildos established in the Havana and Matanzas provinces had both sociocultural and political functions, serving as clubs and mutual aid societies [...] for Kongo peoples. David Brown records that urban slaves, especially, "had the advantages of mobility, greater labor options, wider liberty in social and sexual conduct, access to certain legal protections ... and the organized presence of the African nations in the *cabildo* system"; these resulted in much stronger African institutions in those centers.[37] Among the cabildo groups that became famous and well known throughout Cuba during the colonial period, perhaps the most notable was the "Congas Reales." It had some of "the most striking regalia and musical performance at the traditional epiphany festivities in Havana."[38] Kongo cabildos, in some communities, were referred to euphemistically as "kingdoms of the forest" because, on their Day of the Kings, the "festivities were exceedingly good, the best; no expense was spared on items of luxury. The King wore a frock coat and a sword and sat on a throne beside his Queen, surrounded by [their] courtiers. There, they ruled in the African style";[39] this, notwithstanding their captive condition and the fact that Kongo "royal and military attributes and processionals were regarded as mere imitations, as if the participants were impostors and buffoons playing at prestige and authority on their one day of the year to be king—their 'only day of freedom'"[40] and revelry.

Like the cabildos of Santeria, these allowed Kongo peoples to remain organized and unified in true African fashion, yet still distinct in their various groups. This was the people's main outlet for cultural spontaneity, creativity, and identity. Through the organized cabildos, the Congas were better able to reconstruct, enact, and remember their lost cultures, religion, and "ethnic nations." According to Matory, "The late 18th and 19th centuries were in fact a time when both American territorial units (such as Brazil, Cuba, and British colonial North America) and transoceanically dispersed black ethnic groups (such as the Nago, Jeje, Angola and Congo) were becoming 'nations' for themselves,"[41] but they did so in a context of distress. Accommodated since the sixteenth century as an extended arm of the Catholic Church, Conga *cofradias* were in their heyday in the eighteenth to nineteenth centuries. At that time, the "sticks" or fragments of the spirit of Palo thrived under the pennant of African culture, the church, and the Spanish flag. On days of celebration, Cuban Kongo Flag bearers, dancers, and singers paraded in jubilation, honoring country, god(s), and African culture.

In spite of the measurable success and role of the cabildos [...], Afro-Cuban identity and religious expressions were complex and tenuous peculiarities in a highly stratified colonial Cuban society. Brown captures the essence of this anomaly when he writes of Havana's leader of the Kongo cabildos, the enslaved King Siliman, who, during the French War of 1808, addressed his *afrocubanos* constituency as men (Senores) of "*Conga, Luango, Lucumi, Arara, Macua, Fanti, Mandinga, Mina, Brichi, Mondongo, and Intuanza,*" passionately urging them to support Spain, Cuba, Christianity, and their ATRs against Napoleon's imperialistic ambitions:

> The esteemed royal head of a *cabildo* of the Congo nation (*nacion*), Siliman. ... A historically conscious participant in a global struggle for the New World, Siliman officially identified himself as a passionate royal subject, the servant of a vast, divinely sanctioned chain of authority called the Bourbon Empire (Spain, God, Jesus Christ, The Church, King Ferdinand VII, along with Cuba ... and its African nations), which seemed threatened by Napoleon and his godless armies. Yet, Siliman's unique vision of future freedom carefully balances a series of goods and rights on parity with the whites, with specific markers of African cultural and social continuity. ...[42]

This is reminiscent of African Americans being spurred to defend the Union and to preserve its religious, cultural, and political traditions in 1776, 1812, and 1861 while the said institutions held them enslaved. Both African groups saw their future freedoms intertwined with the preservation of the sovereignty and liberties of the state—that is, preserve the one to obtain the other.

On the eve of the Wars of Independence, however, ATRs were forbidden, and Palo, like Lucumi, lost an important cultural, spiritual, and political forum and vehicle. State censorship and persecution followed the wars. After a short hiatus (about three decades), the state resumed its persecution of Afro-Cuban religions. Brown notes:

> After 1875, increasingly in the 1880s, and with an unprecedented ferocity between the first American occupation of the island (1899–1902) and the early 1920s, the government not only scrutinized but also attacked the "internal essence" of Afro-Cuban organizations. This took the direct form of state "persecution against *naniguismo* and other religious customs of African origin." ... Havana's

Lucumi and Palo practitioners did not fare well. From the end of the nineteenth century, the houses of Lucumi and Palo Monte priests ... were the special targets of ferocious police raids intended to stamp out *brujeria* (witchcraft).[43]

In addition to the bad fate Kongo fraternities suffered, the "specter of *cabildo* royalty may have provoked a certain anxiety in observers who could not reconcile" it with the participants' servitude.[44] The despised institutions therefore languished under political, ecclesiastical, and other restrictions and persecutions. As a result, Palo and other African religions went underground.

In modern Cuba, Africans again contend with their tenuous situation and unpredictable accommodation within restrictions imposed by Castro's Revolutionary Government. At first, the revolution advocated elimination of all class structures and institutional and cultural racism through the promotion of *cubanidad,* a single Cuban identity regardless of class, race, national origin or ethnicity, as propounded earlier by the nationalist "hero/institution" Jose Marti. Afro-Cuban religions and cultures were, on the surface, assimilated as, according to Palmie, "creolised manifestations ... into the project of building a synthetically conceived national identity" [45] early in the revolution. This welcomed accommodation was very brief. Shortly after 1959, and well into the mid 1990s, as Erica Moret discovered, faith-based practices were disinclined and greatly restricted, "largely because of a supposed incompatibility of religion with Marxism"; the "restrictions on religious practices extended to prohibitions on the use of plants in Afro-Cuban religions and cults—typically suppressed through arguments relating to the use of 'witchcraft' or *brujeria.*" [46] Practitioners of Afro-Cuban religions, again, had to find innovative means for their religious expression; so they formed smaller "houses" that could survive away from the watchful gaze of Castro's political informants.

In post-Soviet Cuba, intimates Moret, the Government took a reverse course, as it was forced to initiate "widespread economic restructuring" in the late 1980s and 1990s to deal with a crisis of unprecedented proportion in Cuba's health-care system. Led by the head of the Armed Forces and the Ministry of Health, Rual Castro, the government—as did the World Health Organization and the Ghanian government in the mid-1980s—sought to utilize "domestic and 'traditional' forms of knowledge" to address its medical crisis.[47] Cuba's government initiated a nationwide shift in health-care provision that would embrace traditional medicine. Moret reports that "as a consequence, ethnobotanical knowledge underwent a dramatic process of state-ordained validation ... throughout the island. The government began to encourage the use and cultivation of medical plants in homes, schools, hospitals, work places and medical facilities." [48] Although the Castro regime kept African religions on its restricted list, the knowledge of pharmacopeia by African ritual specialists' was suddenly at a premium and the religions had a respite.

Palo Cosmology

Zambi (Nsambi)

No pantheon of divinities cross-dressing as Catholic saints exists in Palo. Followers venerate and court the help of one god and many spirits of ancestors, nature, and the dead—summoned in special ways, depending on the occasion and on what ceremonies Kongo groups and individual practitioners are observing. God, or *Zambi*, who created and governs the world, is the highest and most powerful spiritual entity. Outside of this central deity is the diverse array of ancestral and nature spirits termed *minkisi inquics* and *mpungas* (also called *mfumbe*, *fumbe*, or *muertos*), each of which has a special name designation.[49] Minkisi are powerful spirits of ancestors resembling the orisha and the Vodou lwa. Palo does not entertain a pantheon of deities, but some avatars and their spiritual communities give their nkisi divine characteristics adopted from Cuban orishas. The most popular minkisi are *tiembla tierra* (a spirit who helps rule the world); *madre agua* (a female spirit who mothers waters and new life); *mama chola* (a spirit of beauty, libidinous love, and rivers); *lucero* (a joker or prankster messenger of God); *zarabanda* (a spirit of metal and conflict or battle); *centella* (a spirit of grave yards); and *siete rayos* (a spirit of fire, lightning, electricity, and other dangerous elements). This cosmology is not common in all Palo houses, or *munaso(s)*. The nature spirits and the ancestral spirits inhabit, or are lodged in, various vessels given the multivalent name nganga, which possess nkisi charms and divine force or spiritual power, the equivalence of *axe* in the Yoruba-influenced religions of Santeria, Orisha, and Candomble.

Mpungus

It is a tribute to their resilience that, despite the borrowing and sharing that took place—and that involved the characteristics of the Yoruba pantheon of spirits, the forms of spiritual practice in Santeria, and the influence of the surrounding Catholicism—the Cuban Kongo people kept their cosmology separate from that of their African counterparts and different from that of colonial Christianity. Palo's cosmology incorporates God, spirits of nature and of the dead, humans, and other creatures and things in the phenomenal world. The Palo spirits are generally referred to by several names: a name in the Palo tradition, a creole or Kongo-Cuban name, a name in the Yoruba-based Lucumi, and a name in Cuban Spanish. For example, *mpungas*, "spirits of deceased ancestors and forces of nature," are given names such as *Nsasi*, *Sarabanda*, and *Baluande*.[50] These have characteristic traits that give them the aura of individual deities. Some *mpungu* are associated with objects, like a clay pot, iron and steel, and colors. The mpungu is awakened and summoned, by the smoke from lighted gun powder, to participate in a ceremony. When mpungu and nkisi "axe"—drawn from animals, herbs, fossils, or a special type of soil—combines with the nganga, they are said to produce or channel powerful forces to be harnessed by the palero in magic and healing.

Tata-Palero

A practitioner of Palo who communicates with God, the spirits, and the phenomenal world is known as a palero; the term denotes someone who follows the religion as well as one who functions as a leader. Initiates affectionately called the priests *tata* ("papa") and *yaya* ("mama"), and the place of their ritual activity is a *munanso* ("house"). *Palero* is a Cuban creole designation that parallels and replicates the roles of the Kongo *kitomi*, a public religious leader, and the nganga, the private spiritualist.[51] Not much difference exists between the Cuban palero and the West African traditional priest, who are both adepts at employing receptacles of power in rituals and at procuring healing for the well-being of clients. Conga groups are lead by a master of divination, known affectionately as tata nganga, essentially the palero, a keeper of the traditions. This avatar directs the spiritual operation as the village shaman or priest would. Although there is a spiritual hierarchy within each temple, ultimately practitioners function independently of each other or in accord with oral traditions inherited from their forebears or ancestors. Since Palo, as "sticks of the forest," envisions different spirits thought to inhabit sacred objects from nature, or the forest, its leader "works with the earth, forest branches, stones, animals and all kinds of plants and objects. They assist him in the spells that he uses to save his clients. ... These elements are the vehicles through which the palero can articulate his ritual language"[52] both to communicate with the spirit and to mystify or aid adherents.

Most paleros command a limited Kikango vocabulary, used in the weekly rituals and divinatory sessions they conduct. According to van Wetering and van Velzen, the fact that adepts have to perform ceremonies to the spirits provides paleros and priests opportunities to give speeches using "sacred" Kikango words. Their competence in the language may vary and the words they speak are often equivocal, "glossed over, or unduly accelerated, but a command of the sacred idiom is nevertheless a way of gaining prestige and a sign of belonging to this network of male devotees."[53] In the same vein, the names of the deities, "sacred objects, and the recurrent phrases of invocation are made common knowledge through songs that resound through the three wards in the town where most adepts live"[54] and operate in Cuba. Paleros do not form a distinct group like santeros "in any strict sense, but are recruited as individuals, and they are predominantly men. They come from diverse social backgrounds, often do not know each other, and are highly mixed ethnically"[55] and socially.

Summoning the Spirits

A palero has a different relationship with the spirit than that of a santero or santera. Palo spiritualists attempt to control the actions of spiritual powers (except the Creator God), including spirits of the deceased. While Santeria requires a continuous commitment or marriage to a divinity, Palo negotiates a "more occasional and intermittent sacred pact with a spirit. The spirit is summoned when needed, being a magical enforcer who carries out one's will."[56] When required, paleros call directly on the spirits of nature and the dead to do their bidding: these spirits can be summoned for healing purposes, considered either nocuous or beneficent. Palo's spirit engagement shares a similarity with Santeria in that its magic can be either constructive or malicious, but the manner and frequency with which the paleros call on the spirit constitutes a significant difference between the two. They summon the spirit more erratically and, although possession plays an important role in Palo's ceremony, its leader, representing the Kongo nganga, does not seek to be possessed or controlled by a spirit, as do priests and priestesses in Santeria. Instead, *perros* (mediums called "dogs" or servants) are the ones that experience possession. Similar to Santeria, temples have members who are initiated to become *perros* or *criados* ("servants") of the spirit.

Paleros control and dominate the small spiritual world signified in the nganga (the cauldron made of clay or iron). Legend has it that the *kiyumba,* or human skull, regarded as essential and a most potent aspect of many ngangas, controls all the herbal plants and animals that are associated with the receptacle. "The *mayombero* or palero, in turn, rules the kiyumba, who obeys his orders like a faithful dog. The kiyumba is the slave for the mayombero and it is always waiting inside the cauldron or the *macuto* to carry out his commands."[57] This master-servant-dog relationship seems to echo a lingering vestige of the slave colonial culture in Cuba. The characterization shows also a view of the palero as a sorcerer, manipulating the spirits in order to get his way. Other sources reveal a complex relationship between the palero and the spirit; or go a step further and describe an act of veneration of the various divinities with which they are in contact. Thus, the palero exhibits at least three dispositions: (1) he has mutual relations with the spirit, (2) venerates the highest being, and (3) dominates the spirit housed inside the nganga to his own ends. A palero specializes in performing healing with the use of magic charms and is regarded as the owner of the nganga (in fact, he is often called the nganga) that produces the magical charms. After a ritual ceremony, it is believed that a spirit of the dead is captured in this caldron of charms; the owner of the pot becomes the master and the spirit does the master's will, performing either good or punitive deeds.

Participation/Initiation

Participation

Palo has evolved into a loosely organized institution with great fluidity in the constituency of its membership. Groups are formed around a temple house (*munanso*) and a tata or palero, but one "adopts the religion and its values in an individualistic manner, relying on his own personal viewpoint, and on the traditions of his family or clan."[58] A follower establishes a relationship directly with the power he or she venerates. Implicit in this design are ways in which individual perspectives function in interpreting exactly what it means to become a follower of Palo. A tata nganga may be involved in the process of attracting someone to the traditions, and one's family ancestry may influence one's participation, but in the end, the personal relationship between a practitioner and the spirit is of paramount importance. As Bettelheim records, "The 'rayados,' those sworn into the

Congo Reglas ... consider themselves united by a sacred bond of mystical kinship and, like them, speak and pray in their language," both Yoruba and Kongo.[59]

It has already been noted here that Palo and Santeria participants cross the religious lines with ease. Some paleros are knowledgeable of Santeria's ritual practices and its veneration of Catholic saints, and participate in both religions. Often, little difference is seen among followers of both faiths. As Brown records, tata gaitan, "a priest of the Lucumi hunter-deity, Ochosi," was "also a powerful Tata Nkisi, a priest of the Regla de Congo or Palo Monte. During the late nineteenth century, ... 'many *babalawos* had their *prendas* [Congo sacred cauldrons] in order to protect themselves' "[60] from harmful forces. Brown interjects that tata gaitan has a huge property and a home with guest quarters

> for scores of *babalawo* colleagues, and Ocha, Ifa, and Palo godchildren, who [travel] from as far as Palmira, in Cuba's interior, to undergo initiation and work the religion in Guanabacoa. Undoubtedly, Tata was multilingual: he not only spoke Spanish, but also utilized the Lucumi, Congo, and Abakua Bricamo languages, as well as communicated in bozal with living African-born inhabitants or creoles and the spirits of the dead who would posses their mediums.[61]

This fluidity of membership in various African religions poses no problem to one's participation in Palo. Juan Boza, a priest in Kongo religion and an artist from Camaguey, Cuba, reports that he, like many others, grew up with a variety of religious influences and traditions that formed his ritual and cultural "aesthetics" and identity. Boza confesses, "The patrimony of my religion through the language of Yoruba, the Congo, and Carabaldi are united and incarnated through different rituals. The bilingualism compounded by existential secretiveness is inevitably called upon at the time of sacred creation."[62] As Arturo Lindsay records, Jose Bedia, another Cuban American artist and emblematic Palo initiate, acknowledges that, like other Cubans, he also experienced Lucumi[63] without any conflict of interest or concerns. Participation in Palo is open to followers of other faiths, but initiation is essential for avatars.

Initiation

As practiced in most religions, initiation is the most fundamental and important ceremony for a *rayado* or *ngueyo* in Palo; a *rayado* or ngueyo is sometimes labeled a "*bozal*."[64] Among the important ritual symbols that Palo adopted from Santeria, and which are employed in initiation, the *ndungui* ("coconut rind") and *chamalongos* ("shells") oracles stand out. Like santeros, paleros employ those symbolic oracles for divination: to arrive at answers to questions they inquire of the spirit, to prognosticate or reveal hidden secrets, and to divine one's condition, fate or destiny. A Santeria ritual expert occasionally refers clients to a Palo specialist for consultation or healing therapy. At an initial meeting before initiation, the tata performs a consultation by tossing the four pieces of coconut rinds. This is one of three types of divinatory oracles, employed on the basis of the kind of questions posed on behalf of an initiate-to-be. Cowrie shells (adopted from Lucumi) and gunpowder are also used as divinatory oracles. "This initial divination session determines if one is going to become a ngueyo, the first level of initiated participation in Palo, or a tata, the highest level." [65]

Often, the tata-palero's divinatory science, called Kongo magic, is little more than guesswork; it is a luck-and-chance tossing of the coconut rinds, or objects catching fire from other objects. For the practitioners and clients, however, they are efficacious enough to engage the tata in performance. The tata performs the initiation of the ngueyo or *bozal*, which requires necessary preparation and ritual paraphernalia. During the periods of state persecution, followers greeted each other in codes, the initiation was performed in secrecy, and the area of the *munanso* or *casa-templo* ("temple house") had to be protected from the police and political informants. The *casa-templo* must be guarded ritually against contamination. This is done by situating small packets called *makutos* and *masango* at the four corners of the sacred precinct. *Masango*, made of corn husk, earth from the four cardinal directions, and extract from the nganga cauldron, are ritually cleansed before they are lodged in the four corners of the sacred property. [66]

Before the initiation ceremony commences fully, the *munanso* and *casatemplo* are made sacred through a symbolic ritual of the drawing of a *firma* ("a signature, a composite name, a cosmogram") on the wall or the ground floor of the house, in front of the cauldron. [67] "These firmas often incorporate Kongo-derived references to the circling of the sun around the earth and to the Kalunga line, or horizon line," as symbolized in the Kongo yowa cross, and "to the Kalunga line, or the horizon line, the division between heaven and earth." [68] The firma includes a combination of arrows, circles, crosses, lines, and other parts representing the physical universe, such as the sun and the moon. These symbolic designs come together to give the firma its ritual power. The firma, resembling "the veve of Haitian Vodou in form and function, is an essential act in the ritual. Without the firma, the *mpungus* do not have a path into the ceremony, and communication with them will not occur"; [69] therefore worship will not be effectual.

Firmas seem pervasive. Each *casa-templo* has a specific firma to be used by a ngueyo initiated into that house. Every *mpungu* has its personal firma, which is appealed to when the spirit or its nganga is actively summoned. Each palero also has his own firma representation. Other firmas are personal and must not be copied, or else negative consequences result. The devotees believe that the act of drawing firmas on the back and chest of an initiate during the ceremony puts the ngueyo at the center of life's force and power. As is done in a Santeria initiation, the ngueyo must learn the signs and complex meanings of the firmas and other receptacles of power. The initiation ceremony, which last at least seven days, is fraught with rituals and symbolism. The initiate is purified with a ritual cleansing bath called the *limpieza* or *omiero*, made of seven, fourteen, and twenty-one special herbal leaves mixed in water; the multiples of sevens and the naming of the bath are patterned after the Santeria iyawo initiation ritual. During the herbal bath, the ngueyo is stripped, and walks in a circular motion while he or she is washed from the neck down. The tata-palero rips the initiate's clothes and ritually discards them, as a sign of the dying of the old self. According to Bettelheim, twenty-one "palos" are "placed around the circumference of an nganga"; and "twenty-one paths of energy" are said to emanate from firmas "drawn as an arrow with twenty-one intersecting marks."[70]

A stick and a machete are used to mark the location of incisions that the initiate will later receive on the chest and back. Then the ngueyo is led into the initiation room proper for the next phase of the ceremony, the *rayamiento,* which he submits to while blindfolded to prove sincerity, commitment, and courage. When the ngueyo opens his eyes at the conclusion of the ceremony, the first thing he should see is a reflection of his new self in a mirror. The ngueyo rises from his knees to be greeted by the tata-palero and those who assisted him. In Jose Bedia's initiation, which Bettelheim narrates, the tata and his assistants welcomed their new member "with the special Palo handshake, saying: Salaam malekum! malekum salaam!" This Muslim greeting opened and concluded the ceremony,[71] in that *casa-templo.* The initiate is admitted to the faith at the climax of the initiation and accepts a spirit of the nganga pot or prenda*;* this is a vital receptacle of spiritual power in which his very personal nkisi is lodged.[72] The tata-palero prepares the newly initiated for service as a medium who allows the spirit to use him or her as a vessel of communication and a source of spiritual power.

Receptacles of Power

An interconnectedness between spirit, nature, ancestors, and flesh, or humans, is at the heart of Palo and is contained in, as well as communicated through, many spirit power-generating receptacles. All spiritual activities and actions—whether initiations, divinations, healings, spirit possessions, or the procuring of charms—are channeled through these sacred objects. They function as indispensable mythic and putative symbols of the religion. The most popular receptacles of power are nkisi or minkisi (objects of sacred charms); nganga (a pot or cauldron); *funza* (sacred medicines); *fula* (gunpowder); *ndungui* (a coconut); firmas (magic symbols); prenda (a divination receptacle); *vititi mensu* (a small mirror); *miyumba* (a human skull); and *macuto* (a form of pot), among others. Practitioners and initiates own objects which, in turn, provide them with a source or avenue to power and a means of spiritual communication.

Negotiating Palo Power

Nkisi

Among the African Kongo, nkisi (plural minkisi) or *masango* were object-charms that practitioners held sacrosanct because they were charged with spiritual power for defense.[73] Wyatt MacGaffey notes that their visible form, intended to signify the presence of controlled masked forces, took the form of "an anthropomorphic or zoomorphic figure, an animal horn, a clay pot, a basket, and many others. The container itself is a mere object, until animated by 'medicines,' " and can adopt personal mannerisms: it can be flattered, petitioned, actuated, insulted, and humiliated.[74] According to African scholar T. J. Desch-Obi, in pre-colonial Africa these were used as charms that offered protection against certain forces and misfortune. Among these were "group charms, such as the Imbangala *maji minkisi*," and sacred medicines "given by God the creator"; Africans took these "to protect themselves from sorcerers (*ndoki*) who used witchcraft to effect evil in the world."[75] Legend has it that "the first *nkisi* called Funza originated in God, and Funza came with a great number of *minkisi*, which he distributed throughout the country [of Congo], each with its respective powers, governing" its specific domain.[76]

Desch-Obi believes that enslaved Africans and their descendants, trained in the martial arts, "held on to this understanding of spiritual preparation for combat" in the Americas. "Group combat preparation rituals were an important part of many slave revolts such as the Haitian Revolution"; they were "influenced by Kongo-Angolan martial technologies" used in battle. It "began with spiritual preparation, referred to as *wanga* charms, and ritual specialists accompanied the troops."[77] A Palo nkisi object is a symbolic representation and metaphor for the harnessing and use of spiritual force to avenge hostile acts or to defend one against such malicious actions. This scheme is often effectuated by psychological angst, rather than by actual medical harm, because minkisi are not always noxious; a good nkisi brings good fortune.

Nganga

As for the physical manifestation, where flesh meets spirit in Palo, the nganga (or *cazuela*) or prenda, the cauldron that supposedly houses the spirits, is at the epicenter of spiritual force. This Kongo signifying object is Palo's main receptacle of power; here, "poles, grasses, earth, animal and human remains, pieces of iron, stones, signs, objects, spirits and deities are arranged in a sort of summoning up of the cosmos."[78] Back in the Kongo, a nganga was a private individual spiritualist, or diviner, who had sacred powers to work secret magic and sorcery but could function occasionally in public roles [...]. In addition to assisting individuals in dealing with hardship, the nganga often acted as a rainmaker, supposedly procured cures for epidemics, gave assurances of good luck, and performed other functions on behalf of the community at large. He was seen as a type of priest, although there were "differences in ceremonial usage between a *nganga a ngombo's* activities for private persons and those of the public."[79] Since a nganga could make foreboding magic, he was kept at a distance and treated with respect as well as dread. Beatriz Morales holds that "Congolese magicians and sorcerers developed a powerful role. ... The ability to communicate with the dead, and to use medicine to cure and harm, made them major figures in maintaining social harmony, but also in disrupting the social order."[80] For this they were greatly feared. Christian missionaries to the Kongo viewed minkisi with derision and prohibited converted nganga from possessing or retaining the sacred objects, which were believed to be symbols of evil African paganism and witchcraft.

In Cuba, nganga amassed a baffling array of significations and meanings. The name symbolizes the spirit itself, the pot used to house the spirit, the objects that act as "signifiers," and the symbols of a religious role and role player in the religion, among others. Nganga is a spirit, a deceased individual, a supernatural power or force, a receptacle, ornamental rapping around the cauldron, and even "a sack of Russian cloth ... in which is deposited a skull and human bones, earth from the cemetery ... sticks, herbs, bowls, bones of birds and animals."[81] Nganga is also the precinct where the practitioners house and ritually utilize the objects they have collected; they arrange them in a symbolic manner that will aide in summoning the spirit to action. While the nganga refers to the pot itself, as well as to "the power of the pot," it is also the one who owns the pot. "It is a word in miniature, and when one is initiated into the final level in Palo, one receives a personal nganga. Thus, initiation makes nganga—both the priest and the pot." [82] In Cuba, "the most carefully preserved, and the most respected and feared Kongo element, is that of magic. The main source of this magical power is the palero's ability to make contact with the spirit of a dead person and to control it and make it work for him,"[83] or his client and *perros*, with the use of nganga.

The nganga is the most focal point of the palero's practice. From one perspective, the Cuban prenda represents the knowledge that paleros acquired from those who initiated them into the Palo religion. A Cuban tale holds that these nganga*s* or prenda*s* were the only inheritance the ancestors could leave their children because they "had no wealth, land, or property. ... The only possession they had was their culture—the knowledge of their rituals, the use of herbs," and the divination systems that are "symbolized by the prenda."[84] Prendas and ngangas are unique to each individual practitioner; once one is initiated, the initiate is given an individually owned nganga, which can be "born" only from a previously existing one. According to Bettelheim, "In the service of Palo Monte, the initiate accumulates power through the objects he or she deposits in the nganga."[85] By creating and using a nganga, a practitioner is entering into an agreement with the spirit held therein. Although the nature of the relationship, and the way it is interpreted, differ from person to person, there is a general understanding that the spirit will be helpful, or will "work" for the palero in some unique ways. The Cuban nganga fits the profile of the Kongo private spiritualist as well as the sorcerer, but his work and role in Palo are creole; they are best seen in the palero and in the healing and making of magic charms.[86]

Symbolic Oracles

Cuban Cosmographic Yowa Cross

Perhaps the most intriguing ritual signification in Palo is its preservation of the multivalent Bakongo cross. This cosmographic symbol, prominent in African Kongo death rites, portends a cosmological reality and existence in the world of the deceased, guided by the spirits, for the extension of life in the beyond. MacGaffey records that in Palo, as in the African Kongo, practitioners symbolize the cosmos as this encircled spherical cross showing four equal portions cleaved and clearly marked and having a time clock at the fulcrum. They label the four points of the cross in cardinal and elemental directions, exactly as was done in Mayombe Congo. The position pointing upward to the sky is *nsulu (ku zulu)*. The *ensiafua*, or *kumangongo*, points to "the deep of the earth," or the "land of the dead." The *nototo*, "the earth," is the position on the cross that corresponds to 6:00 P.M. on the clock. The *kalunga*, "the ocean," is the opposite point of the cross that corresponds to 6:00 A.M. on the clock.[87]

Since the cross predates the Christian era, and is present in the ancient Greek and Roman civilizations, Dianne Stewart thinks it is probably one of the oldest religious cultural icons in Africa. It "symbolizes the holistic spiritual and philosophical orientation regarding [the] visible-invisible sacred cosmos, which is normative for many classical African societies." [88] Of the cross in Kongo religion, Robert Ferris Thompson writes: "The simplest ritual space is a Greek cross [+] marked on the ground, as for oath-taking. One line represents the boundary; the other is ambivalently both the path leading across the boundary, as to the cemetery; and the vertical path of power linking 'the above' with the 'below.' " [89] Thompson proffers the view that the circle around "the Kongo cross refers to the everlasting continuity of all righteous men and women" in the mystery of life.[90] The special import that the *yowa* cross served in Mayombe Kongo seems preserved in Cuba, although creole elements have been added to its multivalent meaning. Scholars suspect that the taking of oaths in some Afro-Caribbean religions was influenced by the Kongo *yowa* cross signification. In addition to being used in the swearing of oats and the pledging of allegiance, the cross as symbol points to the memory of ancestral spirits in the land of the beyond and represents the summoning of invisible mystical powers in the visible world through ritual. Thus the cross may function to attract and focus the spirit in the ceremonies, the same way that drawing the firma in Palo and the vive of Haitian Vodou focus the power.

Vititi Mensu

Other oracles unique to Palo are the *fula* ("gunpowder"), the *vititi mensu* ("small mirror"), and the *macuto*. Maria Valez explains how the *fula* is used: the priest places a number of "small piles of gunpowder over a board, or over the floor, in a ritually separate space. A question is formulated, and the palero sets one of the pile bundles on fire; according to the number of piles that catch fire, the answer to the question is considered positive or negative."[91] The other oracle, *vititi mensu* (*mpuka mensu*)—a receptacle of the "power of Kongo, made of an animal horn filled with religious substances and covered by a mirror"—is said to "reproduce … the flesh of the spirit"[92] that situates the palero in contact with the world of spiritual power and gives him a glimpse into the other world. The palero reads the *vititi mensu* by filling the mirror with smoke soot from a candle, and proceeding to interpret the various shapes formed from it.[93] Descriptions like these demonstrate the diverse practices in Palo as a whole, but they also illuminate some similarities and differences between it and Santeria.

Makutos

Other components of Palo important to its ritual function are those of music and two sets of magical symbols called *macuto* or *makuto*. Music plays a significant role in the religion's celebrations, initiations, funerary rites, and rituals, where its sacrifices are performed to feed the *mpungas*, or the spirits associated with objects made from iron or steel.[94] As the ceremonies themselves are generally less elaborate than those of Santeria, the music is also less complex; it does not revolve around special rhythms, chants, and dances for each spirit or deity. The palero has a collection of *mambos* ("chants") that are sung by a leader during rituals, as well as special drums unique to Palo ritual music.[95] As in other religions, the drums summon the spirits, announce their arrival, and dispatch them at the appropriate time.

A Palo *macuto*, like the nganga, is a complex symbolic oracle. In its simplest form, it is a small sacrosanct bundle made of vegetable and other ingredients ritually sanctified and imbued with protective medicines. In its superstitious world, many taboos surround the *macuto's* efficaciousness. A *macuto* is also an individually owned receptacle of the spirit of empowerment that manifests in ways pertinent to an initiate's pressing circumstances. Commenting on Marta Maria Perez's *macuto* receptacle of power, demonstrated in a 1991 art photo of a woman clasping an object across her unclothed breast, artist Gerardo Mosquera writes, "She gathers within the object the two dolls she has used in earlier works to represent her twin girls, using her chest as a hierophanic space, sacralized by means of one of those ritual drawings of Palo Monte," seen "so often in Bedia's works."[96] Mosquera concludes, "In this case, it is the 'sign of the four moments of the sun,' 'sign of signs,' foundation of everything: a graphic synthesis of *yowa* or Kongo cosmogony, which serves to activate the center of power, marking the very eye of the cosmos, [a uniquely] privileged point where the object that is prepared may acquire force."[97] Here symbol and auricle converge in ritual space to generate spiritual power and deep religious meaning.

Conclusion

Palo and its Cuban cognates are undoubtedly among the most distinctly Kongo religious traditions in the Caribbean. The religion's language and vocabulary, philosophical concepts, and religious practices are so different from Yorubabased religion (and Christianity) that for a long time it remained less popular, less known, more suspect, and more greatly suppressed as *brujeria* than Lucumi was. Like other Afro-Cuban religions, persecution sent Palo underground and contributed to its national isolation, but also to its cultural preservation. After Castro's regime lifted its ban on Afro-Cuban religions as a means of dealing with its mammoth economic and health crises at the end of the last millennium, the religion reemerged to be among the now popularly sought "forbidden African religions." As Moret observes, Cubans and foreigners alike seek initiation and pharmacopeia from "*paleros, santeros, babalawos,* and *espiritista*." Under state-organized "folkloric" tours, tourist are now enthusiastically ferried to the once damned Palo *casa-templo* in Palmira (as elsewhere) "to experience mocked-religious ceremonies, or, according to a *Ruta del Esclavo* [slave route] museum guide, a consultation with a local babalawo" [98] or palero. Because of practitioners' creative artistic expression, the religion is also a huge source of attraction for "culturalists" and art historians' articulation of Cuban culture. Art exhibitions on Palo and other Afro-Cuban religions are now educational staples of diversity in our cultural diets, brought into most world communities through the omnipresent Internet and the economic gods of international cooperation. In Cuba, Palo Monte Mayombe and Congas Reglas will continue to compete for cultural space and appreciation with the well-established Santeria and more newly arrived traditions, such as Espiritismo and Rastafari.

Notes

1. Judith Bettelheim, "Palo Monte Mayombe and Its Influence on Cuban Contemporary Art," *African Arts* 34, no. 2 (Summer 2001): 2; also available at EBSCOhost.com.

2. "Palo (religion)," available at Wikipedia.org/wiki/Palo-Myombe, 1 (accessed October 2, 2008). The popular but marginally reliable encyclopedia points to a study done by Eric M. Miletti on Palo Monte.

3. Dianne Stewart of Emory University (2005), Terry Rey (who gave a trenchant and insightful review of my manuscript), Kenneth Bilby (at the Smithsonian Institution), two other scholars who participated in the blind review process of my manuscript, and others.

4. Kenneth Bilby, "Review of Jesus Fuentes Guerra and Armin Schweler, *Legua y ritos del Palo Monte Mayombe: dioses cubanos y sus fuentes africanas,*" *Journal of the Royal Anthropological Institute* (N.S.) 12: 957–1003 (2006): 979; also available at EBSCOhost.com, 979.

5. Fu Kiau Bunseki, interview with Dianne Stewart, Atlanta, Ga., April 23, 2004; Dianne M. Stewart, *Three Eyes for the Journey: African Dimensions of the Jamaican Religious Experience* (New York: Oxford University Press, 2005), 50–51, 256.

6. Bettelheim, "Palo Monte Mayombe," 2.

7. Mary Ann Clark, *Where Men Are Wives and Mothers Rule: Santeria Ritual Practices and Their Gender Implications* (Gainesville: University Press of Florida, 2005), 79; Stephen Palmie, *Wizards and Scientists: Explorations in Afro-Cuban Modernity and Tradition* (Chapel Hill, N.C.: Duke University Press, 2002), 162.

8. David H. Brown, *Santeria Enthroned: Art, Ritual, and Innovation in an Afro-Cuban Religion* (Chicago: University of Chicago Press, 2003), 29–30.

9. Erica Moret, "Afro-Cuban Religion, Ethnobotany and Healthcare in the Context of Global Political and Economic Change," *Bulletin of Latin American Research* 27, no. 3 (2008): 341.

10. Bilby, "Review of Fuentes Guerra," 979.

11. Ibid., 980.

12. W. van Wetering and H.U.E. Thoden van Velzen, "Lengua y ritos del Palo Monte Mayombe: Dioses cubanos y sus fuentes africanas," ed. Jesus Fuentes Guerra and Armin Schegler (Frankfurt am Main: Vervuert, 2005); Review in *Nieuwe West-Indische Gidsvol.* 80, nos. 3–4 (2006): 301.

13. Palmie, *Wizards and Scientists*, 25. Cited also in Margarite Fernandez Olmos and Lizabeth Paravisini-Gebert, *Creole Religions: An Introduction from Vodou and Santeria to Obeah and Espiritismo* (New York: New York University Press, 2003), 78.

14. Bilby, "Review of Fuentes Guerra," 980; van Wetering and van Velzen, "Lingua y ritos del Palo Monte Mayombe," 300.

15. Miguel Barnet, *Afro-Caribbean Religions* (Princeton, N.J.: Marcus wiener Publishers, 2001), 74.

16. Robert Farris Thompson, *Flash of the Spirit: African and Afro-American Art and Philosophy* (New York: Vintage Press, 1984), 103. Cited by Olmos and Paravisini-Gebert, *Creole Religions*, 78; also J. Lorand Matory, *Black Atlantic Religion: Tradition, Transnationalism, and Matriarchy in the Afro-Brazilian Candomble* (Princeton, N.J.: Princeton University Press, 2005), passim.

17. Matory, *Black Atlantic Religion*, 43. See also Jan Vansina, *African History* (Boston: Little, Brown, 1978), 25–30.

18. Erica Moret and others put the number at 850,000 enslaved Africans, most of whom came "from the Bantu-speaking region of western central Africa" ("Afro-Cuban Religion," 339–340).

19. Of course, Bettelheim found that "Oyo-Yoruba gods are the core of a ... lingua franca" that dominates African religious thought in Cuba ("Palo Monte Mayombe," 2).

20. Barnet, *Afro-Caribbean Religions*, 73.

21. Moret, "Afro-Cuban Religion," 339.

22. Barnet, *Afro-Caribbean Religions*, 83.

23. Bilby, "Review of Fuentes Guerra," 979.

24. Palmie, *Wizards and Scientists,* 193.

25. Ibid., 165. Referenced by Mary Ann Clark (*Where Men Are Wives*, 80–81) as a precursor to discussing gender relations in Santeria and Palo Monte.

26. Patrick Bellegarde-Smith, ed., *Fragments of Bone: Neo-African Religions in the New World* (Chicago: University of Illinois Press), 2005.

27. Gerardo Mosquera, "Eleggua at the (Post?)Modern Crossroads: The Presence of Africa in the Visual Art of Cuba," in *Santeria Aesthetics in Contemporary Latin American Art,* ed. Arturo Lindsay (Washington, D. C.: Smithsonian Institution Press, 1992/1996), 226–227; Eugenio Matibag, *Afro-Cuban Religious Experience: Cultural Reflections in Narrative* (Gainesville: University Press of Florida, 1996), chap. 5; Jorge Castellanos and Isabel Castellanos, *Cultura Afrocubana 1 (El Negro en Cuba, 1492–1944)* (Miami, Fla.: Ediciones Universal, 1992), 3.

28. Matory, *Black Atlantic Religion*, 13. See also Palmie, *Wizards and Scientists*, 25.

29. Brown, *Santeria Enthroned*, 28, 71. See also Bettelheim, "Palo Monte Mayombe,"1–3.

30. Brown, *Santeria Enthroned*, 187.

31. Olmos and Paravisini-Gebert, *Creole Religions*, 86.

32. Maria Teresa Velez, *Drumming for the Gods: The Life and Times of Felipe Garcia Villamil, Santero, Palero, and Abakua* (Philadelphia: Temple University Press, 2000), 30.

33. Mosquera, "The Presence of Africa in the Visual Art of Cuba," 227.

34. Fernando Oritz, "Los Cabildos Afrocubanos," *Revista Bimestre Cubana* 16 (January–February, 1921): 5.

35. Miguel Barnet, *Afro-Cuban Religions*, trans. from Spanish by Christine Renita Ayorinde (Princeton, N.J.: Markus Wiener Publishers, 2001), 74, 76.

36. Ibid, 76.

37. Brown, *Santeria Enthroned*, 30, 34.

38. Barnet, *Afro-Cuban Religions*, 74.

39. Ibid., 78. Cited from Lydia Cabrera, *Reglas de Congo, Palo Monte, Mayombe* (Miami, Fla.: Peninsular Printing, 1979), 15–16.

40. Brown, *Santeria Enthroned*, 44. Cited of Fernando Oritz, *La antigua fiesta afrocubana "del dia de reyes"* (Havana: Ministerio de Relaciones Exteriores, Departmento de Asuntos Culturales, Division de Publicaciones, [1920] 1960), 15.

41. Matory, *Black Atlantic Religion*, 9.

42. Brown, *Santeria Enthroned*, 26. See also Isabel Mercedes Castellanos, "The Use of Language in Afro-Cuban Religion" (PhD Dissertation: Georgetown University, 1977), and her "Grammatical Structure, Historical Development, and Religious Usage of Afro-Cuban Bozal Speech," *Folklore Forum* 23, nos. 1, 2 (1990): 57–84; Fernando Oritz, *Los Negros Esclavos* (Havana: Editorial de Ciencias Sociales, 1916/1987), 40–59.

43. Brown, *Santeria Enthroned*, 57.

44. Ibid., 44.

45. Stephen Palmie, "Against Syncretism: 'Africanising' and 'Cubanising' Discourses in North American *Orisha* Worship," in *Counterworks: Managing the Diversity of Knowledge*, ed. R. Fardon (London: Routledge, 1995), 77, 96. Cited by Moret, "Afro-Cuban Religions," 341. See also G. Girardi, *El ahora de Cuba: Tras el derrumble del comunismo y tras el viaje de Juan Pablo 11* (Madrid: Nueva Utopia, 1994), 287.

46. Moret, "Afro-Cuban Religion," 340. See also Girardi, *El ahora de Cuba.*

47. Moret, "Afro-Cuban Religion," 340.

48. Ibid., 339.

49. Bettelheim, "Palo Monte Mayombe," 2.

50. Ibid., 2–3. On the idea of the absence of a pantheon in Palo Monte, see also Olmos and Paravisini-Gebert, *Creole Religions*, 79.

51. Bettelheim, "Palo Monte Mayombe, 2

52. Barnet, *Afro-Cuban Religions*, 95. Avatars of Palo Monte depend on the natural reserve for their ritual paraphernalia and are thus environmentally sensitive.

53. van Wetering and van Velzen, "Lengua y ritos del Palo Monte Mayombe," 301.

54. Ibid. The desire to impress communicants with linguistic acumen is a common pastime of clerics in most religions, especially those with sacred texts in an earlier language, whether written or oral.

55. van Wetering and van Velzen, "Lengua y ritos del Palo Monte," 300.

56. Olmos and Paravisini-Gerbert, *Creole Religions*, 78. Also van Wetering and van Velzen, "Lengua y Ritos del Palo Monte," 300.

57. Olmos and Paravisini-Gebert, *Creole Religions*, 80. See also Migene Gonzalez-Wippler, *Santeria: The Religion* (New York: Harmony Books, 1989), 246.

58. Barnet, *Afro-Caribbean Religions*, 79.

59. Bettelheim, "Palo Monte Mayombe," 2.

60. Brown, *Santeria Enthroned*, 71–72.

61. Ibid. Cited from Cabrera, *Reglas de Congo, Palo Monte, Mayombe* (Miami, Fla.: Coleccion del Chicheriki, 1979).

62. Ricardo A. Viera and Randall Morris, "Juan Boza: Travails of an Artist-Priest, 1941–1991," in *Santeria Aesthetics in Contemporary Latin American Art*, 171–172.

63. Arturo Lindsay, "Living Gods in Contemporary Latino Art," in *Santeria Aesthetics in Contemporary Latin American Art*, 216. See also Bettelheim, "Palo Monte Mayombe," 6–10.

64. In Cuba, *bozal* is a novice or new inquirer, but it also names a creole language: "arriving Africans who could not speak Spanish were called *bozales* ('raw')" or new (Brown, *Santeria Enthroned*, 30).

65. Bettelheim, "Palo Monte Mayombe," 6.

66. Ibid., 5.

67. Velez, *Drumming for the Gods*, 16.

68. Bettelheim, "Palo Monte Mayombe," 6.

69. Ibid., 4.

70. Ibid., 6–7.

71. Ibid., 7. Since Islam's influence in Central Africa was not prominent in the seventeenth and eighteenth centuries, this greeting was probably not Kongo in origin but learned from enslaved Muslim in Cuba.

72. van Wetering and van Velzen, "Lingua y ritos del Palo Monte Mayombe," 301. See also Jesus Fuentes Guerra and Armin Schwegler, *Lengua y ritos del Palo Monte Mayombe: Dioses cubanos y sus fuentes africanas* (Madrid: Iberoamericana/Frankfurt am Main, Vervuert, 2005).

73. John K. Thornton, *The Kingdom of Kongo: Civil War and Transition 1641–1718* (Madison: University of Wisconsin Press, 1983), 62.

74. Wyatt MacGaffey, "Art and Spirituality," in *African Spirituality, Forms, Meanings, and Expressions*, ed. Jacob K. Olupona (New York: Crossroad, 2000), 231–232.

75. T. J. Desch-Obi, "Deadly Dances: The Spiritual Dimensions of Kongo-Angolan Martial Art Traditions in the New World," in *Fragments of Bone*, 76. See also Thompson, *Flash of the Spirit*, 103 and passim.

76. Desch-Obi, "Deadly Dances," 76. Quoted also from Thompson, *Flash of the Spirit*, 117.

77. Ibid. Quoted from John Thornton, "African Soldiers in the Haitian Revolution," *Journal of Caribbean History* 25 no. 1 (1994): 71–72.

78. Mosquera, "The Presence of Africa in the Visual Art of Cuba," 230.

79. Thornton, *The Kingdom of Kongo*, 59. Thornton states, "The public role of mediating between society and nature belonged typically to the *kitomi*," whom missionaries likened to the Christian bishop. See also Wyatt MacGaffey, "The Religious Commissions of the Bakongo," *Man, New Series* 5 (1970): 28–36.

80. Beatrix Morales, "Afro-Cuban Religious Transformation: A Comparative Study of Lucumi Religion and the Tradition of Spirit Belief" (PhD Dissertation: City University of New York, 1990), 107–108. See also Olmos and Paravisini-Gebert, *Creole Religions*, 79.

81. Bettelheim, "Palo Monte Mayombe," 3. See Lydia Cabrera, *La medicina popular de Cuba: Medicos de antano, curanderos, santeros y paleros de hogano* (Miami, Fla.: Coleccion del Chichereku, 1984/1986), 126.

82. Bettelheim, "Palo Monte Mayombe," 3.

83. Olmos and Paravisini-Gebert, *Creole Religions*, 79.

84. Velez, *Drumming for the Gods*, 32.

85. Bettelheim, "Palo Monte Mayombe," 3.

86. Olmos and Paravisini-Gebert contend that "healing rituals of the *quimbandeiros* [healing sorcerer], are strongly linked to the mysteries of the jungle; and the preeminence of the sorcerer or *nganguleros* [makers of magic charms or *ngangos* of the villages in the interior zones of the Congo Basin ...]. All of this is mixed together ... gives rise in the Caribbean to a new product without necessarily in this case ... a clash with Christianity as an indispensable condition" (*Creole Religions*, 229).

87. Wyatt MacGaffey, *Religion and Society in Central Africa: The BaKongo of Lower Zaire* (Chicago: University of Chicago Press, 1986), 46. See interpretation in Stewart, *Three Eyes for the Journey*, 158–159.

88. Stewart, *Three Eyes for the Journey*, 158. See MacGaffey, *Religion and Society in Central Africa*, 46–47; Thompson, *Flash of the Spirit*, 108.

89. Thompson, *Flash of the Spirit*, 108. Cited also in Stewart, *Three Eyes for the Journey*, 159.

90. Thompson, *Flash of the Spirit*, 108.

91. Velez, *Drumming for the Gods*, 15.

92. Mosquera, "The Presence of Africa in the Visual Art of Cuba," 253.

93. Velez, Drumming for the Gods, 15.

94. Bettelheim, "Palo Monte Mayombe," 3.

95. Velez, *Drumming for the Gods*, 16, 64.

96. Mosquera, "The Presence of Africa in the Visual Art of Cuba," 254.

97. Ibid. See also "Mosquera References Robert Farris Thompson and Joseph Cornet," *The Four Moments of the Sun: Kongo Art in Two Worlds* (Washington, D.C.: National Art Gallery of Art, 1981), 43–52; Thompson, *Flash of the Spirit*, 108–116; MacGaffey, *Religion and Society in Central Africa*, 42–51; A.

Fu-Kiau Kia Bunsiki-Luminisa, *Le Mukongo et le Monde qui l'Entourait: Crosmogonie Kongo* (Kinshasa: n.p., 1969), 2, 8–11, 17–29.

98. Moret, "Afro-Cuban Religion," 343–344. See also Katherine J. Hagedorn, *Divine Utterances: The Performance of Afro-Cuban Santeria* (Washington, D.C.: Smithsonian Institution Press, 2001).

Wicca and Neo-Paganism

A Primer for Counselors

Jeffry L. Moe, Keith Cates, and Victoria Sepulveda

···

W iccans and Neo-Pagans are a growing and historically marginalized group, yet little scholarship is available that addresses their specific counseling needs. The authors discuss the
origins of Wicca and Neo-Paganism, population characteristics of Wiccans and Neo-Pagans in the
United States, important terminology, and common themes of Wiccan and Neo-Pagan belief based on
review of the literature. Also discussed are implications for how counselors can incorporate awareness
of these knowledge domains into competent practice with Wiccan and Neo-Pagan clients.

According to the U.S. Census Bureau (2011) there are approximately 682,000 self-identified
Wiccans and Neo-Pagans living in the United States. The number of Wiccans and Neo-Pagans
recorded by the census doubled between the years 2000 and 2008 (Kosmin & Keysar, 2008). Ezzy
and Berger (2009) asserted that this figure underestimates the number of self-identified Wiccans
and Neo-Pagans and also excludes members of this population who are not open about their beliefs.
Wiccan and Neo-Pagan communities have grown in part due to increased representation in popular
media such as television and cinema (Berger & Ezzy, 2009) and the increase of information on
Neo-Paganism available on the Internet (Adler, 2006). Wicca and Neo-Paganism are recognized as
religions in the United States, and there are several national-level organizations recognized by the
U.S. government to ordain Wiccan and Neo-Pagan ministers (Reuther, 2005). Scholarly research
dedicated to this group has increased in the past two decades (Adler, 2006), affording counselors the
chance to develop greater understanding of the needs of Wiccan and Neo-Pagan clients (Yardley,
2008). Spirituality and religion have implications for well-being and for improved client outcomes
(Worthington, Hook, Davis, & McDaniel, 2011), yet little counseling scholarship has focused on
Neo-Pagan spirituality or Neo-Pagans (including Wiccans) as a growing and historically marginalized
group.

Highlighting how counselors can better serve Neo-Pagan clients is warranted given the
extent of the Neo-Pagan population within the United States (U.S. Census Bureau, 2011) and

Jeffry L. Moe, Keith Cates, and Victoria Sepulveda, "Wicca and Neo-Paganism: A Primer for Counselors," *Journal of Professional
Counseling, Practice, Theory, & Research*, vol. 40, no. 1, pp. 38-48. Copyright © 2013 by Texas Counseling Association. Reprinted
with permission. Provided by ProQuest LLC. All rights reserved.

trends signifying that interest in and adherence to Wiccan and Neo-Pagan beliefs is increasing, particularly among youth and young adults (Ezzy & Berger, 2009). These trends also intersect with the principles of multicultural counseling competence (Arredondo et al., 1996), spiritual and religious competence (Association for Spiritual, Ethical, & Religious Values in Counseling, 2009; Powers, 2005), and the American Counseling Association (ACA) *Code of Ethics* (2005) to support the development of competency to work with clients of diverse backgrounds and worldviews. This text is not intended to be an exhaustive analysis but rather an overview of: (a) the origins of Wicca and Neo-Paganism, (b) common terminology, (c) population characteristics of Wiccans and Neo-Pagans, (d) common Wiccan and Neo-Pagan beliefs, and (e) how integration of these knowledge domains can help facilitate counselors' awareness and rapport-building skills with Wiccan and Neo-Pagan clients.

Origins and Definitions

During the Christianization of continental Europe, people who kept beliefs or rituals related to pre-Christian religions began to be referred to as pagans, from the Latin *paganus*, meaning country-person (Albrecht, 2007). The extent to which pre-Christian religions continued to be formally practiced within Europe is not fully known (Cornish, 2009; Hutton, 2007) but it is generally agreed that interest in pre-Christian pagan beliefs experienced a revival in Great Britain and the United States during the early 20th century (Berger, Leach, & Shaeffer, 2003). In the 1930s anthropologist Margaret Murray proposed her controversial theory that remnants of pre-Christian religions survived in Britain and other parts of Europe in the form of secret and group-oriented worship and that the European witch trials were an attempt to extinguish these practices (White, 2010). Though disputed by scholars to this day (Hutton, 2007), interest in Murray's theory spurred the formation of groups in Great Britain dedicated to a religious system that came to be called *Wicca* (White, 2010). The Old Anglo-Saxon word *wicca* itself is the origin of the English word *witch* (White, 2010), and by the 1950s adherents of the Wiccan movement began using the term witch to describe themselves and the term *Witchcraft* to describe their religion.

As the terms witch and Wicca became popularized within the Wiccan movement, so too did the terms Pagan or *Neo-Pagan* as promulgated by those interested in pre-Christian religions who sought to dissociate themselves from the negative connotations attributed to the words witch or witchcraft (Jensen & Thompson, 2008). The word witch is considered by many Wiccans to be synonymous with the words priestess or priest, and can connote formal initiation into the beliefs and rituals of a specific Wiccan tradition (Pike, 2004). Adherents of other Neo-Pagan traditions may use the terms priestess or priest, or may use other titles such as *druid* or *elder* (Pike, 2004). Wiccans adopted the term *coven* to describe groups of adherents associated by shared beliefs and the collective enactment of important rituals (Tairu, 2010), while those identifying as Neo-Pagan began using the term *circle* to refer to similar groups (Yardley, 2008).

Development to Present Day

Interest in Wicca and Neo-Paganism continued to grow in the 1960s and 1970s, especially in the United States (Jorgensen & Russell, 1999). Other movements such as environmentalism and feminism influenced the growing Wiccan and Neo-Pagan communities (Jensen & Thompson, 2008). The concept of Goddess-worship itself was seen as a radical alternative to mainstream religions (Coleman, 2005) and incited further growth in the 1970s and 1980s of increasingly diverse groups of Wiccan and Neo-Pagan practitioners (Jorgensen & Russell, 1999). The term *solitary* emerged to represent individuals who adhere to a Neo-Pagan worldview but are not affiliated with a local coven or circle, usually due to isolation from and lack of access to other Neo-Pagans (Berger et al., 2003).

The ascendency of the Internet facilitated access to other practitioners and to knowledge about Wicca and Neo-Paganism (Ezzy & Berger, 2009). Neo-Pagan groups continued to diversify, with devotion to specific deities, emphasis on shared cultural heritages, and involvement in political movements serving as inspirations for group formation and identity (Rigoglioso, 2005). One way practitioners signify this diversity is by using the terms *path* or *tradition* to distinguish between individuals and groups that adopt a Wiccan or Neo-Pagan worldview but emphasize different beliefs and practices as more central (Pike, 2004). An example would be the difference between the *Gardnerian* Wiccan tradition whose adherents emphasize the contributions of Gerald Gardner and his cohorts (White, 2010), and the *Dianic* Wiccan tradition founded by Zsuzsanna Budapest whose adherents emphasize female empowerment and female-centered worship (Coleman, 2005). Today, Wicca is viewed as a distinct faith tradition within Neo-Paganism and approximately half of self-identified Neo-Pagans are followers of Wicca (US Census Bureau, 2011). Other prominent Neo-Pagan traditions include Druidism (based on ancient Celtic mythology), Goddess-worshippers (who seek to distance themselves from the terms witch and witchcraft), and traditions rooted in other distinct ethno-cultural heritages such as Scandinavian (i.e. Viking) culture or the culture of ancient Egypt (Pike, 2004). There are also several eclectic Wiccan and Neo-Pagan groups operating at the national level in the United States that welcome adherents from across the various Wiccan and Neo-Pagan traditions (Reuther, 2005).

Population Characteristics

Self-identified Wiccans and Neo-Pagans are more commonly of Northern European heritage (Jensen & Thompson, 2008) and more likely to reside in urban areas (Jorgensen & Russell, 1999) than the general U.S. population. Jensen and Thompson (2008) found that Wiccans and Neo-Pagans were more likely to reside in communities where interests in religion, spirituality, and environmentalism were high across the general citizenry. Berger et al. (2003) found Wiccans and Neo-Pagans are more likely to be college-educated, to have been raised within a mainstream religion such as Catholicism (which they subsequently rejected), and to endorse anti-authoritarian attitudes. Smith and Simmons (2006) found adherents of alternative religions (including Wicca and Neo-Paganism) viewed counseling in a favorable light, holding similar help-seeking attitudes in this regard to both adherents of mainstream religions and participants who indicated they held no religious beliefs.

Wiccans and Neo-Pagans face marginalization as followers of minority or non-mainstream religions (Tairu, 2010) and due to the persistent inaccurate conflation of Neo-Paganism with Satan-worship (Emerson & Syron, 1995; Tairu, 2010). Scholars report that Neo-Pagans face challenges such as overt discrimination in the workplace (Jorgensen & Russell, 1999) including termination due to their beliefs (Cookson, 1997), being denied custody of children (Cookson, 1997; Yardley, 2008), and alienation from family and other community members (Jenson & Thompson, 2008). Children and adolescents who express interest in or whose parents adhere to Neo-Paganism face harassment and bullying at school (Kermani, 2009). Neo-Pagans in the military lack access to Neo-Pagan chaplains (Harrow, 2005), and veterans who identify as Wiccan or Neo-Pagan may be denied the use of the symbols of their faith in funerals and on grave markers should they be killed in the line of duty (Learning, 2006). While Neo-Pagans are more likely to be college-educated, this does not translate to financial security in part due to the effects of gender-based wage discrimination as the majority of self-identified Neo-Pagans are female (Jensen & Thompson, 2008).

It is important to note the scholarly distinction between spirituality and religion. While both are viewed as systems that facilitate engagement with transcendent levels of symbolic meaning (Berger & Ezzy, 2009), the former is viewed as more personal and sometimes idiosyncratic while the latter is viewed as more group-oriented and standardized across adherents (Worthington et al., 2011). While useful for developing awareness of spiritual and religious experiences, this distinction itself is sometimes used to trivialize Neo-Pagan beliefs precisely because there is no recognized central authority that standardizes practice across all Neo-Pagan groups (Tairu, 2010). If counselors believe religions must include such over-arching institutions, this may bias them against accepting Neo-Paganism as both a spiritual system and as a religion. Given the recognition at the federal level in the United States of several Wiccan and Neo-Pagan organizations as religious bodies, the authors encourage counselors to conceptualize Neo-Pagan beliefs as both spiritual and religious in nature.

Wiccans and Neo-Pagans value and affirm diversity of belief in terms of relating to adherents of different paths or traditions (Harwood, 2007). Individual creativity and personal engagement with aspects of the Neo-Pagan worldview are generally valued more by members of this population than precise historical reconstruction of their religious or spiritual beliefs (Berger & Ezzy, 2009; Cornish, 2009). Though diversity of belief is valued, Wiccans and Neo-Pagans are likely to construct their respective spiritual worldviews within common dimensions or themes of belief. These dimensions include: (a) the concept of immanent divinity and universal interconnectedness (Harwood, 2007),

(b) the view that divinity is both male and female (Coleman, 2005), (c) seeing the earth and nature as sacred (Rigoglioso, 2005), and (d) belief that humans can experience the divine directly through ritual and/or the practice of magic (Hume, 1998). Counselors should be aware that adherents of different traditions may emphasize some beliefs over or to the exclusion of others (Tairu, 2010).

Wiccan and Neo-Pagan Beliefs

Immanent Divinity and Interconnectedness

One dimension of belief important to the Neo-Pagan worldview is that divinity is immanent, meaning that the sacred, including conceptions of deity, is infused into both natural and supernatural levels of reality (Starhawk, 1999). While not unique to Wicca or Neo-Paganism, the view that divinity is immanent is often used to contrast these spiritual-religious orientations with other orientations that differentiate the spiritual, sacred, and holy from the physical, profane, and worldly (Tairu, 2010). The concept of immanent divinity is related to belief in universal interconnectedness (Harwood, 2007), or the sense that humans, animals, nature, and divinity are interconnected and exist within dynamic, mutually influential relationships (Wise, 2004). One axiom associated with Wicca that is based on the principles of immanent divinity and of interconnectedness is known as the *Wiccan Rede,* usually formulated as "and it harm none, do as you will" (Harwood, 2007, p. 381). Fostering healthy relationships with others is seen as a means to honor the sacred that infuses all existence and that exists within all people (Harwood, 2007).

Earth-Based Spirituality

One way Wiccans and Neo-Pagans engage with the concept of immanent divinity is through the honoring of the earth and/or nature as sacred (Harwood, 2007). Sometimes referred to as *earth-based spirituality,* viewing the earth or nature as sacred is often represented as a web of interconnected elements associated with different aspects of existence (Wise, 2004). The most common elements identified within the web model are earth (representing stability, physicality, and death), air (creativity and intellect), fire (change and movement), water (emotions and intuition), and spirit (essence and unity) (Yardley, 2008). The veneration of nature also includes celebrating solstices and equinoxes, the changing of seasons and phases of the moon, and the agricultural cycle (Pike, 2004). These nature-based events symbolize the phenomena of birth, growth, decline, death, and re-birth, sometimes viewed as re-incarnation, and are honored as sacred and endlessly repeating processes (Starhawk, 1999). Group-based observances of the natural cycle are highly stylized forms of veneration, often incorporating elements from mythology, and may involve symbolic instruments and attire, chanting, dancing, and drumming (Albrecht, 2007). Viewing the earth and nature as sacred sometimes translates into political activism for environmental conservation and sustainability (Jensen & Thompson, 2008), though this is by no means universal across Neo-Pagans (Ezzy, 2006).

Divinity Encompasses Female and Male

Another important theme of Neo-Pagan and Wiccan belief is the idea that divinity is both female and male (Tairu, 2010). Conceptualizing divinity as female is seen as divergent from the official theology of mainstream religions in Western (-ized) societies (Rigoglioso, 2005) and as particularly empowering to women in the United States and Great Britain (Coleman, 2005). Divinity is often conceptualized either as an omnipotent and omnipresent Goddess or as a Goddess paired with a God as divine consort (Pike, 2004). This concept intersects with the veneration of nature and translates into viewing sexuality, fertility, and the body as sacred (Coleman, 2005). Honoring the divine as both female and male or as the Goddess singularly is a common dimension of belief, but Wiccans and Neo-Pagans will view this as more or less important depending on their tradition and personal views (Pike, 2004).

Ritual and Magic

One of the most misunderstood features of modern Neo-Paganism is the practice of magic. From a Wiccan or Neo-Pagan perspective, magic is the practice of focusing intention, aligning with nature, and using symbolic representations in order to deepen and broaden awareness of the sacred that infuses all reality (Wise, 2004). Wicca is closely associated with the practice of magic (Wise, 2004) either as a solitary, as part of a coven, or as part of a public ritual to honor the natural cycle and other occasions such as initiations and marriage ceremonies (Berger et al., 2003). A spell as an act of magic is a ritualized practice involving specific symbolic elements related to the intentions and desires of the practitioner (Wise, 2004). Elements of magic and ritual common across Wiccan and Neo-Pagan traditions include: (a) grounding and centering energy, which includes stating or acknowledging intentions (Adler, 2006; Starhawk, 1999), (b) raising and directing energy (Pike, 2004; Adler, 2006), and (c) visualization of divine or sacred forces that practitioners have a personal connection to or that represent symbolically the focus of desired changes (Adler, 2006; Starhawk, 1999). It also is common to clearly demarcate both the physical spaces and the time periods wherein ritual or magic is practiced (Adler, 2006), sometimes by thanking the presence of divinity (Hume, 1998) or using guided reflection upon participants' experience of a ritual or magical act (Wise, 2004).

Magic is not in and of itself harmful according to the Wiccan and Neo-Pagan worldview (Wise, 2004), and distinctions between so-called white and black magic arise more from popular media and folk-beliefs about magic than from Wiccan or Neo-Pagan thought (Adler, 2006). Intentions are, however, an important consideration when engaging in magic or ritual (Harwood, 2007), and one important principle used to guide magical practice involves what is commonly known as the Three-fold Law (Harwood, 2007). The *Three-fold Law* stipulates that whatever good or harm a Wiccan or Neo-Pagan might do will come back to them threefold, meaning that Wiccans and Neo-Pagans should strive to avoid harming others so as to avoid harming themselves (Harwood, 2007).

It is important for counselors to distinguish magical thinking from the Neo-Pagan belief in magic. Neo-Pagan and Wiccan views on magic involve a coherent set of beliefs related to valuing ritual, creativity, nature, and interconnectedness (Wise, 2004). Magical thinking involves loosely associated beliefs that a person causes or controls unrelated events in their social world. A Wiccan who participates in a ritual on the full-moon with his or her coven, who invokes images related to renewal and creativity, and who sees a connection between this ritual and his or her own renewed sense of vitality would be narrating their experiences in accordance with the Wiccan or Neo-Pagan worldview. In contrast, a person who thinks that he or she has developed the ability to control the thoughts of other people is demonstrating magical thinking instead.

Implications

Counselors can synthesize what is currently known about Wiccan and Neo-Pagan traditions, summarized here, in order to develop competence for work with Wiccan or Neo-Pagan clients. This includes further study on the different Neo-Pagan traditions and these faiths' historic and current relationships to each other, as well as investigating what specific Neo-Pagan groups and resources exist in counselors' local areas. Web-sites such as The Witch's Voice at www.witchvox.com (Walker & Jung, 2011) and organizations like Covenant of the Goddess at www.cog.org (Reuther, 2005) are excellent resources to learn more about Neo-Pagan resources and communities.

It is important for counselors to assess how the Wiccan or Neo-Pagan client identifies and to what path or tradition the client belongs. Powers (2005) and Parker (2011) both recommend using informal attending along with formal interviews to develop richer understanding of clients' spiritual and religious worldviews. Yardley (2008) recommends using neutral but affirming and open-ended language to explore Wiccan and Neo-Pagan clients' beliefs once the topic of spirituality has been broached. Counselors should also determine whether a Wiccan or Neo-Pagan client practices as a solitary or is affiliated with a local coven or circle, as this will indicate what sources of community and support the client may have. Wiccans and Neo-Pagans appear to share concerns about privacy and disclosing their beliefs to potentially biased non-believers (Tairu, 2010); therefore, therefore counselors should be aware that Wiccan and Neo-Pagan clients may be cautious about disclosing or discussing their beliefs (Adler, 2006) and that this does not signify an unhealthy level of paranoia.

Given the history of stigma attached to self-identification as Neo-Pagan it is vital that counselors acknowledge their own assumptions and potential biases before engaging in work with Neo-Pagan clients (ACA, 2005; ASERVIC, 2009). M. M. Kocet (personal communication, October 27, 2011) encourages counselors to engage in *bracketing*, or the intentional reflection upon personal values and biases in order to avoid imposing preconceived notions onto clients. Counselors also should reflect upon the dimensions of belief stated above, and process their reflections with peers knowledgeable about Wicca, Neo-Paganism, or working with spiritual-religious clients. Counselors should specifically avoid confusing Wicca and Neo-Paganism with Satan-worship, black magic, and other negative cultural stereotypes, as these do not relate to the Wiccan and Neo-Pagan worldview (Adler, 2006).

Wiccans and Neo-Pagans may come to counseling due to stress, anxiety, and depressive feelings related to the cognitive dissonance that members of marginalized groups cope with on a daily basis (Salazar & Abrams, 2005). Helping clients recognize and address this dissonance is a common feature of counseling with members of marginalized groups, and may involve consideration of how multiple identities intersect or are in conflict within the client's life (Salazar & Abrams, 2005). Clients who adhere to Wiccan or Neo-Pagan beliefs and who belong to cultural groups with strongly negative views of witchcraft, magic, and occultism may experience added dissonance as they struggle to integrate different aspects of their own identities.

Since most Wiccans and Neo-Pagans in the United States are raised in families where majority culture religions are practiced (Berger et al., 2003), issues pertaining to a sense of alienation from family of origin may be common as well. Wiccans and Neo-Pagans may feel close affinity with others of their faith especially if they are affiliated with a coven or circle; the coven or circle becomes a source of social support in tandem with or even in place of the Wiccan or Neo-Pagan client's family of origin. Maintaining relationships with members of the Wiccan or Neo-Pagan client's coven or circle may be an important focus for counseling. Other relational issues, such as making or keeping friends who are not Wiccan or Neo-Pagan and the decision to raise children within a Neo-Pagan tradition (Kermani, 2009) may also serve as sources of stress that Wiccan and Neo-Pagan clients may focus on during counseling.

Wiccans and Neo-Pagans may also struggle with spiritual or faith development in similar fashion to members of other spiritual-religious orientations. Parker (2011) suggested that counselors: (a) assess how a client's faith development may be impacting the presenting issue, including facilitating client identification of the benefits and strengths that faith is providing to the client, (b) collaborate with clients to differentiate non-spiritual life crises from crises of faith, and (c) facilitate client's exploration of and linkage to resources that will help promote continued faith development if warranted. This would include referrals to local Wiccan and Neo-Pagan groups as well as encouraging clients to connect with peers and community elders.

Conclusion

Wiccans and Neo-Pagans, despite experiencing stigma and marginalization for their beliefs, are a growing population in the United States. Counselors must familiarize themselves with accurate information and identify approaches that have been effective in order to work with this client population. In addition, research that further explicates issues and concerns specific to Wiccans and Neo-Pagans is needed. For instance, qualitative approaches that focus on describing aspects of lived experience from a Wiccan or Neo-Pagan perspective could serve to improve understanding of how adherents of these faith traditions define concepts such as wellness, mental health, and therapeutic rapport. Further study on different developmental aspects of Wiccan and Neo-Pagan experience, such as transitioning between different life phases, is also warranted. Spirituality and religious belief are important aspects of human existence, and counselors should be prepared to offer sensitive and effective services to Wiccan and Neo-Pagan clients. Affirming the beliefs and worldviews of Wiccan and Neo-Pagan clients is consonant with the ACA (2005) *Code of Ethics* and calls by scholars for counselors to be more attentive to spirituality and religion within the context of the counseling relationship. Awareness of the history, development, and themes of Wiccan and Neo-Pagan belief can serve as a foundation for competent, sensitive, and affirmative counseling with Wiccan and Neo-Pagan clients.

References

Adler, M. (2006). *Drawing down the moon: Witches, druids, goddess-worshippers and other pagans in America* (Rev. ed.). London: Penguin.

Albrecht, R. (2007). The Virgin, The Princess, and The Goddess: A field report and analysis of Pagan and Christian symbolism in a Roman Catholic religious celebration of northern Chile. Atlantic *Journal of Communication, 15,* 171–193. doi:10.1080/15456870701316152

American Counseling Association (ACA). (2005). *Code of Ethics.* Alexandria, VA: Author.

Arredondo, P., Toporek, R., Brown, S. P., Sanchez, J., Locke, D. C., Sanchez, J., & Stadler, H. (1996). Operationalization of the multicultural counseling competencies. *Journal of Multicultural Counseling & Development, 24,* 42–78.

Association for Spiritual, Ethical, and Religious Values in Counseling [ASERVIC]. (2009). *Competencies for addressing spiritual and religious issues in counseling.* Alexandria, VA: Author. Retrieved from www.aservic.org /resources/spiritual-competencies/

Berger, H., & Ezzy, D. (2009). Mass media and religious identity: A case study of young witches. *Journal for the Scientific Study of Religion,* 48, 501–514.

Berger, H., Leach, E., & Shaffer, L. (2003). *Voices from the pagan census: A national survey of witches and neo-pagans in the United States.* Columbia, SC: University of South Carolina Press.

Coleman, K. (2005). Why 'God' as 'She' provokes us: Semiotically [sic] speaking: The significance of the divine feminine. *Pomegranate, 7,* 117–127.

Cookson, C. (1997). Reports from the trenches: A case study of religious freedom issues faced by Wiccans practicing in the United States. *Journal of Church & State, 39,* 723–748.

Cornish, H. (2009). Spelling out history: Transforming witchcraft past and present. *Pomegranate, 11,* 14–28. doi:10.1558/pome.v11i1.14.

Emerson, S., & Syron, Y. (1995). Adolescent Satanism: Rebellion masquerading as religion. *Counseling & Values, 39,* 145–159.

Ezzy, D. (2006). Popular witchcraft and environmentalism. *Pomegranate, 8,* 29–53.

Ezzy, D., & Berger, H. (2009). Witchcraft: Changing patterns of participation in the early twenty-first century. *Pomegranate, 11,* 165–180. Doi: 10.1558/pome.v11i2.165

Harrow, J. (2005). To me, it was magic: Nature mysticism and feminist power in a woman's military career. *Gender Issues, 22*(4), 56–70.

Harwood, B. (2007). Beyond poetry and magic: The core elements of Wiccan morality. *Journal of Contemporary Religion, 22,* 375–390.

Hume, L. (1998). Creating sacred space: Outer expression of inner worlds in modern Wicca. *Journal of Contemporary Religion, 13,* 309–319.

Hutton, R. (2007). The status of witchcraft in the modern world. *Pomegranate, 9,* 121–131. doi:10.1558/pome.v9i2.121.

Jensen, G., & Thompson, A. (2008). 'Out of the broom closet': The social ecology of American Wicca. *Journal for the Scientific Study of Religion, 47,* 753–766.

Jorgensen, D., & Russell, S. (1999). American Neo-paganism: The participants' social identities. *Journal for the Scientific Study of Religion, 38,* 325–338.

Kermani, Z. (2009). Don't eat the incense: Children's participation in contemporary Pagan practice. *Pomegranate, 11,* 181–196.

Kosmin, B. A., & Keysar, A. (2008). *American Religious Identification Survey* (ARIS), Hartford, Connecticut: Trinity College. Retrieved March 19th, 2011 from http://www.americanreligionsurvey-aris.org/reports/ARIS_Report_2008.pdf.

Learning, J. (2006). Pentacle quest. *Church & State, 59,* 10–13.

Pike, S. M. (2004). *New Age and Neo-pagan religions in America:* Columbia University Press.

Powers, R. (2005). Counseling and spirituality: A historical review. *Counseling & Values, 49,* 217–225.

Rigoglioso, M. (2005). Interview with Starhawk. *Feminist Theology, 13,* 173–183.

Smith, A., & Simmonds, J. (2006). Help-seeking and paranormal beliefs in adherents of mainstream religion, alternative religion, and no religion. *Counselling Psychology Quarterly, 19,* 331–341.

Starhawk. (1999). The spiral dance: *The rebirth of the ancient religion of the great Goddess 20th anniversary edition.* San Francisco: Harper Collins Publishers, Inc.

Tairu, T. (2010). Religion as a discursive technique: The politics of classifying Wicca. *Journal of Contemporary Religion, 25,* 379–394.

United States Census Bureau. (2011). *Statistical abstract of the United States 2011.* Washington D.C.: Author. Retrieved February 7th from www.census.gov/compendia/statab/2011/tables/11s0075.pdf

Walker, W., & Jung, F. (2011, November 9th). Re: WitchVox site map directory [Welcome posted to on-line forum]. Retrieved from http://www.witchvox.com/xmap.html

White, E. (2010). The meaning of "Wicca": A study in etymology, history, and Pagan politics. *Pomegranate, 12,* 185–207. doi:10.1558/pome.v12i2.184.

Wise, C. (2004). A process epistemology of Wiccan occult knowledge. *Pomegranate, 6,* 199–211.

Worthington, E., Hook, J., Davis, D., & McDaniel, M. (2011). Religion and spirituality. *Journal of Clinical Psychology, 67,* 204–214. doi:10.1002/jclp .20760.

Yardley, M. (2008). Social work practice with Pagans, Witches, and Wiccans: Guidelines for practice with children and youth. *Social Work, 53,* 329–336.

PART VIII

New Religious Movements

From *Star Wars* to Jediism

The Emergence of Fiction-Based Religion

Markus Altena Davidsen

....

May the Force Be with You

When Luke Skywalker takes off in his space fighter to attack the Death Star, the seemingly uncon-querable imperial space station, Princess Leia wishes him good luck with the words "May the Force be with you." The heroes in *Star Wars* believe that the Force will aid those who combat evil. Those who fight on the side of the Force can overcome even a vastly superior foe—and of course the mission succeeds. In the crucial moment Luke turns off his ship's targeting computer, lets the Force direct his actions, and manages to strike the Death Star at its only weak point. The Force is with him and secures him the victory.

Many *Star Wars* fans playfully greet each other with the phrase "May the Force be with you" and sign their posts on online discussion forums with the abbreviation "mtfbwy." Nevertheless, these fans attribute the Force existence only within the fictional *Star Wars* universe. They do not anticipate that the Force could actually intervene in their own world, the empirical world. By contrast, there is a movement based on *Star Wars* that explicitly distances itself from the mainstream fan culture and in fact does postulate the existence of the Force in the empirical world. The members of Jediism, as this movement is called, not only believe in the Force but also ritually interact with it, mostly through meditation.

The present essay has three aims: (1) to present an overview of the core elements (Force teachings, ritual practices, and legitimization strategies) of Jediism;[1] (2) to compare Jediism with *Star Wars* fan culture and argue that Jediism must be classified as a religion, whereas fan culture must not, because Jediism substitutes ritual and belief for the play and fascination of fan culture; and (3) to introduce the category "fiction-based religion" and establish Jediism as a member of this subcategory of religion.

Jediism as Religion

Inspired by Steve Bruce, I consider religion to constitute any activity (i.e., cognition, communica-tion, or action) that assumes the existence of transempirical realities (e.g., other worlds, Heaven), supernatural entities with power of action (e.g., gods, spirits), and/or impersonal processes or principles possessed of moral purpose (e.g., karma, *ma'at*).[2] According to this definition, Jediism must be categorized as a religion because its ideas and concerns are formulated with reference to a supernatural power (the Force) and the core of Jediist practice is ritual interaction with the Force (through meditation and, in some cases, prayer and various rites of transition). Jediism is not formally organized into a churchlike institution but is developed, maintained, and transmitted by a network of individuals and groups. Members mostly use the Internet as their medium of communication, but some also meet face to face. They have no physical places of worship, but some Jediists express a wish to build temples in the future.

Fiction-Based Religions

Jediism is a new religion. The world premiere of the first *Star Wars* film in 1977 can be taken as its absolute beginning, but not until the rise of mass access to the Internet in the mid-1990s did it develop into a visible, organized, and extensive movement. Jediism is, however, interesting for the study of religion not only because it is a new religion but also because it represents a new form of religion, which I suggest calling "fiction-based religion."[3] In my understanding, a fiction-based religion is a religion that uses fictional texts as its main authoritative, religious texts. That a text is authoritative for a religion means that its members use terminology, beliefs, practices, roles, and/or social organization derived from the authoritative text as a model for their own real-world religion. The term *fiction* refers to a narrative that an author presents without any aspiration to refer to events that have taken place in the real world prior to their enshrinement in a text.[4] In some cases fiction-based religions are grounded in what we can call "fictional religions," that is, religions within fictional narratives, invented by the author and practiced by fictional characters. The Force religion of the Jedi Knights in *Star Wars* is an example of a fictional religion. Jediism, the fiction-based real-world religion, is modeled on the fictional Force religion. Even though the members of Jediism, the Jediists, see *Star Wars* in general as fiction, they consider the theology and practice of the Force religion to be valid in the empirical world.

There are many other examples of (partly) fiction-based religions that all use fictional narratives (science fiction, fantasy, horror) as authoritative texts. One well-known science fiction example is the neo-pagan movement the Church of All Worlds, which is modeled on the organization of the same name in Robert Heinlein's novel *Stranger in a Strange Land*, from 1961. From the fictional religion in Heinlein's novel, the Church of All Worlds has taken over the water-sharing ritual, polyamory, and the recognition of the divine within all human beings, which they express with the greeting "Thou art God/dess."[5] H. P. Lovecraft's horror story "The Call of Cthulhu," from 1928, and other short stories from his "Cthulhu Mythos" have inspired both Anton Szandor LaVey's Church of Satan and groups of chaos magicians. LaVey explains in *The Satanic Rituals* how one can call upon Cthulhu, Nyarlathotep, and other of Lovecraft's monster gods, and chaos magicians claim to be possessed by these gods, though they still stress their fictionality.[6] A spiritual milieu exists based on J. R. R. Tolkien's fantasy works. Its members believe that Middle-earth is a real place, being either a prehistory to our world or existing on another plane, and communicate ritually with the Valar, the Powers or "gods" of Tolkien's narrative world.[7] Some also believe themselves to be Elves, and in the 1990s the Internet-based Otherkin movement developed out of the Tolkien-inspired Elven community. The Otherkin believe themselves to be nonhumans, such as werewolves, dragons, or angels.[8] Jediism is thus not the only example of a fiction-based religion, but it is probably the largest of its kind and therefore suitable as a case through which to examine more closely this new type of religion.

Star Wars

The Star Wars Narrative

The opening roll-up of all six *Star Wars* movies begins with the same formulaic phrase:[9] "A long time ago in a galaxy far, far away ... ." This is obviously a transformation of the traditional fairy-tale introduction "Once upon a time in a land far, far away," and *Star Wars* certainly shares a number of traits with fairy tales. The main character and hero, Luke Skywalker, has been raised by foster parents on a desolate farm in the Outer Rim of the galaxy and does not know the truth about his special ancestry and extraordinary powers. The story is full of princesses, noble warriors (Jedi Knights), evil villains, and all kinds of fantastic creatures. When George Lucas, script writer and producer of *Star Wars*, was interviewed around the time of the release of the first movie in 1977, he therefore never referred to his movie as "science fiction" (understood as dystopian anticipation of the future) but always as a "space opera" or "space fantasy." In these terms, *Star Wars* should resemble *Flash Gordon*, not *2001: A Space Odyssey*.

Star Wars is about the battle between good and evil. The peaceful Galactic Republic has become a tyrannical empire, ruled over by a Sith Lord, a kind of evil wizard who can manipulate the Force. A small band of rebels fights for the freedom of the galaxy. Among them is Luke Skywalker, who in the course of the film is initiated into the order of the Jedi Knights, warrior monks inspired by samurai warriors, Franciscans, and Arthurian knights. The Jedi Knights also use the Force, but only in the service of good. The Force gives the Jedi telepathic and telekinetic abilities and stimulates their perception, cognition, and skill, especially when they use their intuition and let themselves be guided by the Force.

In *A New Hope*, the old Jedi Knight Obi-Wan Kenobi introduces the Force to young Luke Skywalker with the following words: "The Force is what gives a Jedi his power. It's an energy field created by all living things. It surrounds us and penetrates us. It binds the galaxy together."[10] Put briefly, the Force is a nonpersonified divine energy. It takes special training to be able to sense the Force itself, but its effects (levitation, lightning bolts shot from one's fingertips, etc.) are visible to everybody, leaving the reality of the Force unquestionable within the *Star Wars* universe. The existence of the Force is a matter of fact, but its deeper nature remains a mystery into which one can gain (partial) insight only through meditation.

Star Wars *Fandom*

For most fans, *Star Wars* is first and foremost a fairy tale, and fans see the *Star Wars* universe as a fascinating world in which one can playfully immerse oneself. A twenty-year-old woman with the user name Dust from the Danish *Star Wars* fan club skywalker.dk expresses it like this:

> The Jedi, the Force, and the light-sabre battles are probably the things that cap-
> tivate me the most about the *Star Wars* universe. I have always loved fantasy and
> love to immerse myself in other worlds or to dream that this boring, commonplace
> world will turn out to contain something more magical and exciting. I find the
> idea of a universal Force that binds us all together and gives us supernatural
> powers deeply fascinating.[11]

Entering the colorful and detailed universe of *Star Wars* is an important aspect of being a fan. Not only do fans like to discuss movies and books, to watch them again and again, and to collect heaps of merchandise and an encyclopedic knowledge of the fictional universe, they also play role-playing games within the *Star Wars* universe, dress up and fight with light sabres, compose their own fan fiction, draw and paint fan art, and so on. They enter the universe, explore it, and expand it.[12]

For many *Star Wars* fans, however, being a fan is not only about entering the fictional world from the empirical world, but also about how elements from the fictional world can enter the empirical world. It is the values of the *Star Wars* narrative, in particular, that are transferred from fictional space to everyday life. These values include an ideal of personal growth, a religious involvement, and a social ethic. The social ethic is emphasized by many fans, who either claim to have changed their ethical views after watching *Star Wars* or report seeing their own values confirmed in the choices and actions of the *Star Wars* heroes. Will Brooker cites several fans who talk about the ethical impact of *Star Wars* on their lives. One fan formulates it as follows:

> Yoda's theme song calms me from a day and gives me strength to continue helping
> others in a warm and caring way. He, Obi-Wan, Qui-Gon and Luke are such
> respectable figures that some of us can't help but aspire to be like them. Sure, we
> may not be able to lift droids, rocks or X-Wings, but we could "Use the Force"
> in other ways such as helping, loving, caring and supporting, and be our own
> personal Jedi.[13]

The four characters named here, Master Yoda, Obi-Wan Kenobi, Qui-Gon Jinn, and Luke Sky-walker, are all Jedi Knights. This fan denies that the Force and the supernatural powers of the Jedi have a counterpart in the real world, but he perceives the social ethic of the Jedi ("helping, loving, caring and supporting") as equally valid and important in the real world and in the world of fiction.

Jediism takes its point of departure from the fascination with the Force and the identification with the Jedi Knights as role models that are common in fan culture, although there are, of course, many *Star Wars* fans who are not at all interested in Jedi ethics and Force theology.

"Jedi" as Religious Self-Identification

Surprisingly many people are prepared to identify themselves as "Jedi" in a religious context. In the summer of 2009, the *Washington Post* reported that "Jedi" was the tenth most common religious self-identification globally on Facebook.[14] Better known, however, is the "Jedi Census Phenomenon," which has its own entry on Wikipedia. Before the 2001 census in Great Britain, Canada, New Zealand, and Australia, an e-mail circulated urging people to report their religious affiliation as "Jedi." The e-mail was probably a combination of practical joke, a test of the power of e-mail as medium, and political protest against the religious affiliation tick box (even though reporting one's religion was not mandatory). The result was that more than 500,000 people in the four countries reported themselves to be "Jedi." With more than 390,000 self-identified adherents, Jediism emerged as the fourth-largest religion in Great Britain. The largest concentration of Jedi proved, however, to be in New Zealand, where they made up 1.3 percent of the total population.[15] There was no e-mail campaign prior to the following census in 2006, and the number of Jedi dropped dramatically. In New Zealand, for instance, it dropped from 53,715 to 20,262.[16] More remarkable than the fall-off, however, is the fact that so many people continued to state their religious affiliation as "Jedi."

No researcher has attempted to establish how many of the self-identified Jedi Knights on Facebook and in the census really practice a Force-directed spirituality. The president of the Australian Star Wars Appreciation Society estimated in a newspaper interview in 2002, just after the publication of the census results, that of the 70,000 Australian Jedi, 50,000 had identified themselves as Jedi just for fun; 15,000 aimed to "give the government a bit of curry"; and 5,000 "would be hard-core people that would believe the Jedi religion," though for the most part probably only "at a metaphorical level."[17] If we generalize to all countries that participated in the census his approximation that between 5 and 10 percent of self-identified "Jedi" are serious Jediists, we get an estimated 30,000 Jediists in Great Britain, Canada, Australia, and New Zealand combined. To this figure should be added an even greater number in the United States, but so far such figures are pure speculations.

The Mythologization of *Star Wars*

Star Wars has not achieved its status as myth and cult solely because of its content and its fans. It has also benefited from a process of mythologization orchestrated by film critics, journalists, and George Lucas himself.[18] Though Lucas does not consider himself a Jediist, he has explicitly stated that *Star Wars* can legitimately be viewed as a spiritual resource.

The mythologization process began with the reviews of the second *Star Wars* film, *The Empire Strikes Back*, in 1980. Steven Hart describes the new rhetoric as follows:

> Associate editor [of *Time* magazine] Gerald Clarke, who had praised the original flick for its light-hearted refusal to offer anything like a serious message, now finds "a moral dimension that touches us much more deeply than one-dimensional action adventures can." A sidebar, ponderously headlined "In the Footsteps of Ulysses," cites everything from "The Odyssey" to "Pilgrim's Progress" before concluding that the "*Star Wars*" films "draw from the same deep wells of mythology, the unconscious themes that have always dominated history on the planet."[19]

Since then, Lucas has himself actively participated in the construction of *Star Wars* as a myth. In a famous interview with the journalist Bill Moyers, Lucas explains at length his view of the mythical and religious elements in *Star Wars* and formulates the following programmatic statement:

> I put the Force into the movie in order to awaken a certain kind of spirituality in young people—more a belief in God than a belief in any particular religious system. I wanted to make it so that young people would begin to ask questions about the mystery. ... I didn't want to invent a religion. I wanted to try to explain in a different way the religions that have already existed. I wanted to express it all. ... I'm telling an old myth in a new way.[20]

During the interview, Lucas makes three points. First, he considers *Star Wars* to be a "myth" because the narrative carries certain basic values. Second, he asserts that he has let religion and faith play a central role in *Star Wars* because he deems the authentic human life to be a religious life and because he takes the existence of a divine power for granted: "I think there is a God, no question."[21] Third, he makes clear that even though *Star Wars* is inspired by "real" religions, the movies are fundamentally human-made entertainment and not the result of divine revelation. Therefore, they are unsuitable as the foundation of a religion. When confronted with the fact that young people today draw inspiration for how to live their lives from films, including *Star Wars*, rather than from organized religions, he therefore answers, "Well, I hope that doesn't end up being the course this whole thing takes, because I think there's definitely a place for organized religion. I would hate to find ourselves in a completely secular world where entertainment was passing for some kind of religious experience."[22] According to Lucas, it is desirable for entertainment, including *Star Wars*, to awaken a religious interest, but he sees this interest as no substitute for organized religion.

The Force Religion of the Jedi Knights: The Fictional Religion in *Star Wars*

Mythic narratives play almost no role in the "Force religion," by which I mean the system of theological teachings, ritual practices, and ethical rules of the Jedi Knights in the *Star Wars* universe.[23] Instead, it focuses on theology, social ethics, and spiritual practice. The sources of this fictional religion are the canonical films and their "extended universe," which comprises official comics, computer games, and more than two hundred novels. The central metaphysical power in the Force religion is, obviously, the Force. In the extended universe, it becomes clear that many different schools have fought over how to understand its true nature. Here I shall briefly touch on just two themes in these theological or, more precisely, dynamological debates. One central theme is the question whether the Force is monistic or dualistic in nature. The Force is usually represented as dualistic, with both a light side (Ashla) and a dark side (Bogan). This dualism is always moral insofar as the light side is good whereas the dark side is evil. The real question concerns the ontological status of the dualism. It is generally agreed that one can either follow the light side and do good or let oneself be seduced by the dark side and work evil. Jedi Masters debate whether a turn to the dark side should be understood as the corruption in an individual of an essentially monistic and good Force, or whether the dark side has its own extra-psychic, cosmological existence. The dominant theology is an intra-psychic dualism (the individual is free to choose between good and evil) encapsulated in a cosmological monism (the Force itself is essentially good). The other important theme is the question of whether the Force is an independent agent. One position views the Force as a passive, dynamistic energy that can be manipulated, whereas according to another viewpoint the Force is a semi-personal, active, and animistic will power with a project of salvation. The second view is implicitly expressed in the common farewell greeting "May the Force be with you."

As a member of the Jedi Order, a Jedi Knight is obliged to live by the Jedi Code. One of the novels summarizes the code in this way:

> Jedi are the guardians of peace in the galaxy.
> Jedi use their powers to defend and to protect.
> Jedi respect all life, in any form.
> Jedi serve others rather than ruling over them, for the good of the galaxy.
> Jedi seek to improve themselves through knowledge and training.[24]

Here an ideal of physical and spiritual self-development is combined with a social commitment to serve, protect, and help others. The last line of the code deserves comment. Jedi Knights are required to acquire knowledge and to train. They have to practice fighting and investigative skills, for the Jedi Order forms a kind of intelligence agency in the Galactic Republic. But through study, meditative contemplation, and guidance by a master, they are also required to gain insight in the Force and learn to interact with it ritually. In doing so they become capable of being guided by the Force and of using it to perform seemingly supernatural acts like clairvoyance, levitation, and the influencing of weaker minds, the so-called "Jedi mind trick."

Jediism: The Fiction-Based Religion

Outside the *Star Wars* universe, the fictional Force religion serves as the basis for a loosely organized religious movement that is made up of several small, independent, but networked groups. Although throughout this essay I have used "Jediism" to designate the entire movement and "Jediists" to refer to all its members, several different terms are in use. Some members prefer to name their religion "Jedi Realism" or "Jedi Philosophy" and to self-identify as "True Jedi," "Real Jedi," or "Jedi Realists" (to emphasis the difference between the fictional Jedi and themselves) or simply as "Jedi" (to emphasize their likeness to the fictional Jedi). Jediists use the different terms in order to position themselves in relation to each other, but the particle *Jedi* is used in them all. The ideas and practices of Jediism stem primarily from *Star Wars*, but are also inspired by other religious traditions, such as Christianity and Westernized Buddhism and Taoism.

In April and May 2008 and February 2010, I visited the homepages and discussion forums of seven Jediist groups: the Temple of the Jedi Order, the Jedi Foundation, the Jedi Church, the Jediism Way, the Jedi Sanctuary, the Force Academy, and the Ashla Knights. The Jedi Church is based in New Zealand, the Force Academy in Great Britain, and the rest in the United States. All use the English language, but participants in the online discussions can in principle live anywhere in the world. In my analysis of the homepages, I aimed to answer the following four questions: (1) How does the group categorize itself? (2) How does the group view the Force? (3) How does the group legitimate the fact that its religion is based on a fictional text? and (4) What are the practices of the group? Based on this source material, I can sketch what a collection of elite Jediists (homepage owners and active online discussants) understand to be the most important Jediist ideas and practices and how they position themselves in relation to fans and more conventional religions. The data collected do not allow me to say anything conclusive about whether common group members (let alone solitary Jediists) share these points of view or anything about their social backgrounds. Since I used only online sources, my knowledge of offline practices was limited. With these reservations in mind, let me present a sketch of Jediism as a religion in the empirical world.[25]

Dissociation from Fandom and Self-Identification as "Religion" or "Spirituality"

Jediists describe the *Star Wars* films as "wonderful,"[26] and they display an extensive knowledge of the *Star Wars* universe in their discussions—traits that normally characterize fans. Nevertheless, they find it imperative to distance themselves from general *Star Wars* fandom and to emphasize their own seriousness and sincerity in opposition to the playful and ironic fans. Accordingly, interested visitors on the Jedi Sanctuary site are addressed as follows: "Some of you might think that the Jedi Sanctuary is like a SW fan club, or just a joke. It's not. It's a real path that we follow, and we take it seriously. When we say, 'May the Force be with you,' we believe it and mean it."[27]

In opposition to the category "fan club," three of the seven groups I have analyzed define Jediism as a "religion" (or "church"). The Jedi Church does not speak of Jediism, but simply of "the Jedi religion,"[28] and the Temple of the Jedi Order considers Jediism "a real living, breathing religion."[29] Both groups are legally authorized to perform marriages, and since December 14, 2005, the Temple of the Jedi Order has been recognized as a nonprofit religious and educational corporation under Texas law, granting members the right to deduct contributions from their tax bill.[30] The Temple of the Jedi Order clearly considers a high degree of institutionalization and official recognition as a prerequisite for counting as a real religion. The Jedi Church and the Jediism Way, by contrast, see no problem in combining self-description as religion/church with dissociation from the dogmatic and collective aspects of institutionalized religion. The former stresses that the "Jedi church has no official doctrine or scripture,"[31] and the Jediism Way explains that it is a religion because of its members' shared belief in the Force despite the absence of collective rituals.[32]

In the other four groups, Jediism is more often referred to as a "spirituality," "philosophy," "path," or "way," and these terms are all used in opposition to "religion" understood as a collective and institutionalized (and therefore inhibited and alienated) engagement with the divine. As one Jediist formulates it in a post on the Jedi Sanctuary's forum, Jediism is a spirituality and not a religion because Jediism is not "the unthinking following of dogma."[33] Later in the same thread, one of the leaders of the group adds, "I don't consider the Jedi Path a religion, as far as traditional religions are viewed. When I think of religion, I think of an organized set of rituals, public worship conducted according to certain rules, incense burning, religious symbols, group prayers, etc. ... I think Jedi believe in a more intimate connection to the Force than what organized religion offers."[34] These groups understand Jediism as an essentially individualistic, free, authentic, and mystical spirituality.

Teachings about the Force

Whether Jediist groups define Jediism as religion or spirituality, they do so with reference to their belief in the Force—even though different groups understand the Force differently. These dynamological differences stem partly from the fact that the individual groups typically stress one of the two Force conceptions in *Star Wars*, the dynamistic or the animistic, and partly from their inspiration from other religions.

The four self-identified "spiritual" groups, the Ashla Knights, the Force Academy, the Jedi Sanctuary, and the Jedi Foundation, are inspired by Eastern religions and holistic spirituality ("New Age") in addition to *Star Wars*. These groups all tend to view the Force in dynamistic terms. For them the Force is thus a vitalistic power or life energy. The Force Academy, the Ashla Knights, and the Jedi Sanctuary compare the Force to Eastern concepts like *qi* and *prana* and observe similarities between their own practice and taiji, aikido, and zen.[35] The Jedi Foundation believes the Force to be "essentially a 'by-product' of life—a side effect, if you will, yet symbiotic,"[36] and considers "the study of science and other beliefs and practices on energy" as different paths to knowledge of the Force.[37]

The three self-identified "religious" groups view the Force in *animistic* terms as an independent agent, sometimes interpreting the Force through a more or less Christian lens as a kind of Holy Spirit. The Jediism Way declares, "We believe the guidance of the Force will bring us to a course of right action," but still stresses that the Force is no person.[38] The Temple of the Jedi Order has a similar vision and refers to the Force as an active "living Force."[39] The Jedi Church is open to both dynamistic and animistic understandings of the Force.[40]

The Relation to *Star Wars*

As we have seen, the groups' self-identification as religion or spirituality corresponds with their conception of the Force as either a semi-personified agent or an impersonal energy. Along another axis, the seven Jediists groups can be divided into two groups depending on whether they seek to explicitly affirm that their spirituality is based on *Star Wars* or whether they dissociate themselves from *Star Wars* as a means of legitimation.

Three groups—the Jedi Sanctuary, the Jediism Way, and the Jedi Foundation—all stress that their ideas and practices come from *Star Wars*. The Jediism Way simply understands "the community of Jediism" as "those who connected with the stories in Star Wars, share the belief in an open concept of divine power known as 'the Force' … [and aspire to live their] lives similarly to that which they connected with in these tales."[41] The Jedi Foundation joins in with the following statement:

> Jedi [Jediists] strive to emulate those [Jedi Knights] seen in the movies, but we
> are aware of the differences from fiction to reality. This site takes a lot of [its]
> views from three main sources, *The Star Wars Power of the Jedi Sourcebook* [a
> source book for the *Star Wars* role-playing game], The *Jedi Apprentice* series
> [three novels that tell of Luke Skywalker's reinstigation of the Jedi Order after
> the movie storyline], and the Movies. We use these as guides, to explore, learn
> from and more importantly expand from. As *Star Wars* Jedi are what inspired
> us, it is what we chose to look towards.[42]

The members of the Jediism Way and the Jedi Foundation feel no need to legitimate and defend the fact that Jediism is based on the fictional *Star Wars* movies, but the Jedi Sanctuary refers to Joseph Campbell, who has supposedly said, "I've heard youngsters use some of George Lucas's terms—'The Force' and 'The dark side'. So it must be hitting somewhere. It's a good sound teaching, I would say."[43] The quote is regarded as Campbell's acknowledgment of *Star Wars*' status as a myth and thus by implication as his recognition of Jediism as a religion/spirituality.

In all seven groups, but strongest in the Temple of the Jedi Order, the Jedi Church, the Ashla Knights, and the Force Academy, one encounters a contrasting strategy, namely, disassociation from *Star Wars* and the claim that the *real* source of inspiration for Jediism is not *Star Wars* itself but the religions that inspired George Lucas to make it. The Ashla Knights and the Force Academy claim to build on "real world philosophies and influences" or "life force philosophies,"[44] namely, different forms of Eastern philosophy, religion, and martial arts. The Jedi Church and the Temple of the Jedi Order claim to base themselves not only on Eastern religion but on universal truths shared by all religions:

> The Jedi Church makes no denial that its name and terminology originate from a fictitious past, but the concepts and ideals that are identified by Jedi followers are known for their innate truth. … The Jedi religion … existed before a popular movie gave it a name, and now that it has a name, people all over the world can share their experiences of the Jedi religion, here in the Jedi Church.[45]
>
> Jediism is a syncretistic religion—a faith involving elements from two or more religions including Taoism, Shintoism, Buddhism, Christianity, Mysticism, and many other Religions' universal truths and a combination of martial arts and the Code of Chivalry. These philosophies [the different religions] are the heart of Jediism; not the wonderful Star Wars movies themselves except to serve as parables.[46]

Because the Temple of the Jedi Order equates Jediism with the true essence of all religion as such, Jediism can be seen as ancient, and the line of "Masters of Jediism" can count "Buddha, Jesus, LaoTsu, St. Francis of Assisi, Gandhi, Martin Luther King, and so many others."[47]

In Table 15.1, I have plotted the seven groups into a matrix with self-identification/dynamology on one axis and the place of *Star Wars* in their legitimation strategy on the other. Groups that are no longer active in September 2012 are marked by italics. It would seem that the combination of dissociation from *Star Wars* and "religious" Jediism makes for the "fittest" form of Jediism, or at least for the most stable Jediist communities.

Table 15.1

	"Spiritual"/dynamistic	"Religious"/animist
affirmative toward *Star Wars*	Jedi Foundation *Jedi Sanctuary*	Jediism Way
dissociative from *Star Wars*	Ashla Knights *Force Academy*	Jedi Church Temple of the Jedi Order

Practice and Ethics

All Jediist groups emphasize physical and spiritual self-development, but this aspect is particularly dominant in the Jediism Way, the Jedi Sanctuary, the Jedi Foundation, and the Ashla Knights. As the leader of the Jediism Way formulates it, "I don't pray to the Force or worship it every day in the traditional sense, but I meditate and do other things [to] strengthen my connection to it every day!!"[48] Similarly, the Jedi Sanctuary emphasizes that the group does not have rituals, but instead aims to "discuss all aspects of being a Jedi, fitness, meditation, conflict resolution, negotiation, staying positive, making good decisions, having healthy relationships, trusting in the Force, and personal growth."[49]

The Ashla Knights has a comparable vision,[50] and the Jedi Foundation focuses on:

> Physical Well-Being (diet, exercise, and practical self-defense), Mental Well-Being (stress-relief, conflict resolution, and learning new subjects such as different philosophies that exist), and Spiritual Well-Being (meditation, self-awareness and self-honesty, learning about the Force). The Jedi work towards self-betterment.[51]

The homepage for the Jedi Church gives no information about the practice of the group, and in the Force Academy the practice depends on which "path" the member belongs to—whether he or she is a "Light Jedi," "Dark Jedi," or "Shadow Jedi."

While some groups deny that social ethics founded on the idea of charity should have anything to do with Jediism (e.g., the Jedi Foundation),[52] others see no contradiction between the ideals of self-development and charity (e.g., the Jedi Sanctuary).[53] In the Temple of the Jedi Order, which downplays the self-development aspect, it is emphasized that "love and compassion are central to our lives. We must love each other as we love ourselves."[54]

A social ethics formulated in terms of charity is not the only loan from Christianity in the Temple of the Jedi Order. We are also told that Jediists "believe in the eternal life,"[55] and the homepage contains a modified version of one of Francis of Assisi's prayers under the title "Jedi Creed."[56] One of the functions of the forum is that members can present personal problems and ask other members to pray for them. Such calls for intercessory prayer get answers like "I will keep you in my thoughts and meditations."[57] The group also has a clergy and a "Clergy Ceremonies and Rituals Committee" that is responsible for the development of "the Temple of the Jedi Order Clergy Handbook," with rituals for "baptisms, naming, weddings, and funerals."[58] The Temple of the Jedi Order is thus clearly the Jediist group that to the largest extent models itself on a conventional religion (denominational Christianity), which entails institutionalization, public recognition, and the development of collective rituals.

***

We have seen that *Star Wars* includes a fictional religion, the Force religion of the Jedi Knights, and that both *Star Wars* fans and Jediists are interested in the dynamology, practice, and ethics of this fictional religion and see parallels between the *Star Wars* universe and the empirical world. On these grounds, and using a broad, functionalistic definition of religion, John Lyden has argued that both *Star Wars* itself (as a film conveying values) and *Star Wars* fandom (as a community sharing a "canonical" myth) constitute religious phenomena.[59] Such a conclusion is confusing and misleading, however, for it obscures real differences between *Star Wars* fandom and Jediism, differences that justify labeling the latter, but not the former, as religion according to a substantive definition.

For fans the *Star Wars* universe is first and foremost a fascinating place that one can playfully enter and leave again. Many fans see such visits to the *Star Wars* universe as inspiring and edifying because *Star Wars* confirms basic values in their own world. Jediists differ from mainstream fans by claiming that not only the ethics of the Jedi Knights, but also their dynamology and religious practice, are valid models for real world religious activity. Despite disagreements over self-identification, dynamology, and legitimization strategies, Jediists agree on two things: first, that a divine power guarantees the order of existence and that this power is the Force; and second, that being a Jediist is defined by belief in and ritual interaction with this Force through meditation and sometimes additional ritual techniques. The fictional religion of the Jedi Knights, which is merely an object for play within fan culture, is here transformed into a real religion, Jediism. Despite the facts that some groups distance themselves from *Star Wars* in an attempt to legitimate Jediism as a "real" religion and that all Jediist groups to a smaller or larger extent integrate ideas and practices from other religions, the Force religion from *Star Wars* remains the main source of inspiration and terminology for Jediism. Because its main authoritative text is a fictional narrative, Jediism can therefore be categorized as a fiction-based religion.

Jediism and other fiction-based religions constitute the institutionalized tip of a much larger iceberg of religious ideas and practices created and maintained by popular culture.[60] Popular cultural narratives with religious themes or embedded fictional religions—narratives such as *Star Wars*, *The Lord of the Rings*, *Battlestar Galactica*, *Buffy the Vampire Slayer*, *The X-Files*, and *Discworld*—are today very important sources of religious knowledge and edification for many (especially young) people. Just as *Star Wars* mixes material from the religious past—from Christianity and Eastern religions—other popular cultural narratives recombine and revitalize elements from both organized religion and folk belief. By influencing the religious beliefs and practices of their readers and viewers, these narratives contribute to the transmission and transformation of the religious past into a fiction-mediated religious future.

Notes

An earlier version of this article was published in Danish as "Fiktionsbaseret religion: Fra *Star Wars* til jediisme," *Religionsvidenskabeligt Tidsskrift* 55 (2010): 3–21.

1. Jediism has received some scholarly attention, but earlier studies have focused on the "Jedi Census Phenomenon" of 2001 (see the section "'Jedi' as Religious Self-identification" in this essay) rather than on organized Jediism; see Adam Possamai, "Alternative Spiritualities, New Religious Movements and Jediism in Australia," *Australian Religion Studies Review* 16, no. 2 (2003): 69–86; Possamai, *Religion and Popular Culture: A Hyper-real Testament* (Brussels: P.I.E.–Peter Lang, 2005), 72–76; Jennifer Porter, "'I Am a Jedi': *Star Wars* Fandom, Religious Belief and the 2001 Census," in *Finding the Force of the "Star Wars" Franchise: Fans, Merchandise and Critics*, ed. Matthew Wilhelm Kapell and John Shelton Lawrence (New York: Peter Lang, 2006), 95–112. Readers might want to compare the present essay with Debra McCormick's treatment of Jediism in "The Sanctification of *Star Wars*: From Fans to Followers," in *Handbook of Hyper-real Religions*, ed. Adam Possamai (Leiden: Brill, 2012), 165–84; see also Markus Davidsen, "Jediism: A Convergence of *Star Wars* Fan Culture and Salad Bar Spirituality," *De Filosoof* 51 (2011): 24.

2. Bruce defines religion as "beliefs, actions and institutions which assume the existence of supernatural entities with powers of action, or impersonal powers or processes possessed of moral purpose"; see Steve Bruce, "Defining Religion: A Practical Response," *International Review of Sociology: Revue Internationale de Sociologie* 21, no. 1 (2011): 112.

3. Adam Possamai speaks about "hyper-real religions," with reference to Jean Baudrillard's concept of the hyper-real. For Possamai, new religions based on fiction are "hyper-real" because they attribute the status of reality to a virtual that usurps the empirically real. So far as I can see, hyper-reality in this sense is a common feature of all religions. I therefore prefer the more descriptive term *fiction-based religion*; cf. Possamai, *Religion and Popular Culture*, and Adam Possamai, "Yoda Goes to Glastonbury: An Introduction to Hyper-real Religions," in *Handbook of Hyper-real Religions*, ed. Adam Possamai (Leiden: Brill, 2012), 1–21.

4. This understanding of fiction as being dependent on the author's intention of (partial) nonreference follows Dorrit Cohn, *The Distinction of Fiction* (Baltimore: Johns Hopkins University Press, 1999), 12.

5. See Carole M. Cusack, *Invented Religions: Imagination, Fiction and Faith* (Farnham, UK: Ashgate, 2010), 53–82.

6. Anton Szandor LaVey, *The Satanic Rituals: Companion to The Satanic Bible* (New York: Avon, 1972), 173–201. On chaos magicians and Lovecraft, see Wouter Hanegraaff, "Fiction in the Desert of the Real: Lovecraft's Cthulhu Mythos," *Aries* 7 (2007): 105.

7. See Markus Altena Davidsen, "The Spiritual Milieu Based on J. R. R. Tolkien's Literary Mythology," in *Handbook of Hyper-real Religions*, ed. Adam Possamai (Leiden: Brill, 2012), 185–204.

8. See Danielle Kirby, "From Pulp Fiction to Revealed Text: A Study of the Role of the Text in the Otherkin Community," in *Exploring Religion and the Sacred in the Media Age*, ed. Christopher Deacy and Elisabeth Arweck (Farnham, UK: Ashgate, 2009), 141–54; Kirby, "Alternative Worlds: Metaphysical Questing and Virtual Community Amongst the Otherkin," in *Handbook of Hyperreal Religions*, ed. Adam Possamai

(Leiden: Brill, 2012), 129–40; Joseph Laycock, "'We Are Spirits of Another Sort': Ontological Rebellion and Religious Dimensions," *Nova Religio: The Journal of Alternative and Emergent Religions* 15, no. 3 (2012): 65–90. Many new religious movements that are not, strictly speaking, fiction-based are still inspired by trends in fictional literature. This is especially clear in the well-documented influence of fantasy literature on all strands of the neo-pagan movement (witchcraft, heathenry, the goddess movement, etc.); see, e.g., Graham Harvey, "Discworld and Otherworld: The Imaginative Use of Fantasy Literature among Pagans," in *Popular Spiritualities: The Politics of Contemporary Enchantment*, ed. Lynne Hume and Kathleen McPhillips (Aldershot: Ashgate 2006), 41–52. For more examples of new religions inspired by or based on fiction, see Adam Possamai, ed., *Handbook of Hyper-real Religions* (Leiden: Brill, 2012).

9. The corpus of *Star Wars* texts (films, novels, computer games, etc.) is enormous, but the core is the six "canonical" movies, which were all written and produced (but not all directed) by George Lucas. The six movies comprise two relatively independent trilogies. The storyline in the second, "prequel" trilogy takes place before the events in the "original" trilogy. In order of production, the canonical movies are: *Star Wars Episode IV: A New Hope* (1977), *Star Wars Episode V: The Empire Strikes Back* (1980), *Star Wars Episode VI: Return of the Jedi* (1983), *Star Wars Episode I: The Phantom Menace* (1999), *Star Wars Episode II: Attack of the Clones* (2002), and *Star Wars Episode III: Revenge of the Sith* (2005).

10. George Lucas, *Star Wars Episode IV: A New Hope*, Lucasfilm, Ltd., 1977.

11. Dust, personal e-mail, May 22, 2008; translated from Danish.

12. The active, "poaching" character of fandom, as opposed to earlier stereotypes of fans as passive consumers, has been acknowledged since Henry Jenkins, *Textual Poachers: Television Fans and Participatory Culture* (New York: Routledge, 1992). The playful aspect of fan cultures in general is emphasized in fan research, especially by scholars who are themselves fans; see, e.g., Matt Hills, *Fan Cultures* (London: Routledge, 2002), chap. 4.

13. Will Brooker, *Using the Force: Creativity, Community and "Star Wars" Fans* (New York: Continuum, 2002), 6.

14. The ten most common self-identifications were Christian, Islam, Atheist, Agnostic, Buddhist, Hindu, Jewish, Spiritual, Sikh, and Jedi. In the category "Christian" were included the following self-identifications: Catholic, Protestant, Episcopalian, Presbyterian, Methodist, LDS, and Mormon; William Wan, "Soul-searching on Facebook," *Washington Post*, August 30, 2009, available at http://www.washingtonpost.com; accessed September 2, 2012.

15. Porter, "I Am a Jedi," 96–98.

16. Jedi Church: Census, http://www.jedichurch.org. In the menu "Learn," choose "News/Videos." Choose the news item "NZ Census Capitulates—Jedi Stats for New Zealand 2006 Census"; accessed September 2, 2012.

17. Agence France-Presse, "Jedi Census Ploy a Success," *The Australian IT*, August 28, 2002, cited in Possamai, *Religion and Popular Culture*, 72–73.

18. George Lucas's inspiration by Joseph Campbell, especially *The Hero with a Thousand Faces*, is an issue unto itself; see John Shelton Lawrence, "Joseph Campbell, George Lucas, and the Monomyth," in *Finding the Force of the "Star Wars" Franchise: Fans, Merchandise and Critics*, ed. Matthew Wilhelm Kapell and John Shelton Lawrence (New York: Peter Lang, 2006), 21–33.

19. Steven Hart, *A Galactic Gasbag*, 2002, http://www.salon.com/2002/04/10/lucas_5/; accessed September 2, 2012.

20. Bill Moyers, "Of Myth and Men: A Conversation Between Bill Moyers and George Lucas about the Meaning of the Force and the True Theology of *Star Wars*," *Time*, April 26, 1999.

21. Ibid.

22. Ibid.

23. This section draws on the articles "Force," "The Light Side," "The Dark Side," "Jedi Code," and "Jedi Order" from *Wookieepedia*, the *Star Wars* wikia. *Wookieepedia*, http://www.starwars.wikia.com; accessed March 5, 2009.

24. *Wookieepedia*, "Jedi Code"; accessed March 5, 2009.

25. I follow the standard practice in the study of social groups on the Internet of quoting anonymously from discussion forums, though with full reference to homepages; see, e.g., Storm A. King, "Researching Internet Communities: Proposed Ethical Guidelines for Reporting of the Results," *Information Society* 12, no. 2 (1996): 119–27. However, I do quote with full reference to sections of forums with an official character, such as the group's FAQ.

26. Temple of the Jedi Order: Doctrine, http://www.templeofthejediorder.org/home/doctrine; accessed September 2, 2012.

27. Jedi Sanctuary: Fan club, http://www.jedisanctuary.org/articles/index.php?page=not-afan-club; accessed May 2008; no longer available.

28. Jedi Church: Doctrine, http://www.jedichurch.org/jedi-doctrine.html; accessed September 2, 2012.

29. Temple of the Jedi Order: Main, http://www.templeofthejediorder.org; accessed February 3, 2010; the quote is no longer available.

30. Ibid.; accessed September 2, 2012.

31. Jedi Church: Doctrine.

32. Jediism Way: Welcome, http://www.thejediismway.org/index.php/topic,1.0.html; accessed February 3, 2010; no longer available.

33. The forum was located at Jedi Sanctuary, http://www.jedisanctuary.org; accessed April 2008; no longer available.

34. Ibid.

35. Force Academy: Force, http://www.forceacademy.com/theforce_menu.htm; accessed February 3, 2010; no longer available; Ashla Knights: Force, http://www.ashlaknights.net, subpage "So you want to be a Jedi"; accessed June 9, 2009; no longer available; and Jedi Sanctuary: Force, http://www.jedisanctuary.org/pages/force/origin-of-force.htm; accessed February 3, 2010; no longer available.

36. Jedi Foundation: FAQ, http://www.jediacademyonline.com/faq.html; accessed September 3, 2012.

37. Jedi Foundation: Main, http://www.jediacademyonline.com; accessed June 9, 2009; the quote is no longer available.

38. Jediism Way: About, http://www.thejediismway.org/index.php/topic,35.0.html; accessed February 3, 2010; no longer available.

39. Temple of the Jedi Order: Main; accessed February 3, 2010; quote no longer available.

40. Jedi Church: Doctrine.

41. Jediism Way: Welcome.

42. Jedi Foundation: FAQ.

43. Jedi Sanctuary: Campbell, http://www.jedisanctuary.org/pages/philo/joseph-campbell.htm; accessed February 3, 2010; no longer available.

44. Ashla Knights: Force; Force Academy: Force.

45. Jedi Church: Doctrine.

46. Temple of the Jedi Order: Doctrine.

47. Ibid.

48. Jediism Way: About.

49. Jedi Sanctuary: Welcome, http://www.jedisanctuary.org/pages/about/welcome.htm; accessed February 3, 2010; no longer available.

50. Ashla Knights: Practice, http://www.ashlaknights.net. Choose "Academy" in the top menu and then "Practice of Ashla" in the right menu; accessed February 3, 2010.

51. Jedi Foundation: Main; accessed June 9, 2009; the quote is no longer available.

52. Jedi Foundation: Circle, http://www.jediacademyonline.com/jcircle.html; accessed September 3, 2012.

53. Jedi Sanctuary: Teachings, http://www.jedisanctuary.org/pages/teachings/teachings-from -starwars-p2. htm; accessed February 3, 2010; no longer available.

54. Temple of the Jedi Order: Doctrine.

55. Ibid.

56. Ibid.

57. The forum is located at Temple of the Jedi Order, http://www.templeofthejediorder.org; accessed April 2008.

58. Temple of the Jedi Order: Clergy, http://www.templeofthejediorder.org. In the forum section "Commit-tees," choose the section "Ceremonies and Rituals" and then the thread "Clergy Ceremonies and Rituals Committee"; accessed February 3, 2010.

59. On *Star Wars* as religion, see John C. Lyden, *Film as Religion: Myths, Morals, and Rituals* (New York: New York University Press, 2003), 216–25. On *Star Wars* fandom as religion, see John C. Lyden, "Whose Film Is It, Anyway? Canonicity and Authority in *Star Wars* Fandom," *Journal of the American Academy of Religion* 80, no. 3 (2012): 775–86. Lyden's identification of *Star Wars* fandom as religion continues a tradition initiated by Michael Jindra; see Jindra, "Star Trek Fandom as a Religious Phenomenon," *Sociology of Religion* 55, no. 1 (1994): 27–51.

60. See, e.g., Christopher Partridge, *The Re-enchantment of the West: Alternative Spiritualities, Sacralization, Popular Culture and Occulture*, vol. 1 (London: T. & T. Clark, 2004), chap. 6.

Scientology

History, Beliefs, Practices

Douglas Cowan

···

O perating in more than 150 countries and claiming as many as ten million members worldwide, the Church of Scientology regularly presents itself as "the fastest growing religious movement on Earth" and "the only great religion to emerge in the twentieth century." In North America, although it is known for the entertainment celebrities it counts among the faithful—Tom Cruise, John Travolta, Kelly Preston, Kirstie Alley, and Isaac Hayes, to name just a few—it has also been the target of trenchant popular satire, most notably on the adult cartoon programs *The Simpsons* and *South Park*. In Europe, on the other hand, principally in France, Germany, and Greece, the Church of Scientology has fought a bitter, continual battle for social legitimacy and legal acceptance. In other parts of the world, the experience of the church varies between these two extremes.

History

Now over fifty years old, the Church of Scientology began with a pulp science fiction writer from Tilden, Nebraska, named L. Ron Hubbard (1911–86). In 1950 Hubbard published *Dianetics: The Modern Science of Mental Health*, the seminal text of what became Scientology. The text appeared both in much abbreviated form in the pulp magazine *Astounding Science Fiction* and as a full-length book. The church claims that within a few years more than 750 groups were practicing Hubbard's method of Dianetics counseling. In 1954, Hubbard formed the Church of Scientology and devoted the rest of his life to expanding and systematizing what he called the religion of Scientology.

The church is represented by a vast and complicated bureaucratic structure, each unit of which is responsible for reaching particular performance targets and each of which is guided in its operation down to the smallest detail. Called "orgs," these units range from the Church of Scientology International, the "Mother Church," to the Flag Service Organization in Clearwater, Florida, and from the MV "Freewinds," where elite Scientologists practice upper-level auditing (see below), to local storefront missions in cities and towns around the world. Wherever they are, each org is dedicated to

Douglas Cowan, "Scientology: History, Beliefs, Practices," *Handbook of Religion: A Christian Engagement With Traditions, Teachings, and Practices*, ed. Terry C. Muck, Harold A. Netland, and Gerald R. McDermott, pp. 608-614. Copyright © 2014 by Baker Publishing Group. Reprinted with permission.

one of three principal goals: Scientology practice and training; application of the "tech," as Hubbard's educational methods are known; or social reform and betterment.

Beliefs

Although he is not worshiped as a divine figure, Hubbard is the author of Scientology's voluminous scriptures, the touchstone of belief and practice, and the guarantor of authority and salvation for practitioners. For those unacquainted with Scientology, the church appears as an often confusing welter of categories, organizations, neologisms, acronyms, and terms (many of which are defined differently than in common discourse). Hubbard was a prodigious writer, and the church has preserved even the minutiae of his output, turning it into the equivalent of sacred writ. To grasp a basic understanding of Scientological beliefs, however, one must be familiar with relatively few key concepts: thetan, MEST, mind, time track, engram, Clear, and Operating Thetan.

Like many other religious traditions, Scientology regards the human person as the product of three distinct but interdependent constituents: the body, the mind, and the spirit, which is known among Scientologists as the thetan, the basic energetic force animating all life. Rather than simply having thetans, though, Scientologists believe that human beings *are* thetans. That is, we are incarnate spiritual beings, not physical beings equipped with some form of spiritual adjunct. Moreover, since the thetan exists outside the normal frames of spatial and temporal reference, it is not a thing per se. According to Hubbard, "it is the creator of things." Among the thetans' most basic creations is the material universe, which Scientologists know as MEST—matter, energy, space, and time.

Hubbard trifurcates the mind into somatic, analytic, and reactive components or modalities. Governing involuntary bodily functions and autonomic responses to stimuli, the somatic mind receives comparatively little discussion in Hubbard's works, most of which are concerned with the analytic and reactive modalities. The analytic mind is the thinking mind, the individual's rational command-and-control center that is responsible for observation, interpretation, analysis, and behavior. Hubbard taught that, unencumbered, the analytic mind functions efficiently and infallibly in the service of the principal goal of all life, which is to survive. Unfortunately, over the course of millions of years spent in the MEST universe, untold numbers of negative experiences—which are neither recorded nor processed by the analytic mind—accumulate in the thetan and dissociate it from both the facility and the skills to survive.

Down to the smallest sensory detail, these negative experiences are stored in the reactive mind, "a stimulus-response mechanism" that records each experience as a separate mental image, called an engram. Gathered together from a thetan's multitude of lives—the time track—and housed in the reactive mind, the totality of one's negative experiences constitutes a person's engram bank, which, according to Scientology, is "the source of all travail, unwanted fears, emotions, pains, and psychosomatic illnesses." Whenever we encounter a situation similar to a trauma experienced in

The Creed of the Church of Scientology

The Creed of the Church of Scientology was written by L. Ron Hubbard shortly after the church was formed in Los Angeles on February 18, 1954.

We of the Church believe:

That all men of whatever race, color or creed were created with equal rights.

That all men have inalienable rights to their own religious practices and their performance.

That all men have inalienable rights to their own lives.

That all men have inalienable rights to their sanity.

That all men have inalienable rights to their own defense.

That all men have inalienable rights to conceive, choose, assist or support their own organizations, churches and governments.

That all men have inalienable rights to think freely, to talk freely, to write freely their own opinions and to counter or utter or write upon the opinions of others.

That all men have inalienable rights to the creation of their own kind.

That the souls of men have the rights of men.

That the study of the Mind and the healing of mentally caused ills should not be alienated from religion or condoned in nonreligious fields.

And that no agency less than God has the power to suspend or set aside these rights, overtly or covertly.

And we of the Church believe:

That Man is basically good.

That he is seeking to Survive.

That his survival depends upon himself and upon his fellows and his attainment of brotherhood with the Universe.

And we of the Church believe that the laws of God forbid Man

To destroy his own kind.

To destroy the sanity of another.

To destroy or enslave another's soul.

To destroy or reduce the survival of one's companions or one's group.

And we of the Church believe

That the spirit can be saved.

And that the spirit alone may save or heal the body.

any of our lifetimes, the engram associated with that experience is reactivated. We feel the same fear, anger, guilt, pain, sorrow, or whatever emotion was imprinted during the initial experience, and we are prevented from moving forward until the blockage created by the engram is cleared.

Resolving the internal conflict and external manifestations of one's accumulated engram bank is the first order of business for a beginning Scientologist, who is known as a "preclear." After a number of initial courses of auditing offered by the Church of Scientology (see below), practitioners are declared "Clear" of these amassed engrams and are free to continue their journey up what Hubbard called "the Bridge to Total Freedom." In addition to various adjunct courses and "rundowns," the Bridge beyond Clear consists of numerous courses of auditing designed to take practitioners through the fifteen levels of Operating Thetan. For Scientologists, salvation is progressive and is achieved as individual practitioners make their way up the Bridge and successfully complete a series of increasingly complex (and expensive) courses of auditing—the principal practice of Scientology.

Not unlike Abraham Maslow's well-known hierarchy of needs, Scientologists believe that the will to survival exists by degrees or levels, and our ability to participate in successive degrees is reflected in our progress up the Bridge. Called the Eight Dynamics, these levels involve the survival of (1) the individual, (2) the family unit, (3) social groups, (4) the human species, (5) all life-forms, (6) the physical universe (MEST), (7) the individual as a spiritual entity, and (8) survival through infinity. In the service of these dynamics, one of Scientology's stated goals is to "Clear the Planet"—that is, to bring every person on Earth to at least the state of Clear, and hopefully beyond.

Practices

Many Scientology orgs offer Sunday services, which follow a liturgy similar to that found in main-line Protestant churches (see entry on Christian interaction with Scientology): hymns; prayers; a recitation of the Scientology creed; an inspirational message drawn from Hubbard's writings and read verbatim by the presiding minister from *The Background, Ministry, Ceremonies and Sermons of the Scientology Religion*; and some form of group process activity. Relatively few Scientologists, however, attend these services. The vast majority of their practice is dedicated to the various courses of auditing and training offered by the church. Unlike many other religious traditions, which appeal to faith as the touchstone of belief and practice, Scientology presents itself as supremely rational, the product of rigorous scientific investigation and refinement. In *What Is Scientology?* the church states that Hubbard's method "works 100 percent of the time when it is properly applied to a person who sincerely desires to improve his life." The effectiveness of the auditing system and sacrality of Hubbard's writings that enshrine it are irrevocably connected, and no deviation from his teachings, however minor, is permitted.

In an auditing session, the practitioner meets his or her auditor around a small machine, the Hubbard Electropsychometer, more commonly known as the E-Meter, and which Scientologists

Scientology Beliefs

Thetan: Spirit, the basic animating force of life. Human beings are thetans.

MEST: Matter, Energy, Space, Time. The material world created by thetans.

Mind: The mind has three parts: somatic, analytic, reactive. Living in MEST inevitably causes negative experiences that result in the reactive mind.

Time track: Many, many lives create a time track, a record of human experiences.

Engram: Each negative experience creates a record in the reactive mind, an engram.

Clear: The conflict created by engrams must be removed. A preclear has not removed all engrams, a Clear has.

Operating Thetan: A Clear who has chosen to go beyond clear on the Bridge to Total Freedom.

regard as a "religious artifact." The E-Meter is essentially a Wheatstone Bridge, a low-voltage skin galvanometer that measures changes in electrical resistance across two electrodes (or "cans") that are held by the practitioner. Registering in a variety of ways on the meter's dial, these changes in resistance are considered proof of the existence of engrammatic blockages in the practitioner. Needle movements are interpreted by the auditor in the context of the questions or exercises engaged by the practitioner. If a particular questions provokes a strong response on the meter, for example, the auditor could conclude that she has encountered a buried engram and will continue to explore that question or experience with the practitioner. Only when the meter's needle no longer moves—when they have together achieved a "floating needle"—is the issue considered resolved, the engram cleared, and the practitioner free to move on in the session. In addition to auditing, several different Training Routines, Objective Processing, and Rundowns are available to Scientologists, all of which are intended to help practitioners apply the principles of Scientology in all areas of daily life.

Organization

The Church of Scientology is one of the most bureaucratically complex new religions in existence. The Church of Scientology International—the "Mother Church"—is the corporate head of the ecclesial structure, while the Religious Technology Center maintains the copyrights for all Dianetics and Scientology trademarks. All matters related to the publication, translation, and copyright of Hubbard's literary estate rest with Author Services, Inc. The Office of Special Affairs, on the other hand, which was known formerly as the Guardian Office, is responsible for coordinating public relations and the legal affairs of the church. The Flag Service Organization, which is located in the restored Fort Harrison Hotel in Clearwater, Florida, provides the highest-level auditing for Scientology's most elite practitioners. Those who wish to dedicate themselves wholly to the church can join the Sea Organization (known as the Sea Org), a high-commitment, quasi-monastic group that requires, among other things, a billion-year contract with its members. One of Scientology's most controversial organizations, which handles the internal discipline of errant Scientologists, is the Rehabilitation Project Force.

The Church of Scientology also operates a number of social service organizations, including Narconon, its network of drug rehabilitation facilities; Criminon, a prison reform and anti-recidivism program; the Volunteer Minister Program, the members of which wear distinctive yellow T-shirts and are often prominent at the site of different social upheavals. The Citizens Commission on Human Rights prosecutes the Church of Scientology's ongoing battle against the psychiatric profession. In the mid-1990s, Scientology was able to purchase the assets of the bankrupt anticult group the Cult Awareness Network, and now operates it as an organization dedicated to the promotion of religious freedom.

Controversy

Controversy has dogged both *Dianetics* and the Church of Scientology almost from their inception. When Hubbard submitted a draft of *Dianetics* to the American Psychiatric Association, his claims were summarily dismissed—something that could account for the virulent antipathy with which Scientology has regarded both psychology and psychiatry ever since. In 1958, the US Food and Drug Administration seized a quantity of E-Meters on the grounds that the church was representing them as a viable treatment for disease. They were eventually returned, but the church was required to use them only in religious practice. In the early 1970s, the Internal Revenue Service revoked the church's 501(c)3 tax exemption, sparking a two-decade-long battle to win it back—which the church did in 1993. In 1995, the death of Scientologist Lisa McPherson while in church care sparked outrage against Scientology, especially when a wrongful death suit brought against the church by her estate was settled for a still-undisclosed amount. In Europe, both France and Germany have included the Church of Scientology in lists of suspect religious groups and subjected the organization to a variety of surveillance and punitive measures.

Further Reading

Church of Scientology International. *Scientology: Theology and Practice of a Contemporary Religion*. Bridge, 2002.

———. *What Is Scientology?* Bridge, 1998.

Douglas E. Cowan and David G. Bromley. *Cults and New Religions: A Brief History*. Blackwell, 2008.

L. Ron Hubbard. *Dianetics: The Modern Science of Mental Health*. Bridge, 1990.

———. *Scientology: The Fundamentals of Thought.* Bridge, 1988.

James R. Lewis, ed. *Scientology.* Oxford University Press, 2009.

J. Gordon Melton. *The Church of Scientology.* Signature, 2000.

Russell Miller. *Bare-Faced Messiah: The True Story of L. Ron Hubbard.* Key Porter, 1987.

Roy Wallis. *The Road to Total Freedom: A Sociological Analysis of Scientology.* Heinemann, 1976.

Printed in the USA
CPSIA information can be obtained
at www.ICGtesting.com
LVHW080821100923
757564LV00019B/26